A History of Bilingual Education in the US

BILINGUAL EDUCATION & BILINGUALISM

Series Editors: **Nancy H. Hornberger** *(University of Pennsylvania, USA)* and **Wayne E. Wright** *(Purdue University, USA)*

Bilingual Education and Bilingualism is an international, multidisciplinary series publishing research on the philosophy, politics, policy, provision and practice of language planning, Indigenous and minority language education, multilingualism, multiculturalism, biliteracy, bilingualism and bilingual education. The series aims to mirror current debates and discussions. New proposals for single-authored, multiple-authored, or edited books in the series are warmly welcomed, in any of the following categories or others authors may propose: overview or introductory texts; course readers or general reference texts; focus books on particular multilingual education program types; school-based case studies; national case studies; collected cases with a clear programmatic or conceptual theme; and professional education manuals.

All books in this series are externally peer-reviewed.

Full details of all the books in this series and of all our other publications can be found on http://www.multilingual-matters.com, or by writing to Multilingual Matters, St Nicholas House, 31-34 High Street, Bristol BS1 2AW, UK.

BILINGUAL EDUCATION & BILINGUALISM: 129

A History of Bilingual Education in the US

Examining the Politics of Language Policymaking

Sarah C.K. Moore

MULTILINGUAL MATTERS
Bristol • Blue Ridge Summit

DOI https://doi.org/10.21832/MOORE4245
Library of Congress Cataloging in Publication Data
A catalog record for this book is available from the Library of Congress.
Names: Moore, Sarah Catherine K. - author.
Title: A History of Bilingual Education in the US: Examining the Politics of Language Policymaking/Sarah C.K. Moore.
Other titles: A history of bilingual education in the United States Description: Blue Ridge Summit: Multilingual Matters, [2021] | Series: Bilingual Education & Bilingualism: 129 | Includes bibliographical references and index. | Summary: "This book traces a history of bilingual education in the US, unveiling the role of politics in policy development and implementation. It introduces readers to past systemic supports for creation of diverse bilingual educational programs and situates particular instances and phases of expansion and decline within related sociopolitical backdrops"—Provided by publisher.
Identifiers: LCCN 2020048467 (print) | LCCN 2020048468 (ebook) | ISBN 9781788924238 (Paperback) | ISBN 9781788924245 (Hardback) | ISBN 9781788924252 (PDF) | ISBN 9781788924269 (ePub) | ISBN 9781788924276 (Kindle Edition) Subjects: LCSH: Education, Bilingual—United States—History.
Classification: LCC LC3731 .M655 2021 (print) | LCC LC3731 (ebook) | DDC 370.117/50973—dc23 LC record available at https://lccn.loc.gov/2020048467
LC ebook record available at https://lccn.loc.gov/2020048468

British Library Cataloguing in Publication Data
A catalogue entry for this book is available from the British Library.

ISBN-13: 978-1-78892-424-5 (hbk)
ISBN-13: 978-1-78892-423-8 (pbk)

Multilingual Matters
UK: St Nicholas House, 31-34 High Street, Bristol BS1 2AW, UK.
USA: NBN, Blue Ridge Summit, PA, USA.

Website: www.multilingual-matters.com
Twitter: Multi_Ling_Mat
Facebook: https://www.facebook.com/multilingualmatters
Blog: www.channelviewpublications.wordpress.com

Copyright © 2021 Sarah C.K. Moore.

All rights reserved. No part of this work may be reproduced in any form or by any means without permission in writing from the publisher.

The policy of Multilingual Matters/Channel View Publications is to use papers that are natural, renewable and recyclable products, made from wood grown in sustainable forests. In the manufacturing process of our books, and to further support our policy, preference is given to printers that have FSC and PEFC Chain of Custody certification. The FSC and/or PEFC logos will appear on those books where full certification has been granted to the printer concerned.

Typeset by Deanta Global Publishing Services, Chennai, India.

Contents

	Acknowledgments	vii
	Preface	ix
	Foreword	xi
	Terrence G. Wiley	
	Introduction	1
1	A Racist White House	4
2	Prequel to the Bilingual Education Act	21
3	Early Bilingual Education and the Sociopolitical Backdrop	50
4	Capacity Building	66
5	Systemic Infrastructure	82
6	Language Ideologies, Politics and Policymaking	98
7	Current Endeavors and Future Possibilities	125
	References	142
	Index	160

Acknowledgments

This book is devoted to advocates for language rights, bilingual education and equity in schooling. The contents were developed based on dialogue and discussion with devoted scholars. Thank you especially to Terry Wiley, who has skillfully and carefully detailed histories of language policy and planning throughout his career. Thank you to Beatriz Arias, whose reminders and contributions have consistently positioned language as a civil right. I appreciate interest, feedback and support from Wayne Wright, with whom I initially shared thoughts about this manuscript at a rainy American Educational Research Association meeting in New York.

Early on in development, I am fortunate that Jim Lyons spoke with me and confirmed my research pursuits were in keeping with his knowledge and lived experience, having lobbied for the National Association for Bilingual Education and worked under the Carter and Reagan administrations to preserve the integrity of the original Bilingual Education Act. Norm Gold, associated with Californians Tomorrow and previously employed by the California State Department of Education, helped to clarify questions after I encountered Bob Cervantes' publication documenting that a key basis for the 1978 Bilingual Education Act reauthorization changes, which constituted the first major shift *away from bilingual* education, 'The AIR Report' federal contract award was depraved and politically generated. David Rogers, of Dual Language Education of New Mexico, provided updates regarding its ongoing activities in the field, recommended the piece used for the book's cover art and graciously committed time and efforts to ensuring agreement for its inclusion. Reynaldo Macías, founding chair of the UCLA César E. Chávez Department of Chicana and Chicano Studies, who worked for the National Institute of Education during time periods covered, provided astute thoughts regarding progress and questions, as I engaged in framing and thinking during revisions, particularly around defining infrastructure.

Throughout research, development, writing, editing and revisions, I regularly referred to the comprehensive *Encyclopedia of Bilingual Education* (2008), edited by renowned scholar Josué M. González. Its contents were instrumental and I thank especially Professor González, as well as its other contributors.

I appreciate time, patience and support from Multilingual Matters, especially Flo McClelland, Laura Longworth and Sarah Williams. Comments and observations from editors, both Wayne Wright and Nancy Hornberger, were valuable and reassuring.

I am thankful for colleagues at the University of Maryland College Park, in the College of Education and Division of Language, Literacy, and Social Inquiry and especially in our Applied Linguistics and Language Education faculty group, who instill intrinsic motivation and impart deep-seated professional and scholarly encouragement.

I am honored and grateful that Jade Leyva shared her art for this book's cover. Originally commissioned by Dual Language Education of New Mexico for its 2019 La Cosecha Annual Conference, its addition is treasured.

Thank you to my parents, who helped with final copyedits, each of whom was a career civil servant and committed policymaker, and brother, whose well-wishes (especially amidst the pandemic) were critical.

Most of all, quips from my stalwart husband, as I struggled with revisions, helped me to push on. To our children, Kevin and Tyler, too fledgling to know the patience they've endured, especially in these past several months, thank you for your youthful reminder that there is a tomorrow and promising future.

Preface

This book was initially submitted to the publisher March 2, 2020; revisions were submitted September 7, 2020. The interim period coincided with the start of a pandemic which dramatically altered the lives of millions. Schools were shut down, shelter-in-place orders introduced and economies crumbled under an uncertain future. In the United States, those working in low-income jobs, Black, Brown, Native and People of Color were acutely and disproportionately impacted by societal shutdowns. At the time of writing, a vaccine for the novel coronavirus of 2019, or COVID-19, seems plausible. Operationalization of its massive distribution less so.

Over Memorial Day weekend, a Black man was executed in the streets of Minneapolis by a white police officer whose knee was used to carry out a 21st-century lynching. Mr George Floyd begged for his mother and repeatedly said, 'I can't breathe'. The murder was recorded by onlookers' cell phones, and across the United States and the world, protests against police brutality and systemic racism in the name of George Floyd erupted. The president's response was to select specific wording echoing an openly racist police chief whose approach to protestors during the Civil Rights era was violence – 'When the looting starts, the shooting starts'.

In response to the president and unrest, Mayor Muriel Bowser created Black Lives Matter Plaza, in clear view from The White House. After decades of challenges and refusals by its owner, the Washington, DC football team finally succumbed to changing its name – chosen in 1932 by its racist founding owner *in jest*. The depiction of a human being as its 'logo' also removed.

Meanwhile, the COVID-19 pandemic rages on, especially across the United States, where it has become a form of weaponized politicking. While writing manuscript revisions, I felt a responsibility to address areas where Africans kidnapped and trafficked into enslavement in the land now referred to as the United States may be pertinent to sociolinguistics and historical language policy. I attempt not to exclude issues of language education for Indigenous and Tribal Language Communities. With hope, this volume situates these and related concerns with sufficient sensitivity and historical reverence to Indigenous, heritage, marginalized, minority and minoritized communities.

Foreword

Terrence G. Wiley
Professor Emeritus
Arizona State University, Tempe

In recent years, there have been several noteworthy strides in language education which have embraced the value of what used to be called 'bilingual' education (BLE). There has been widespread endorsement for 'dual language' education, pervasive interest in promoting 'heritage' languages, welcome enthusiasm for studies on the 'cognitive' benefits of becoming bilingual and pervasive excitement and support for 'translanguaging' practices. In the United States, while there is a sense of freshness to these topics, they are often discussed without reference to the legacy of prior efforts to promote BLE, particularly under the auspices of federally supported BLE. To address this omission, Sarah Moore's latest book on what San Miguel Jr (2004) termed 'contested policy', provides an important and much needed addition to the often forgotten or lesser-known history of the emergence of, and pragmatic efforts to promote, federally supported Title VII BLE.

Many important books deal with policy and the practice of federally supported BLE – too many to list here – as well as those that focus on the consequences of its demise in California and others states. In fact, Moore's (2014) own notable study on the consequences of restrictive policy in Arizona has made an important contribution in this area. What is especially valuable about her current study, however, is her focus on the political and policy climate of federal BLE's implementation as well as what was happening to develop the many elements that were needed for its successful implementation on the ground.

In dealing with the legacy of federally funded BLE, it is important to consider its rise within the context of its times. In addressing this, Moore utilizes a variety of sources, including interviews, policies, documents and legal issues, to describe its rise and development. Among the topics she addresses are BLE policy formation, as well as issues of implementation, administration and the essential problem of resource provision. She describes early programmatic efforts during the 1960s and 1970s and chronicles events and issues leading up to the 1974 authorization. She considers the degree and adequacy of appropriations and details the establishment and functions of the original Office of Bilingual Education, which was necessary to guide implementation. Then, Moore chronicles the backlash against BLE, which had already begun when its implementation was still only in its formative years.

Moore's treatment is keen to focus on the larger sociopolitical context of BLE policymaking against the persistent undertow of anti-immigration and racially biased sentiments that were directed at the minority populations to be served. She notes how criticisms of BLE have often served as surrogates for other forms of discrimination that have more overtly focused on race and immigration. In this connection, she also digresses from her narration of the earlier history of BLE to focus on the problematic nature of the Trump Administration's ideological and policy orientations. This detour is timely, especially given the number of educational challenges that currently face language minority students, not to mention those of detainee children who have been incarcerated along the southern border.

What led to the erasure of the legacy of federally funded BLE? Moore deals with some of the early elements, including the ideological attack that labeled BLE policymaking as 'affirmative ethnicity' (see, for example, her discussion of Noel Epstein's critique). On a deep level, as Moore has noted, there were also historical and ideological antecedents. Foremost among them was the ideological legacy of Americanization, which became hegemonic during the World War I era (see below). During the Great Depression, the US government carried out a forced exodus of possibly a million or more Mexican-Americans, who were 'repatriated' to Mexico. In fact, what was labeled as a repatriation also resulted in the expulsion of American-born citizens (Balderrama & Rodríguez, 2006). As Moore notes, World War II created a labor shortage, so those of Mexican origin were again encouraged to return to labor in what Williams (1939) termed the racialized 'factories in the fields'. And what was the legacy of education for their children?

Among the most important themes in Moore's analysis is that the genesis for federally supported BLE for language minority children was embedded in the historical struggle for educational civil rights. Immigration to the United States increased dramatically after the conclusion of the Civil War in 1865. Initially, large numbers of immigrants came to the country from western Europe. Many from these groups moved into the Midwest, and as Moore notes, BLE was promoted particularly by German immigrants, and initially without opposition in places such as Cincinnati (Toth, 1990). But this migration was soon followed by immigrants from southern and eastern Europe, who became frequently targeted by nativists, who considered the new immigrants culturally and racially less assimilable. Similarly, first Chinese, and then Japanese, and later Filipinos migrated in larger numbers from Asia and faced even stronger opposition. As these groups were targeted, their children also faced discrimination in schooling (Weinberg, 1995, 1997). Legal segregation had already become widespread against African Americans during the Jim Crow era, which was upheld by the US Supreme Court in *Plessy v Ferguson* 163 U.S. 537 (1896). Nativism and anti-immigration advocacy increased in the latter decades of the 19th century, first with a series of Chinese exclusion acts, with other Asians including the Japanese soon targeted. By the early 20th century, the US Congress, through the efforts of the Dillingham Commission (1907–1911), was increasingly fixated on the alleged negative consequences of undesirable immigrants from eastern and southern Europe.

Anti-immigrant activism exacerbated the growing xenophobia during World War I (1914–1918; the United States entered the war in 1917) and 'foreign' language education was restricted. English-only education was promoted under the auspices of the Americanization Movement (1914–1924; see Wiley, 1998). Following World War I, anti-immigration efforts continued and led to the passage of the 1924 Johnson–Reed Immigration Act, which implemented an ethno-racially based national-origins quota system that persisted, with only minimal alterations, until 1965. Former Attorney General Jeff Sessions recently hailed it as a model for contemporary immigration reform (Wiley, in press).

As Moore notes, some states, such as Texas, had had various forms of BLE during the 19th century, but during and following World War I, they became increasingly restrictive (Blanton, 2004). 'Foreign' language restrictions were compounded by separate and unequal schooling for minority children. Texas' segregation and treatment of many Mexican-American and Mexican immigrant children was particularly draconian. As Weinberg (1995: 145) notes, by about 1920, a systematic pattern of discrimination had emerged in Texas involving separate schooling in greatly inferior facilities for Mexican-American students with a 'deliberate refusal to make educational use of the child's cultural heritage, especially the Spanish language' as well as 'a shorter school year'. As early as 1925, language bias was found to be a factor in intelligence testing. Weinberg (1995: 147) notes that in San Antonio when 'Spanish-language tests were administered to Mexican-American children, nearly 70 percent scored higher than they had on an English language test'. Thus, Moore's 'prelude' focus on Texas and the work of George Sánchez (Blanton, 2014) is a fitting introduction to the origins of the struggle for federally supported BLE. As Weinberg (1995) and others have noted, the patterns of discrimination, particularly against children of Mexican heritage, were duplicated in California and throughout the Southwest. Significantly, the patterns of discrimination that began in the early 20th century persisted into the Civil Rights Era of the 1960s when BLE began to catch the attention of policymakers as Moore and others such as San Miguel Jr (2004) have noted.

After a brief period of successes in the incipient period of federal bilingual education during the late 1960s and 1970s, as Moore observes, the policies of the Department of Education, as well as a retreat by the Office of Civil Rights during the Reagan Administration (1981–1989), worked to restrict and redefine what was permissible under Title VII. Simultaneously, this period saw the resurgence of attempts to promote English-only instruction and language restrictionism on a level that had not been seen since the period of Americanization during World War I and the 1920s. The contemporary English-only movement began in the 1970s with the backing of powerful private interests and donors who were linked to anti-immigration efforts and their influence persists with links to the current Trump administration (Wiley, in press). Thus, again, Moore's focus on the Trump administration educational policies is timely.

One of the more important contributions of Moore's history is her focus on the many elements of intellectual and professional support that were necessary for the successful launching and sustainability of bilingual programs. She describes, for example, the development of a national advisory group and the development of the national clearinghouse, which served as a broad-based vehicle for cataloguing and sharing a widely cast net of information and resources ranging from theory and policy to practice. Similarly, Moore describes the important legacy of the federally funded national network of BLE resource centers that helped to support BLE in K-12 settings, as well as the establishment of Title VII fellowship programs, which were critical for the development of professional leadership for a generation of scholars and teachers who would, in turn, go on to mentor the contemporary generation to lead the field, even in the wake of the demise of federal support.

Moore also addresses the role of the Department of Education as an initially constructive force and how, under the Reagan Administration, as well as during the current administration, it became a more reactionary institution that has inhibited BLE and, more recently, continues to fail to promote equitable education for language minority students. During the 1980s, English-only and anti-immigrant efforts were also linked in their efforts to promote a variety of official English, anti-immigrant, anti-affirmative action and anti-BLE propositions in states such as California, which allowed for voter initiatives. Legislative efforts to promote official English at the federal level have, thus far, not been successful. Nevertheless, pro-English organizations still advocate for them. Despite the legacy of resistance to BLE, Moore fittingly concludes her study by focusing on many of the positive developments that have been occurring – most notable among them the 2016 passage of Proposition 58 which paved the way for a stunning reversal of California's restrictive policies dating back to the passage of Proposition 227 in 1998 (see also Wiley, 2019).

Thus, it is important to note positive developments that have been occurring in recent years. Policymakers and professional organizations, for example, now endorse broad-based language education. This represents an ideological shift away from the dominance of English-only practices and the possibility of a reversal of mainstream US educational policy that has been prevalent for the past century. Recall that during the xenophobic period of the World War I era and Americanization movement (1915–1925), 'foreign' language teaching was intentionally constrained in the primary grades to ensure that children would lose their native languages and acquire only English. It was widely assumed that younger children were particularly vulnerable to indoctrination in alien, un-American ideas. Once they were in the upper grades, it was assumed that it would be 'safe' for them to learn their family's native language if it were taught as a 'foreign' language (Wiley, 1998).

Within the contemporary climate of openness toward language education, there are still many reasons to revisit the formative period of federally funded BLE as well as the resistance to it, and Moore's new book provides an important resource in this regard. First, although federally funded BLE was often ridiculed by right-wing pundits at the time as a failed program that was educationally harming children and keeping them from learning English, a review of research studies generated on BLE such as the Ramírez Report (Ramírez, 1992), as well as more recent reviews by Genesee et al. (2005) are still relevant. Secondly, while support for dual immersion, heritage language (HL) education and translanguaging practices are all important in the contemporary context, it is essential to understand the antecedents of many of these areas and prior accomplishments of BLE, which are not always known or acknowledged in the current environment (Wiley, 2020).

Again, today it is common to see arguments for the promotion of language education couched within broad concerns for supporting language development and multilingualism. For example, a recent report by the American Academy of Arts and Sciences' Commission on Language Learning (2017: viii), which was created through a bipartisan effort of the US Congress and brought together by an interdisciplinary team of experts, endorsed promoting 'a national strategy to improve access to as many languages as possible for people of every region, ethnicity, and socioeconomic background ... and that instruction should begin as early in life as possible. Its primary goal, therefore, is for every school in the nation to offer meaningful instruction in world languages as part of their standard curricula'.

Concerning the country's monolingual majority, the commission observed that the United States lags in comparison with European nations and China in helping its citizens develop knowledge and skills in second languages. The commission's recommendations noted the social, economic and cognitive benefits of bilingualism, and it endorses 'heritage' language instruction, particularly for Native Americans in accordance with the Native American Languages Act in 'English-based schools with appropriate curricula and materials' (American Academy of Arts and Sciences' Commission on Language Learning, 2017: x). The commission first framed its arguments for the promotion of languages largely in neoliberal discursive terms. For example, it stressed that language is a resource for the United States in an increasingly globalized world. On the positive side, the commission endorsed improving linguistic access 'for people of every region, ethnicity, and socioeconomic background' (American Academy of Arts and Sciences' Commission on Language Learning, 2017: viii). Languages other than English of the home were largely depicted as 'heritage languages'. In specific reference to HLs, the commission endorsed (1) supporting the intergenerational transition of HLs; (2) encouraging HL speakers to pursue further academic instruction in their languages and more 'learning opportunities for HL speakers in classroom or school settings'; (3) expanding 'efforts to create college and university curricula designed specifically' for them as well as 'course credit for proficiency' in an HL; (4) providing 'targeted support and programming for Native American languages as defined in the Native American Languages Act'; (5) increasing 'support for Native American languages being used as primary languages of education, and for the development of curricula and education materials for such programs'; and (6) providing 'opportunities for Native Americans and others to study Native American languages in English-based schools with appropriate curricula and materials' (American Academy of Arts and Sciences' Commission on Language Learning, 2017: x).

While these recommendations can be taken as positive, especially given the ideological legacies of Americanization and the English Only movements of the prior century, as well as those still being promoted, what is missing in the commission's analysis and from other contemporary language advocacy analyses, is a sense of history on why these steps are necessary, which relates to the lapse of federal BLE, as well as earlier attempts to eradicate Native American languages during the boarding school era (especially between 1879 and 1928, see Adams, 1995).

The absence of an historical perspective also extends to research. All too often, there is a failure to acknowledge and utilize the prior research base that was focused on federally funded BLE. In this regard, although the commission references relatively recent research, for example, on the cognitive benefits of bilingualism by Bialystok (2009), as well as on the effectiveness of 'dual-language' education (Steele *et al.*, 2017), it ignores the legacy of decades of research on Title VII BLE (see Wiley [in press] for elaboration; see also Genesee *et al.* [2005] for a research summary; Ramírez [1992] for a summary of the effectiveness of transitional BLE; as well as Thomas and Collier [2002]).

Another ironic consequence of the erasure of the legacy of federal BLE is that many of those lamenting the weaknesses of current US language policy to promote heritage education seem to miss a major reason for the consequence of its demise. A few years ago, colleagues and I (Fee *et al.*, 2014) analyzed US American Community Survey (ACS) population data by comparing it to the American Council for the Teaching of Foreign Languages (ACTFL) school 'foreign' language enrollment data to get a sense of how many potential heritage learners might be reflected among foreign language learners. The data were quite telling. Based on 2007/2008 ACS data, nationally nearly 9 million school-age children lived in homes where Spanish was spoken. California had the largest single share of the population with slightly over 2.5 million students in homes where Spanish was spoken. When contrasting those numbers with California Spanish language enrollments for 2010, the nearest comparable year, only 617,000 students were enrolled in Spanish statewide, and that total would have included many students who were not living in homes where Spanish was spoken. It is important to remember that, at the time, BLE in California was still being restricted by Proposition 227, and most of the potential 'heritage' learners of Spanish would not have been able to study Spanish bilingually. Obviously, the demise of BLE in California and the lack of availability of Spanish classes in many grades and schools, not only in California, but across the country, greatly affected the opportunity of language minority students to learn through their 'heritage' languages, or have contact with them, as 'foreign' languages (see Fee *et al.*, 2014).

The demise of federally funded BLE has had tremendous consequences for students (Arias & Wiley, 2015; Gándara & Hopkins, 2010; Moore, 2014; Wiley *et al.*, 2009), and the erasure of the legacy of federally funded BLE continues to have important intellectual consequences with implications for language advocacy and language minority rights in the current era. Thus, Moore's efforts to trace the early history of BLE through policy and practice at the ground level provides an important contribution and counterweight to its erasure in policy and scholarly memory. This study offers valuable information to help reconstruct its history. As we strive to promote educational opportunity for a new generation of language minority students by promoting dual language education, translanguaging and educational equity, it is vital that we not forget the legacy of federally funded BLE and utilize its history as a resource.

Introduction

This book is an approach to the history of bilingual education, to revisit its growth and expansion in the United States facilitated by the federal government on a national scale, with the goal of establishing a better understanding of the systemic supports and infrastructure orchestrated through the implementation of Title VII, the Bilingual Education Act (BEA). It is also intended to ensure historical progress is documented and leveraged in future endeavors for the promotion of multilingual language programs by positioning the role of bilingual education as an apparatus for upholding native and heritage language rights.

The contents of the chapters herein represent only a snapshot of the systems created by the countless advocates, parents, communities, stakeholders, researchers, scholars, educators, policymakers, lawyers, legislators, rights activists, civil servants, teachers and students who have contributed since the 1940s to creating schools offering bilingual educational programs (such as the eminent scholar, George I. Sánchez, [to whom I was directed by Terry Wiley]).

In prior research, I and colleagues have focused on the restrictive language policy context in Arizona, where the State Department of Education administered educator professional development referring to 'segregation' of English learners as part of its structured/sheltered English immersion program. Like so many, I never could have imagined that policies comparable to those of Arizona's conservative majority legislature and leadership could ever so closely mirror those that now echo from the White House and its current inhabitant. For this reason and others, in writing Chapter 1, I soon found myself drowning in tracing ties between Donald J. Trump, his administration and white supremacy. However important it is to recognize and be cognizant of these, the critical focus of this endeavor is bilingual education and a humble attempt at understanding the prodigious past contributors and contributions in pursuit of the BEA. To be certain, its priority on bilingual-bicultural education suffered throughout its duration, but it did allow for the introduction of various systemic supports, which in concert, created the first federally administered groundwork for bilingual education.

Bilingual education anything begets racist, hegemonic, monolingual ideologies that favor majoritarian narratives and marginalize the minority (minoritized). Although the immediate utility may be unclear and at the risk of detracting attention from promoting bilingual education, I have therefore retained a review of the relationship between the current White House resident and the white supremacist movement in Chapter 1. It delves deeply into several areas not directly related to bilingual education, also including family border separation; the impact of Trump hate speech in schools among language minority, Latinx, Muslim, LGBTQ and other minority students; and discussion of the president's anti-immigration policies. It also traces the origin of Trump's immigration platform and relationships between related key advisors and white separatism. The contents of the first chapter also include a review of Secretary of Education Betsy DeVos and her family's role in school privatization, the charter school movement and relationships between language minority learners and charters.

In Chapter 2, I attempt to provide an historical review of bilingual education and bilingualism in the United States, from its origins to the 1960s, around the time contemporary bilingual education programs emerged. As with each of the chapters, this second *is not* comprehensive or representative of a history of these topics. It *does not* address the most diverse source of languages in the nation-state which is 'the United States' – Native American, American Indian, Native Hawaiian and Alaska Native languages. It also *does not* address the copious number of African languages spoken by enslaved peoples brought to the continent by English and Spanish inhabitants against their will. It *does not* address the languages brought by other colonizers, such as Spain in the Southwest and France in the Southeast.

Chapter 3 is an effort to describe early bilingual education before the programs actually funded under the BEA – those that existed in the late 1960s and early 1970s, but before the more focused attention on bilingual education in the mid-1970s. It attempts to present for readers a sense of the social, political and policymaking landscape – both in terms of areas of the BEA, and also among presidential administrations and issues leading up to the 1974 BEA reauthorization. Summaries are not comprehensive, but rather demonstrate examples and highlight key areas relevant to bilingual education.

Chapter 4 describes the groundwork that began to be laid in the early 1970s that was more invigorated through the 1974 reauthorization. It provides descriptions of shifts in funding appropriations, the Office of Bilingual Education, a national advisory committee on bilingual education, examples of program types operating just prior to the 1974 reauthorization and program expansion due to 1974 investments. This chapter also captures a glimpse of the fellowship programs that institutionalized the foundation for bilingual educator pipelines.

Chapter 5 revisits the impacts of funding during the 1970s. It describes the genesis and development of the national clearinghouse for bilingual education and provides a window into what a national network of resource centers once looked like. This chapter illustrates how bilingual support centers were once organized, including the distribution of responsibilities for serving bilingual programs on a national scale.

Chapter 6 returns to political debates surrounding bilingual education and related publications from the late 1970s to early 1980s and implications for the viability of bilingual education at the federal level. It also describes the creation of the Department of Education as a new executive agency and its first secretary, prior to the Reagan administration's systemic dismantling of bilingual education throughout the 1980s. It provides an overview and summaries of the English-only movements of the late 1990s and early 2000s.

Chapter 7 reviews progress made in the areas of language education since the passage of English-only initiatives. It *does not* entirely confront and interrogate white monolingual hegemony in the context of bilingual education, yet highlights its intrinsic presence and the critical importance of its exposure. It problematizes the country's current interest in, and expansion of, dual language bilingual programs and discusses future possibilities for repositioning bilingual education on a national scale.

1 A Racist White House

'It's gotten way worse since Trump got elected', said Ashanty Bonilla, 17, a Mexican American high school junior in Idaho who faced so much ridicule from classmates last year that she transferred schools.
'They hear it. They think it's okay. The president says it. ...Why can't they?'

Natanson *et al.* (2020)

Educators in Idaho smiling while posing in Halloween costumes in October 2018 – one group is holding American flags behind a wall (Image 1.1), while the other group is wearing sombreros and ponchos and holding maracas (Image 1.2). These photos were posted to the district's Facebook page (Southern Poverty Law Center [SPLC], 2019: 12).

Image 1.1 Educators make a brick wall wearing American garb with the slogan, Make America Great Again. Source: Southern Poverty Law Center republication of publicly available photos posted on Facebook.

Image 1.2 Educators dress in ponchos and sombreros as part of the larger group costume (wall and immigrants from Mexico). Source: Southern Poverty Law Center republication of publicly available photos posted on Facebook.

The 'Trump Effect'

On April 6, 2018, US Attorney General Jeff Sessions announced the Trump administration's 'zero tolerance' policy on immigration, calling on attorneys general across the country to prosecute 'unlawful entry' to the full extent of the law. In what he claimed was accordance with the law, the new policy sought to separate children from family members for an undetermined period of time. In a May 7 speech, Sessions asserted 'If you are smuggling a child, then we will prosecute you and that child will be separated from you as required by law. If you don't like that, then don't smuggle children over our border' (Department of Justice, 2018).

After investigations conducted by Congress and public outrage bemoaning the callous nature of family separation, as well as deplorable living conditions and reported unconscionable treatment of children – the youngest separated was two months old – Trump signed an Executive Order on June 20, 2018, rescinding the family separation policy (though there is evidence it has continued). On behalf of several families who were detained and separated, the American Civil Liberties Union filed a class action complaint on October 4, 2019, against Sessions and numerous other officials involved in implementation of the policy. Allegations in the lawsuit are stark. The gravity of their accounts is daunting. Families tell of being kept in cells smelling of urine, detained after long journeys through the desert and not offered water, and sleeping on cold cement floors in *las hieleras*, or ice boxes, with only mylar blankets for cover. Perhaps worse in each of the cases is that experiences either preceded or were succeeded by separation from loved ones (in one case for 10 months). The following two accounts demonstrate the conditions children endured while detained and separated:

> When I left, and my dad wasn't with me, they told me not to worry that he would be coming in a moment. I went in the car and felt very relieved and happy that he would follow. But it wasn't like that. He didn't come. I haven't seen him since then.
>
> The way I have been treated makes me feel like I don't matter, like I am trash.
>
> (Sergio, 16-year-old detained for over 45 days after crossing the U.S.-Mexico border with his father [Silva, 2018])

> For breakfast, they gave me a frozen ham sandwich. The ham was black. I took one bite, but did not eat the rest because of the taste.
>
> I was half asleep and they were calling a girl who had a similar first name as me. A male officer kicked me to wake me up to confirm whether or not I was the person they were looking for. I was not. The kick scared me and hurt, although I did not get a bruise.
>
> (Dixiana, 10-year-old from Honduras, detained after crossing the U.S.-Mexico border with her mother [Silva, 2018])

As of October 2020, 545 children who were separated from family at the border remain in care by the US government (Dickerson, 2020).

Image 1.3 MCALLEN, TX - JUNE 12: A two-year-old Honduran asylum seeker cries as her mother is searched and detained near the U.S.-Mexico border on June 12, 2018 in McAllen, Texas. The asylum seekers had rafted across the Rio Grande from Mexico and were detained by U.S. Border Patrol agents before being sent to a processing center for possible separation. Customs and Border Protection (CBP) is executing the Trump administration's 'zero tolerance' policy towards undocumented immigrants. U.S. Attorney General Jeff Sessions also said that domestic and gang violence in immigrants' country of origin would no longer qualify them for political asylum status. (Photo by John Moore via Getty Images)

Trump Rhetoric Seeps into Schools

The bullying Trump demonstrates at rallies, in tweets and public speeches has shifted a general public perspective around decency. Coupled with his polarizing narratives, these have profoundly impacted children's conduct and their experiences in schools. The SPLC conducted two surveys of educators regarding hate speech in schools, finding a significant rise in incidents directed at students of color, lesbian, gay, bisexual, transgender and queer (LGBTQ) students, those perceived to be immigrants, Muslim and Jewish students. A Nebraska teacher reported that 'Students have used the name Trump to taunt others. At times it is telling kids that Trump is going to send them home' (Southern Poverty Law Center, 2019: 16). Illustrative of the ubiquitous, systemic racism entrenched in schools are the Idaho teachers who dressed in costume for Halloween in 2018. One group donned ponchos and sombreros; the other posed behind a wall decorated in red, white and blue, holding American flags and Trump's campaign slogan, 'Make America Great Again'. Although they were widely admonished, a portion of the community defended the Middleton School District educators – over 15,000 people signed a petition to show support

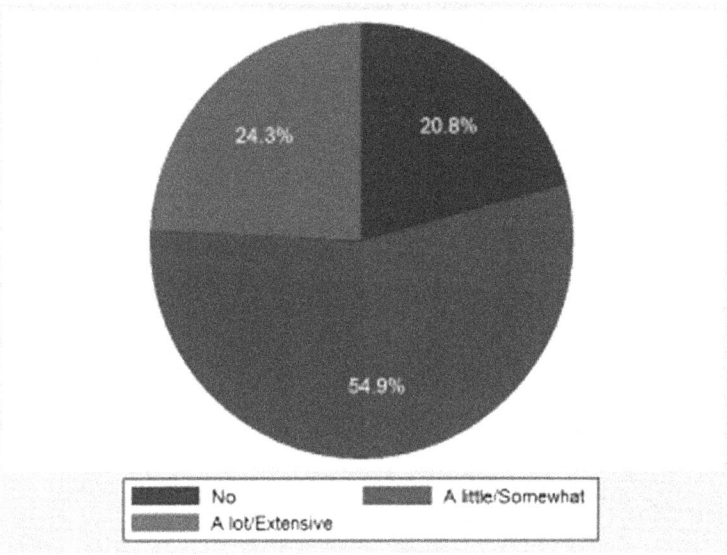

Figure 1.1 Educators' concerns about the influence of immigration enforcement on students

for them. Findings from another Southern Poverty Law Center (2019) survey of 10,000 K-12 educators showed 476 reported cases in which the phrase 'build the wall' was used and 672 mentioned deportation.

The Civil Rights Project/*Proyecto Derechos Civiles* conducted a study on the influence of anti-immigration rhetoric and the expansion of Immigration Control and Enforcement (ICE) raids within schools (Gándara & Ee, 2018). A total of 730 schools in 24 regionally representative districts with 5438 respondents were surveyed. Of those, 73% reported observing the impact of immigration enforcement; 80% indicated behavior or emotional problems among students; and roughly a quarter of respondents reported behavioral or emotional problems resulting from immigration enforcement as a very big problem. Two particularly compelling responses illustrate the gravity schools and teachers face amid fears of deportation (Figure 1.1).

> I had one student who came back the day after prom and would not eat or talk to anyone. I finally found out from one of her friends that she came home from prom to find her mom deported and never had the chance to say good-bye or anything. She was suffering but did not know what to do. (Gándara & Ee, 2018: 10)

> They are worried and scared about the climate of increasing intolerance and bigotry. There has also been an increase in racist graffiti, vandalism, and racial tensions and language on our school campus. I wonder where all this hate comes from? (Gándara & Ee, 2018: 19)

One teacher noted, they 'fear that even though they have worked hard all of their school careers that they will be unable to attend or pay for college'. An Oregon teacher added, 'I have students who were college-bound now questioning if it's worth it, because they don't believe that they could get a job in their field after graduating. They're worried about financial aid…' (Gándara & Ee, 2018).

Increased ICE presence under the Trump administration has had a particular impact on school attendance and heightening absenteeism – 57.4% reported increases in absences from school. A New Jersey administrator wrote:

> The kids are scared and sometimes they hide for days when there are immigration raids in the area. Some of the students have no food or place to live because the parents do not have a job and they go day by day. (Gándara & Ee, 2018: 14)

As Gándara and Ee (2018: 14) note, 'Since school may often be the source of the only meal students will have that day, missing school represents more than just missing class'.

Following the election, the Human Rights Campaign conducted a survey of 50,000 youth between the ages of 13 and 18 in which 70% of respondents reported witnessing bullying; of those, 79% said this bullying increased after the start of the 2016 presidential campaigns (Uddin, 2018).

Pervasive Politics

To many Americans, it was evident that Donald Trump's 2016 path to the presidency was paved with xenophobia and propelled by racist ideologies. In announcing his campaign for the presidency, Trump called immigrants from Mexico 'rapists' who he claimed bring 'drugs' and 'crime' to the United States. For months, many of us were terrified by the possibility that a majority of the electorate would put a flagrant bigot in the White House. Pundits and electoral experts across the country were convinced his opponent, Hillary Clinton, would win the race (*The New York Times* prepared only one backup front page headline, in the event Trump won).

But it happened, and another portion of the electorate collectively searched for some semblance of reason and rationality to help with how to approach this new reality. At the time of this writing, the United States is embarking on the next presidential election cycle and around publication of this volume, the person who will reside in the White House until 2024 may be known (or not, depending on the outcome of massive amounts of mail-in voting during a pandemic). The outcome will be testimony to the ethical state of the majority of US constituencies. The Trump campaign and presidency have been marked by deleterious attacks against any who dare to cross the White House, including Senator Mitt Romney of Massachusetts, the only Republican to vote against one of two impeachment counts put forth by the Democratically controlled House of Representatives.

In response to the election, factions of Americans unified and two arguably bifurcated sociopolitical paths emerged. In one direction, the

Women's March on Washington, which drew millions of attendees from across the country to confront misogyny, promote women's rights and decry transgressions by the new president. Also, the Me Too and Time's Up movements, which gave voice to tens of thousands of victims of sexual violence against women. In part cultivated by these movements, new candidates for local and regional office arose and in the 2018 Congressional election, Democrats won back control of the House of Representatives.

In the shadow of these triumphs, however, numerous hate-based events transpired – white supremacists were both overtly and covertly supported by the president, and human rights violations by his administration escalated immensely, particularly against both legal and undocumented immigrants. In Charlottesville, Virginia, a woman was killed in the summer of 2017 when a neo-Nazi drove his Dodge Challenger into a crowd of counter-protestors during a white nationalist rally.

In fall 2018, the nomination, hearings and, ultimately, swearing-in of Brett Kavanaugh to the Supreme Court occurred, despite accusations by initially one person and later numerous others, of sexual misconduct and assault during his years as a student from secondary through law schools. Beginning in 2019 and culminating in January 2020, the Democratically controlled House of Representatives investigated allegations that Trump withheld critical funds from Ukraine to support its military and war against Russia (which invaded its Crimean region in 2014) in exchange for publicly announcing an investigation into the son of his most prominent political opponent, Joe Biden. Although these momentous movements and appalling events and transgressions may have dominated the president's tenure in office up to March 2020, the details of policies under his administration regarding immigrants, their children, immigration and refugees are far more egregious and deplorable.

The Role of Immigration

The 2016 Trump political campaign was rooted in immigration as its primary rallying cry. The centrality of this issue was deliberate, strategic and the result of years' planning on the part of conservatives opposed to the mainstream Republican establishment, notably Stephen Bannon, who co-founded Breitbart (which he claimed to be the foundation of the alt-right [politically white nationalist-leaning group]). As reported by *The New York Times* (Shear *et al.*, 2018) during the summer of 2018 and the Public Broadcasting System in October 2019, Trump was merely the representative of carefully orchestrated, ideologically divisive politicking derived from several individuals whose backgrounds are inextricably linked with white supremacy and white separatism. The key players were Steve Bannon, Alabama Republican Senator Jeff Sessions and a staffer of his, Stephen Miller. Miller would ultimately play an instrumental role in devising the president's immigration ban and, at the time of this writing, still works as a close Trump advisor in the White House. Bannon,

Sessions and Miller met in 2013 on Capitol Hill at the Breitbart News headquarters and 'bonded over an article titled "The Case of the Missing White Voters"', reported *The Times* (Shear et al., 2018: 2).

In the article, author Sean Trende reports on analyses of voter turnout for the 2012 election (the second election of Barack Obama) by race/ ethnicity as compared with turnout in 2008. He first discusses 'supposed' increases in minority voting as influential in some Republicans' 'renewed need to draw in minority voters, especially Latinos, usually by agreeing to comprehensive immigration reform' (Trende, 2012: 1). Trende (2012: 1) asserts that political strategies designed to win Latino voters away from the Democrats are unlikely to be successful because issues such as income and ideology are what truly 'drive the rift between the GOP and Latinos'. Trende (2012: 2) ruminates on the reasons for, and implications of, the lack of white voter turnout: 'the 2012 elections actually weren't about a demographic explosion with non-white voters. Instead, they were about a large group of white voters not showing up'. For explanation, Trende consults a map of his home state, Ohio, focusing on the counties with the largest decreases in white votes – those in rural areas, which were still feeling the economic consequences of the recession. Trende concludes:

> But in terms of *interpreting* elections, and analyzing the future, the substantial drop-off in the white vote is a significant data point... As it stands, the bigger puzzle for figuring out the path of American politics is who these non-voters are, why they stayed home, and where they might be reactivated in 2016 (by either party). (Trende, 2019: 2)

It was during the meeting at Breitbart headquarters in Washington that Bannon, Sessions and Miller hatched a plan to use immigration as the mechanism for reconciling American conservative politics 'after a string of unexpected Republican congressional defeats' (Todd, 2019). Frontline (PBS/ Frontline, 2020) reported that Bannon came away from the meeting having determined that 'the one and two issues will be immigration and trade'. So, Trende having established that politically speaking *with immigration* is realistically and strategically untenable in competition with Democrats for Republicans, coupled with the need to turn out white 'non-voters' in rural areas, Bannon, Sessions and Miller decided to prioritize going *against immigration*. Todd (2019, n.p.) reports that 'the three men agreed immigration would hit a nerve with the working class, already sore from a collapsing factory job market, and drive its members to the polls in support of candidates who are tough on immigration'.

Jeff Sessions, former Trump administration attorney general

Jeff Sessions' record of prosecuting civil rights activists for voter fraud and supporting the removal of key elements of the Voting Rights Act are demonstrative of his tendencies toward racism and capacity to utilize systemic levers for the calculated deprivation of civil rights. In the

1980s, Sessions prosecuted civil rights activists assisting elderly African Americans to complete mail-in ballots – all were fully acquitted of any wrongdoing (Berman, 2017). As attorney general of Alabama, Sessions tried to stop the prosecution of Ku Klux Klan members who lynched a teenager. Before his 1986 federal confirmation hearings, a former Black employee testified that he was repeatedly called 'boy' by Sessions (Finley, 2017). Another former employee reported that when he shared the rumor that a civil rights lawyer had been called 'a traitor to his race', Sessions replied 'maybe he is' (Hebert, 2016). He also reportedly described the National Association for the Advancement of Colored People (NAACP) and the Civil Liberties Union as 'un-American' (Hebert, 2016). During Sessions' 2017 confirmation hearings, legendary civil rights leader, John Lewis stated before the Senate Judiciary Committee:

> Those who are committed to equal justice in our society wonder whether Senator Sessions' call for law and order will mean today what it meant in Alabama when I was coming up back then… The rule of law was used to violate the human and civil rights of the poor, dispossessed, people of color. (Berman, 2017)

Sessions also has a long history of blocking legislation advocating immigration issues and sponsoring bills related to border restriction.

Stephen Miller, Trump White House aide

Stephen Miller, who remains a senior advisor to President Trump, is originally from Santa Monica, California. At 18, he met David Horowitz, who he has called his mentor (Todd, 2019). While a student at Duke University, he invited Horowitz, author of *The Professors: The 101 Most Dangerous Academics in America*, to be a speaker on campus, which 'provoked outcry by both students and faculty, which included professors named and shamed in Horowitz's book' (Todd, 2019). While at Duke, Miller and white nationalist Richard Spencer coordinated a campus visit and speech by Peter Brimelow. Spencer is attributed with creating the term 'alt-right' (Riley, 2019).

Brimelow founded VDARE (which publishes anti-Semitic and racist content) (Resnick, 2012). On February 9, 2012, Brimelow spoke at the American Conservative Union's Conservative Political Action Conference (CPAC) on a panel entitled 'The Failure of Multiculturalism: How the Pursuit of Diversity is Weakening the American Identity' (Resnick, 2012). Moderated by ProEnglish executive director, Robert Vandervoort, the panel also included Republican House Representative Steve King and Rosalie Pedalino Porter. Porter is historically notable because she is among the most prominent and outspoken proponents for English-only instruction in schools. She was instrumental in the English-only movements that attempted to eradicate bilingual education programs in

California and Arizona in 1998 and 2000. Although California's Proposition 227 was overturned by Proposition 58 in the November 2016 election, the impact of Arizona's Proposition 203 remains devastating. Arizona's implementation of Structured/Sheltered English Immersion (SEI) has been used as a mechanism for promoting segregation in schools and continues to irreparably damage language minority students across the state (see Moore, 2014). During the panel at CPAC, Brimelow 'warned that the U.S. is losing its Anglo identity and spent most of his time talking about what he perceives as a failed system of biculturalism in Canada' (Resnick, 2012). He also claimed that bilingual education and voter translation policies damage the country's non-immigrant middle class (Resnick, 2012).

While at Duke, Miller was also president of Students for Academic Freedom and wrote a controversial bi-weekly column in the university newspaper. In 2006, when a handful of lacrosse players from Duke were accused of raping an African-American woman they had hired as a stripper at an off-campus party, he used the column to decry attacks on the players by what he termed the 'racial left'. Todd (2019) reports that Miller wrote, 'The racial left claimed the lacrosse players got preferential treatment because they were white. In reality, their skin color appeared to earn them something very different—a witchhunt [sic]'.

In January 2020, the SPLC produced email messages sent from Miller to Breitbart news editors in which he promulgated popular white nationalist ideas, such as the 'great replacement'. It is the notion that has permeated politics around the globe – us versus them. Author John Feffer (2019) referred to the great replacement as a 'genocidal playmap', writing:

> If you're not a member of the far right, if you don't subscribe to its YouTube channels or follow its burgeoning Twitter accounts, you might have only scant acquaintance with this story. But once you start looking for it, the great replacement turns out to be omnipresent. (Feffer, 2019: 1)

The demonstrations by white supremacists and white nationalists that resulted in the murder of the counter-protestor in Charlottesville, Virginia, commenced with the demanding, haunting chant, 'You will not replace us!' (Feffer, 2019). Feffer (2019) reported that between 2012 and 2016, 1.5 million tweets referenced the 'great replacement'.

Miller's email interactions also demonstrated affinity for writers such as Jason Richwine. His 2009 Harvard University doctoral dissertation claims 'The average IQ of immigrants in the United States is substantially lower than that of the white native population, and the difference is likely to persist over several generations' (Richwine, 2009: 6). The chair of Richwine's dissertation committee was George J. Borjas, who has linked immigration to a weakened economy. Writing for *Politico* in 2016, Borjas argued that

> Both low- and high-skilled natives are affected by the influx of immigrants. But because a disproportionate percentage of immigrants have

few skills, it is low-skilled American workers, including many blacks and Hispanics, who have suffered most from this wage dip. (Borjas, 2016: 1)

In 2013, Richwine was co-author of a highly critiqued paper published by the Heritage Foundation, which claimed the cost of immigration to the United States was in the millions of dollars. After the media's investigation of his background and discovery of his dissertation, Richwine resigned from the Heritage Foundation. He described author of *The Bell Curve*, Charles Murray as 'my childhood hero' (Beauchamp, 2013). Around the same time Richwine was a student at Harvard, he in fact served as a fellow at the American Enterprise Institute, which then employed Murray. More recently, Richwine (2017a) joined with Sessions and Miller in advocating for passage of the Cotton–Perdue immigration bill, which would favor immigrants with higher levels of English proficiency. In an article published by the Center for Immigration Studies Richwine (2017a: 6) reported on independent analysis of data from the Program for the International Assessment of Adult Competencies (PIAAC), claiming 'that immigrant literacy skills matter beyond the first generation. Although literacy performance of the second generation as a whole rises to match native speakers, U.S.-born Hispanics still lag well behind other natives'. Richwine (2017b: 6) concluded that 'When the United States accepts low-skill immigration, it chooses to accept a multi-generational skills deficit, with all of the socioeconomic challenges that come along with it'.

The Center for Immigration Studies was co-founded by the late John Tanton, a white nationalist and anti-immigration activist, who also founded the pro-eugenics organization, the Society for Genetic Education. According to one obituary, anti-bilingual education supporter Linda Chavez in 2011 called Tanton 'the most influential unknown man in America' (Schudel, 2019: 1). Reporting for *The Washington Post*, Matt Schudel (2019: 1) further described Tanton as 'best known for leading nationwide efforts to make English the official language of the United States and to abolish bilingual education'.

The backgrounds and pursuits of these individuals are demonstrative of the thinly veiled relationship between key figures in the Trump administration, such as Sessions and staff like Miller, and unapologetic white separatist and white nationalist movements. Movements for which anti-immigration stances are not only ordinary, but have also led to the manifestation of accepted false truths, such as those purported in *The Bell Curve* and by eugenicist John Tanton, who may be the most outspoken individual against bilingual education in contemporary politics. These are illustrative of how and why racist ideologies are embedded in Trump's anti-immigration platform.

After the counter-protestor killing in Charlottesville, in reference to the incident Trump noted during a press conference that 'you also had people that were very fine people, on both sides' (Holan, 2019). In the full exchange, reporters identified Bannon as racist, highlighted John McCain's description of the Charlottesville protestors and alt-right as hate groups and insisted on Trump sharing his perspective regarding the neo-Nazi protest. The following is a portion of the exchange:

Reporter: The neo-Nazis started this. They showed up in Charlottesville to protest—
Trump: Excuse me, excuse me. They didn't put themselves—and you had some very bad people in that group, but you also had people that were very fine people, on both sides… You had people in that group that were there to protest the taking down of, to them, a very, very important statue and the renaming of a park from Robert E. Lee to another name.
Reporter: George Washington and Robert E. Lee are not the same.
Trump: George Washington was a slave owner. Was George Washington a slave owner? So will George Washington now lose his status? Are we going to take down—excuse me, are we going to take down statues to George Washington? How about Thomas Jefferson? You like him?
Reporter: I do love Thomas Jefferson

At the 2018 CPAC, event President Trump recounted the metaphorical story he first shared in January 2016 on immigration in the United States, 'The Snake' (Rosenberg, 2018). Reporting on the original source of the story for *The Washington Post*, journalist Eli Rosenberg (2018) described it as 'a crowd-pleaser, part xenophobic fearmongering, part tale told by Grandpa – story time with Trump", as one college supporter said'. The narrative is actually lyrics to a song written by Oscar Brown Junior, an artist, singer, writer and Civil Rights activist. Brown's daughters told CNN (Vales, 2018) that 'The elephant in the room is that Trump is the living embodiment of the snake that my father wrote about in that song'. In commemoration of their father, Maggie and Africa Brown produced a compendium of his works, writing that

> For years, Trump used dad's poem to promote his message of intolerance regarding immigration. We Brown sisters went on national television to defend our father's name against the most powerful man in the world—to let it be known he was misconstruing the context to suit his agenda, and giving credit to the wrong person. (Brown & Brown, 2019: 19)

Among Trump's first actions after taking office as president was to sign an Executive Order creating stringent restrictions on immigration from seven specific countries, which his administration cited as the same that had previously been identified by President Obama as 'sources of terror' (Keilar *et al.*, 2017). The ban evoked outrage across the country, as immigrant families, immigration advocates and others were instantly terrified of separations and shifts in the way of life for transnationals associated with the seven countries. Protestors stormed airports, demanding the release of detainees who happened to be traveling from one of the countries at the time the ban went into effect. Stoking the flames, Rudy

Guliani, a close presidential advisor, and others called the Executive Order a 'Muslim ban', noting that it 'says in the order that Christians are going to be prioritized over Muslims' (Keilar *et al.*, 2017).

Responding to the first major xenophobic-driven campaign promise kept, commentators and policymakers alike surmised that the source of such a ban could be traced back not to established presidential consultants, but rather, individuals with little international or otherwise policymaking experience – notably, Bannon, Sessions and Miller. The president's Principles Committee is a group of insiders who typically advise on intelligence and national security issues, and has traditionally included both the chairman of the Joint Chiefs of Staff and the director of the National Intelligence Agency, each of whom were excused from Trump's Principles Committee and replaced by Bannon and others (Keilar *et al.*, 2017).

Department of Education (ED) Under Trump

Secretary of Education, Betsy DeVos

Among the more controversial presidential agency appointments by Trump was that of Betsy DeVos to ED. DeVos, the product of a wealthy family (her father co-founded the auto parts company, Prince Corp.) from Holland, Michigan, married into the DeVos fortune. *Forbes* writer Chase Peterson-Withorn (2019) estimated that 'together, Betsy DeVos, her husband and their four adult children are worth roughly $2 billion'. The majority of that amount is through stock holdings in Amway, a multi-level marketing company largely accused of functioning as a pyramid scheme. DeVos' brother, Erik Prince, is founder of Blackwater, the military contracting company responsible for attacking a group of 31 unarmed civilians, 14 of whom were killed in Iraq in 2007. Claims have also been made that Prince sought out Russian back-channel connections early on in the Trump administration (see Kirsch, 2018). DeVos' appointment was particularly odd, given that she lacked any time working in public schools, districts or systems of schooling – she has no teaching experience whatsoever.

DeVos and school privatization

In addition to her lack of experience in the field of education, among the most concerning issues related to the DeVos appointment is her family's emboldened promotion of school privatization, particularly through creation of charter schools for 'at risk' youth. Critics claim that her involvement in Detroit's public schools all but froze educational opportunities for school children. In 2001, DeVos founded the Great Lakes Education Project (GLEP), with the goal of 'supporting quality choices in public education for all Michigan students' (Nazaryan, 2017).

In the 2015/2016 school year, California had the highest number of students enrolled in charter schools, followed by Texas, Florida, Arizona and then Michigan (Ballotpedia, n.d.). Since the 2012/2013 school year, in both

Detroit and Flint, Michigan, over half of K-12 student enrollment shares go to public charter schools (National Alliance for Public Charter Schools, 2016). Lake *et al*. (2015) reported that Detroit public schools 'lost two-thirds of its enrollment' between 2005 and 2012. Despite designation as non-profits, schools run by charter school management companies are, to the contrary, more likely to be for-profit businesses, traded on the stock market. For the charter school business, students mean income; as a result of decreased enrollments and the boon of Detroit charter schools following a 2012 law (largely supported by DeVos-founded organizations and backed by their financial support) that eliminated the cap on charters, competition to fill seats was fierce. Lake *et al*. (2015: 22) noted that 'a parent advocate called the competition for students a "snatch and grab"' and 'a district official likened it to "guerilla warfare"'. The charter scenario in Detroit has been further exacerbated by a lack of leadership, very little oversight and few standards for accountability. Lake *et al*. (2015: 24) reported that 'authorizers are free to open schools wherever they choose, regardless of need, and to allow poor-performing schools to remain open'.

According to research conducted by the National Education Policy Center (Miron & Gulosino, 2013), in the 2011/2012 school year, Michigan students made up almost 20% of all charter school students in the country. Further, of those schools, nearly 80% were run by for-profit entities, as compared with 16% nationwide. The National Alliance for Public Charter Schools (Hesla *et al*., 2019) ranked Detroit fifth in the country in terms of charter school enrollment, at 46% of students.

Charter schools

Nationally, the proportion of charter schools to public schools has tripled since 2000 (Author, 2018a). The promotion of charter schools by ED emerged well before DeVos' tenure as Secretary. Under the direction of Secretary Arne Duncan, the Obama administration created several programs that 'gave states strong incentive to reduce or eliminate caps that had previously limited charter school expansion' (Rotberg, 2014: 26). The competitive $4.35 billion Race to the Top program disadvantaged states without charter schools and those with laws limiting their numbers. Obama advocated strongly for charter schools, planning to double funding for them during his time as president. In 2004, only 2% of students attended charter schools, increasing to 3% when Obama took office. By the time he left office in 2016, the number had doubled to 6% (Strauss, 2016). As *Washington Post* reporter Valerie Strauss recounted in 2016:

> as charter schools grow with administration support, charter supporters and opponents are in a scorched-earth war of words, with both sides claiming the civil rights mantle and accusing the other of harming children. When the NAACP, the nation's oldest civil rights organization, last week ratified a referendum calling for a moratorium on new charters until new accountability

measures can be instituted, critics accused of it [sic] being no more than the racist former governor of Alabama, George Wallace. (Strauss, 2016)

Charter schools and language minority students

Navigating charter school systems can be especially challenging for parents of students with special needs and language minority learners. Complex charter systems offer myriad choices for school selection, which require families' acquaintance with the various options. For example, charters may have particular areas of focus, such as science, technology and engineering or the arts. A study of choice schools in areas of Connecticut found that English learners were under-represented across sites (Cotto & Feder, 2014). They found that 76% of charters, 64% of magnets and 56% of technical schools 'had substantially lower ELL enrollment—5 percentage points or fewer below the local public schools' (Cotto & Feder, 2014: 16). Even more troubling, they found divisions more acute in areas with higher percentages of enrolled English learners demographically. In citing factors contributing to the disparity, the authors offer that procedures and required forms may be burdensome and require a certain level of English knowledge and skills to complete. In addition, Connecticut law (in keeping with 1970s-era *Lau* Remedies) may deter the schools themselves because it requires the creation of bilingual programs for cases in which more than 20 students from a shared language background are enrolled in a single school (Cotto & Feder, 2014: 17).

In a 2013 report on findings from a study conducted by the Government Accountability Office (GAO) based on review of data from the 2010/2011 school year, it was not possible to determine English learners' demographic status in charter schools because many sites were not reporting on enrollment. 'Specifically, for over one-third of charter schools, the field for reporting the counts of ELLs enrolled in ELL programs was left blank' (U.S. Government Accountability Office, 2013: 2). Even more troubling, 'In two states generally known to have large numbers of ELLs, New York and New Jersey, over 80 percent of charter schools had blank fields' (U.S. Government Accountability Office, 2013: 5). Figure 1.2 illustrates the percentage of blanks regarding the presence of English learners in charter school reports by state (U.S. Government Accountability Office, 2013: 6).

A study of student demographics in charter schools in Washington, DC's Office of the State Superintendent of Education (equivalent to the state education agency) (a city that consistently ranks within the top five for charter student enrollment numbers) compared data to those of students in District of Columbia Public Schools (DCPS) (Buckley & Schneider, 2005). Researchers found evidence that proportions of English learners are lower in charter schools than DCPS schools. According to data from the National Center for Education Statistics (NCES), as of fall 2016, several of the states with the largest percentages of charters also share educational demographics

A Racist White House 19

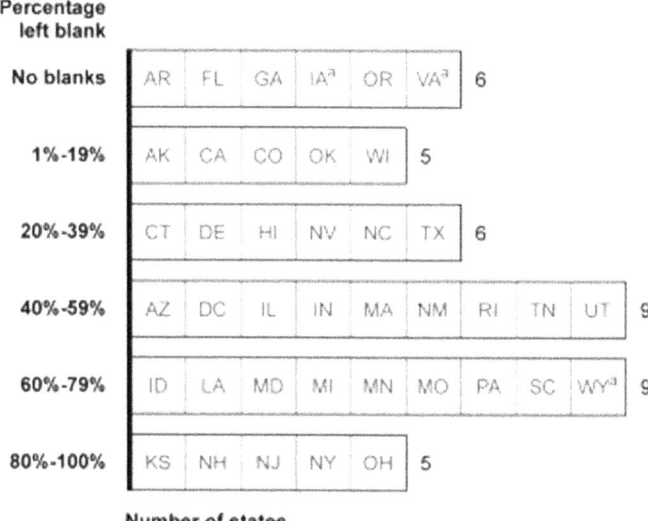

Source: GAO analysis of Education's school-level ELL enrollment data for SY2010-11.

[a]States with less than 5 charter schools operating in school year 2010-11.

Figure 1.2 English learners in charter schools by state

with high enrollments of English learners. A total of 17% of students in Arizona were enrolled in charters, where English learners are 7.5% of overall students. Similarly, 10% of Florida students were enrolled in charters, where 5% of students are identified as English learners.

Failing Government Schools

During the 2020 presidential State of the Union address, on February 4, Trump described the United States' public school system as 'failing government schools'. Highlighting a student in the audience, he pronounced, 'Now, I call on the Congress to give 1 million American children the same opportunity Janiyah has just received. Pass the New Education Freedom Scholarships and Opportunity Act – because no parent should be forced to send their child to a failing government school' (Strauss, 2020: 1). As opposed to Trump's 2016 campaign, in 2020, DeVos was front and center in championing school privatization as part of the president's re-election campaign platform. She traveled with Vice President Pence denouncing Democrats' calls for tuition-free postsecondary education, claiming it would come with strings attached and limits on what students would learn at public universities (Stratford, 2020). At a rally in Pennsylvania on February 6, she decried Democrats' 'socialist' plans for education, pronouncing that 'They want to close every charter school, take away every educational option from low-income families, limit choices everywhere for everyone' (Stratford, 2020: 2). An individual close to DeVos claimed that turning to education may be the next target for the Trump administration, 'it's our turn… We got through the tax cuts, trade deals and immigration' (Stratford, 2020: 3).

The president's FY 2021 budget was released on February 10, 2020. In it, the ED budget is reduced by 8.4% (Rivers, 2020) and elements of the Elementary and Secondary Education Act intended to protect underserved populations, including poor families and those from ethnically and linguistically diverse backgrounds, are consolidated into a single state block program. As part of the consolidation, the 27 programs' funding would be reduced by 19.5% overall (Rivers, 2020) compared with FY 2020. The proposed budget's description reads 'This consolidation would allow those closest to students to meet the needs of their students and families. While increasing flexibility, the new block grant also saves taxpayers $4.7 billion' (Office of Management and Budget, 2020).

Changing Trajectories

Having painted a broad stroke picture of the influence of racism on politics and policymaking and their relationship to language minority schooling, the chapters in this book will lay out how, between 1968 and the mid-1980s, civil and language rights activists successfully created systemic supports for bilingual education. Little data exist regarding the percentage of English learners and heritage language speakers enrolled in bilingual education or dual language educational settings. However, a report of the National Advisory Council for Bilingual Education (1977: 65) cited evidence that '1.3 million school students were of limited English-speaking ability and therefore in need of bilingual education. Of these, only 40 percent were enrolled in bilingual education programs'. By establishing a clear understanding of the political background within which these existed, as well as the mechanisms through which they were enacted into policy and implemented from the federal level to the ground, the field is better prepared for the expansion and enhancement of bilingual and dual language education on a national scale in the United States. Understanding the conditions that led to politicians' support for bilingual education presents the opportunity to strategically and deliberately recreate comparable circumstances. Navigating the politics of policymaking and instituting structures that permeate systems of schooling to ensure smooth and consistently orchestrated language education programs may lead to a new, multilingual reality for future generations.

2 Prequel to the Bilingual Education Act

> A foreign home-language is not a handicap, unless the educational process (informal and formal) makes it so. A foreign mother-tongue can be, and is for many, a decided advantage if properly cultivated—and for centuries we have known that a second language is learned best if the vernacular is developed… Please, do not fall into the common error of attributing all ills of people with a non-English vernacular to 'language handicap.' I remember meeting Albert Einstein—his English left a bit to be desired!
>
> George I. Sánchez, March 6, 1961, quoted in Blanton (2014: 229), 'perhaps the first academic to promote the idea that Mexican American students should be taught in Spanish first. He had been proposing this since 1935' (González, 2011: 34).

American Bilingual Education

Numerous scholars of language and education policy have studied the extent to which languages other than English have been historically incorporated into schooling (Andersson, 1971; Fishman, 1966; Kloss, 1977/1998; Wiley, 1998). Early bilingual schools were established in 1840 in Cincinnati (Schlossman, 1983). Schlossman (1983: 144; citing DeBoer, 1968; Forbes & Lemos, 1981; Kloss, 1977/1978; Wagner, 1981; Wright, 2019) contended 'There is no question that in many one-room, one-teacher rural schools throughout the Midwest, the native tongue was used as the language of instruction to introduce first- and second-generation German children to public schools'. In Cincinnati public schools for example, a German Senior Teachers Association was founded in 1863 and a German-American Teachers Association in 1870 (Kloss, 1977/1998). Table 2.1 shows the increases in pupil enrollment in German schools between 1841 and 1914. In Indianapolis,

> a resolution offered as early as December 1, 1856 in the regular session of the Indianapolis City Council to the effect that a portion of the school fund be appropriated to educate the German children of the city in 'their own language', or for the employment of a German teacher for their instruction, and that the school trustees be instructed to make the necessary investigation and examination into the expenditure consequent upon the same. (Ellis, 1954: 120)

Table 2.1 Cincinnati pupils in German medium schools

Year	Number of pupils
1841	327
1851	1,339
1860	4,788
1870	10,440
1886	16,410
1902	17,200
1914	14,600

Source: Kloss (1977/1998: 203). Reprinted with permission from the Center for Applied Linguistics.

On January 5, 1859, *The Indianapolis Journal* proclaimed that 'A proper knowledge of the German language is important to everyone American or German and German education is all the more valuable' (Ellis, 1954: 122).

In the late 19th and early 20th centuries, privileged children living in Mexican territories, such as California, New Mexico and Texas, attended Catholic colleges, which provided a 'smooth continuity with the Spanish language, culture (sex segregation, for example), and religion distinct from the public universities' (National Park Service, n.d.). Many of these began at the secondary level and articulated into postsecondary instruction, the most prominent of which included 'Santa Clara College in San Jose, California (1851); Saint Michael's College in Santa Fe, New Mexico (1859); ...Notre Dame College in San Jose, California (1868); and Our Lady of the Lake in San Antonio, Texas (1895)' (National Park Service, n.d.). As noted by Macías:

> After Texas and California became states in 1845 and 1850 respectively, measures were introduced to restrict the medium of instruction in the public schools to English. In 1870 the California state legislature enacted a statute providing that all the schools in the state (religious and public) be taught in the English language bringing a crippling blow to the bilingual parochial schools. (Macías, 2015)

When California became a state in 1850, its 1849 Constitution provided that 'All laws, decrees, regulations, and provisions, which from their nature require publication, shall be published in English and Spanish' (Article XI, Miscellaneous Provisions, §21, as cited by Macías, 2014: 45). At the time of its statehood, 18% of students were enrolled in parochial schools (Ewing, 1918; Leibowitz, 1971, cited by Macías, 2014) which 'were usually taught in Spanish, and, of course, consisted mostly of Mexican origin students' (Macías, 2014: 45, citing Sappiens, 1979). Despite these examples of multilingual education (numerous additional cases have been documented, see Kloss, 1977/1998), English-dominant hegemonies and Americanization and anti-immigration movements later led to restrictionist educational language policies.

English monolingualism

The United States has a storied past of using language as a mechanism for power brokering and a proxy for prejudicial, racist and othering ideologies. The notion that immigrants should favor English at the expense of their native language maintenance is historically pervasive. English speaking as a marker of Americanism has been described as the ideology of English monolingualism (Macías, 1985; Wiley, 2000; Wright, 2019). As Wiley (2004: 322) noted, 'the ideology of English monolingualism has a long history, with antecedents dating from the colonial and early nationalist periods in the writings of influential individuals such as Benjamin Franklin and Noah Webster'. Further, Wiley refers to four arguments that aim to justify ideologies promoting societal monolingualism. First, that language minority speakers concede maintenance of their languages in exchange for the privilege of living in the receiving society. Second, because immigrants will benefit economically from life in the new country, they should transition to use of the dominant language. Third, the claim that maintenance of the native language and culture will lead to isolation from the mainstream and majority linguistic and cultural practices; therefore, immigrants will not benefit from opportunities that would be available as English-dominant speakers. And lastly, that language serves as a national unifying force.

Examples of linguistic and human rights violations are prevalent throughout American history. The annihilation of languages and their speakers among Native American, American Indian, Alaska Native and other Indigenous peoples due to the European invasion of the land on which the United States is located 'constituted genocide' (Adams, 1995; Alvarez, 2014; McCarty, 2013). 'Following the European invasion, European-introduced diseases and the seizure of Indigenous lands plunged Native populations – and languages – into drastic decline' (McCarty, 2013: 4). As with federal policies that robbed Indigenous peoples of their land, 'The education policy… was to undermine the culture of the American Indian, by uprooting him or her from the home and forcing a disciplined education process in a boarding school' (Sharpes, 1979: 19). Dr Richard Little Bear, Northern Cheyenne and president and dean of cultural affairs at Chief Dull Knife College, described the history of language loss:

> The cavalrymen, ethnologists, missionaries, anthropologists and linguists who were the first to write Native American languages had their own reasons for doing so, but often they wrote them without any thought whatsoever about saving them, let alone trying to strengthen them. Worse, the U.S. government did its best to, first, try to kill the people who spoke

these languages. When that didn't succeed, it went about, through government dicta, systematically killing the languages themselves and the cultures those languages promoted. (Littlebear, 2001: 5)

As Henrietta Whiteman (1985: 31) reminded, 'Beginning in the year 1568, American Indians were thrust into an alien educational environment in which their languages, the very expressions of their tribal respective cultures, had no relevance or validity from the perspective of their teachers'.

Enslaved Africans forcefully relocated to North America were prohibited from speaking mother tongue languages and forced to speak English only because owners and overseers feared conspiracy and revolt (Wiley & Lukes, 1996). Dyson *et al.* (2020: 358) contend that the cultural tradition of folktales emerged from prohibiting African languages among the enslaved. 'There was no commonly shared African language by which all those enslaved Africans from different groups could understand each other... the plantation system was structured to ensure the widespread adoption of English as the sole language spoken among the slave population'. Expert scholar on the evolution of African-American language, John Rickford, noted in a 2018 National Public Radio interview, 'Slaves were required to learn the language of their masters. That's why black Americans speak English and not Yoruba' (Devarajan, 2018). Enslaved Africans 'spoke Akan, Efik, Fula, Ga, Hausa, Ibibio, Igbo, Kikongo, Kimbundu, Mandingo, Mbundu, Swahili, Temna, Tshiluba, Twi, Wolof, and Yoruba' (Kelley, 2015: 109).

Among the few successful slave revolts, the 1739 Stono Rebellion in South Carolina may have been possible because collaborating Kongolese leaders were highly skilled, with military training and experience using firearms. The tactics employed were reminiscent of warfare methods in Angola in the 17th century, where upper-class community members would have been literate in Portuguese and religiously devout Catholics, likely sending their children to Catholic schools (see Smith, 2001; Thornton, 1991). The multilingual Kongolese may have been secretly communicating with visiting Spanish forces nearby, which offered freedom to escaped slaves in neighboring regions (Smith, 2001; Thornton, 1991).

Until the mid-20th century, children in schools across the Southwest endured corporal punishment for speaking Spanish and were often forced to Anglicize their names (Blanton, 2004; Saldaña, 2013; Skrentny, 2002). Texas, for example, instituted strict English-only policies for the teaching of language minority students, which 'eventually became a functionary branch of all Tejano education' (Blanton, 2004: 80). English-only policies and curricula were implemented 'ruthlessly to Spanish-speaking children to the exclusion of other subjects and in a manner that suggested that knowledge in Spanish was unimportant' (Blanton, 2004: 82). This, despite a 'tangled' (Blanton, 2004) history beginning with 16th-century attempts by the Spanish to convert Native Americans to Christianity.

'One missionary noted that simply overcoming the language barrier was their first and foremost problem' (Blanton, 2004: 12). In fact, in 1871, the first Texas Superintendent of Instruction created policies 'explicitly sanctioning a limited amount of bilingualism in the classroom' in German, French and Spanish (Blanton, 2004: 19). Bilingual schools existed in many parts of Texas through the early 20th century, when they began to suffer due to rise of the Americanization movement.

Eugenics, nativism and the Americanization movement

Defining 'Americanism', national loyalties and the conflation of language use and patriotism has been well documented (Kloss, 1977/1998; Spolsky, 2004; Wiley, 1998, 2004, 2019). The Americanization movement lasted from approximately 1914 to 1925 and was indispensably connected with 'status ascription based on racialization' (Wiley, 2019: 139). In 1909, Ellwood Patterson Cubberley, professor of education at Leland Stanford Junior University asserted that

> southern and eastern Europeans are of a very different type from the north Europeans who preceded them. Illiterate, docile, lacking in self-reliance and initiative, and not possessing the Anglo Teutonic conceptions of law, order, and government, their coming has served to dilute tremendously our national stock, and to corrupt our civic life. (Cubberly, 1909: 15)

As is recounted in Wiley (1998), H.H. Goddard brought the first tests of intelligence (conducted in English) to Ellis Island in 1917, for use in assessing the intellect of arriving immigrants. During this period, nativism and eugenics were each gaining popularity and developing mainstream followings. Goddard later used the same assessment (the Stanford–Binet) to test English literacy levels among military draftees, organizing results based on comparisons of ethnic group background, with Nordics' outcomes highest ranking and Mediterraneans' (Greeks and Italians) lowest (Wiley, 1998: 100). In Texas and across the South, IQ tests were used to justify the segregation of non-white and Mexican-origin students. As Blanton recounted:

> The state of Texas in the early 1920s commissioned IQ research by scholars Helen Lois Koch and Rietta Simmons. Through a host of flawed, methodological practices, they argued that Mexican American children were inherently less intelligent than whites… They took their conclusions so far that, in light of their own admission of a lack of conclusive evidence, they still concluded that darker-skinned Mexican Americans scored lower and were, thus, less intelligent than those of lighter skin. (Blanton, 2004: 71)

Madison Grant, a lawyer, zoologist and eugenicist in New York City wrote *The Passing of the Great Race*, first published in 1917. Hitler closely followed Grant's claims of racial superiority and eugenics; it was a key source for the rationale supporting the genocide of Jews across Europe. Grant wrote:

> The result of unlimited immigration is showing plainly in the rapid decline in the birth rate of native Americans because the poorer classes of colonial stock, where they still exist, will not bring children into the world to compete in the labor market with the Slovak, the Italian, the Syrian and the Jew. The native American is too proud to mix socially with them and is gradually withdrawing from the scene, abandoning to these aliens the land which he conquered and developed. The man of the old stock is being crowded out of many country districts by these foreigners just as he is today being literally driven off the streets of New York City by the swarms of Polish Jews. These immigrants adopt the language of the native American, they wear his clothes, they steal his name and they are beginning to take his women, but they seldom adopt his religion or understand his ideals and while he is being elbowed out of his own home the American looks calmly abroad and urges on others, the suicidal ethics which are exterminating his own race. (Grant, 1917: 81)

Attacks on immigrant identity were not limited to language background or intelligence. Nativists, moreover, called for full *deculturation* – divesting one's cultural and linguistic background entirely in favor of allegiance to the new country. In a speech before the Knights of Columbus in 1915, Theodore Roosevelt lamented 'hyphenated Americanism':

> What is true of creed is no less true of nationality. There is no room in this country for hyphenated Americanism. When I refer to hyphenated Americans, I do not refer to naturalized Americans. Some of the very best Americans I have ever known were naturalized Americans, Americans born abroad. But a hyphenated American is not an American at all. This is just as true of the man who puts 'native' before the hyphen as of the man who puts German or Irish or English or French before the hyphen. Americanism is a matter of the spirit and of the soul. Our allegiance must be purely to the United States. We must unsparingly condemn any man who holds any other allegiance. But if he is heartily and singly loyal to this Republic, then no matter where he was born, he is just as good an American as any one else. (Roosevelt, 1915)

The Americanization movement and nativism ultimately led to the 1924 Immigration Act, which created quotas for immigrants by country, strictly restricting immigrant and refugee entry into the United States.

As Wiley (2019: 138) writes, 'In education policy, this era was the period when Americanization and rapid assimilation became the national formula for social integration, and the use of only English became the litmus test for loyalty and patriotism (Weiss, 1982)'. During World War I, between 1917 and 1922, 34 states passed legislation requiring English-only medium of instruction in schools (Wiley & Wright, 2004; Wright, 2019).

During World War II, the refugee restrictions put in place as part of the Immigration Act were not waived (Pedraza-Bailey & Sullivan, 1979). This meant that Jewish refugees, including children, forced into ghettos in Europe, were effectively trapped, with little chance of escape. During this time, the United States and most of the rest of the world stood strongly against admitting Jewish refugees into other countries. Following a meeting with representatives from around the world in 1938 to discuss the European refugee crisis, the only country that agreed to admit refugees was the Dominican Republic. Then Dictator Rafael Trujillo, a believer of eugenics, hoped that racially Anglican refugees from Europe would improve qualities of the Dominican population (Facing History and Ourselves, n.d.). Following World War II, Truman promulgated an executive decree in 1945 and later pushed for the passage of the 1948 Displaced Persons Act, which again allowed for refugee entry into the United States.

The first 'precedent regarding Mexicans and equal protection law' (Green, 2008: 549) emerged in *Méndez v. Westminster School District* in 1946. *Méndez* was filed against the Westminster, Garden Grove, Santa Ana, and El Modena School Districts in March 1945. In the case 'petitioners argued that the school districts intentionally segregated Mexican heritage school children' (Green, 2008: 549) by denying access to Anglo schools. Judge Paul McCormick concurred with plaintiffs' claims stating, (Green, 2008: 550) '"It is also established by the record that the methods of segregation prevalent in the defendant's school districts foster antagonisms in the children and suggest inferiority among them where none exists"'. It is notable that for purposes of the case, Mexican schoolchildren were identified as 'Caucasian' – meaning discrimination was based not on race, but on national origin. The *Méndez* decision was an important contribution to the future *Brown v. Board of Education* case.

World War II Era

The study of bilingualism in schooling and approaches to instruction for bilinguals was ongoing during the World War II era and later. Tireman (1944) conducted a review of research regarding 'bilingual children', citing numerous studies of bilingual children and students' linguistic development and academic progress. Smith (1942), for example, studied 'correlations between the college aptitude tests and grade point ratios', finding that although bilinguals' college entry scores were impacted, there was no influence on achievement after entrance. Tireman (1944) recounted recommendations from Wooten (1941), whose research concerned hetero versus homogeneous groupings of native English- and Spanish-speaking students, some characteristics of which resonate with contemporary approaches to dual language instruction (apart from language-based division of students). 'She would divide the class [by language background]', reports Tireman.

> The English students should have a Spanish-speaking vocabulary of three hundred words by the end of the first six weeks. The Spanish section should be given work in written Spanish and the correction of errors. 'Every third word is English or an English distortion.' By the third six-weeks period the two groups can be merged, if the Anglo-American group has been given the proper grand work. (Tireman, 1944: 275)

Tireman and Watson (1943) conducted a five-year experiment in a school composed of native Spanish-speaking students in New Mexico, finding 'native Spanish-speaking children will progress as English-speaking children do if proper methods of instruction are used' (as cited in Tireman, 1944: 276):

> The three R's did not suffer and a great deal of additional information was learned about health and conservation. 'Reading Comprehension is close to, or above, the normal expectation in the first five grades' (Tireman & Watson, 1943: 110). This seems to support the point of view that native Spanish-speaking children will progress as English-speaking children do if proper methods of instruction are used.

Pauline Martz Rojas (1946, 1948) was among early advocates for the development of programs specially designed for bilingual children and adults, noting that English should be framed as a foreign language to bilingual children, who therefore should be taught by educators prepared to teach English as a foreign language in US schools and elsewhere. In 1946, Rojas both referenced the illegitimacy of conflating language proficiency with intelligence and lamented school systems' inadequacy to support the needs of bilingual learners.

> All too frequently the child's inability to cope satisfactorily with situations in which language is the prime factor is interpreted as evidence of low intelligence, and foreign-speaking children are frequently catalogued on the basis of scores on intelligence tests of the verbal type. In other cases, the child's inability to handle English adequately is attributed to his perversity, and the attitude is taken that both he and his parents could speak English if they so desired. The failure of teachers

and administrators to understand that the educational problem of the bilingual child is a problem in linguistics is a failure of American education. (Rojas, 1946: 204)

Two years later, Rojas (1948: 322) also highlighted the emergence of 'teacher-training programs in the teaching of English as a foreign language'. She noted barriers to supporting the needs of bilingual learners as rooted in social and economic problems, as well as cultural conflicts, referencing 'racial prejudice and social snobbishness' as explanations for limited expenditures by schools. Further, Rojas (1948: 323) asserted that educational systems' bilingual students' 'cultural background has been ignored along with their linguistic background'. Rojas would later play a pivotal, groundbreaking leadership role in establishing the first federally funded bilingual program for Cuban refugee students in Miami, Florida.

National Defense Education Act

The end of World War II and the start of the Cold War during the 1950s brought new focus on the need for schools in the United State to improve the quality of educational outcomes among Americans for competition against global adversaries. Sputnik was launched by Russia in 1957, sparking national concern that the United States lagged behind global opponents in the race to the moon. Co-sponsored by Senator Ralph Yarborough (who would later be among the strongest advocates for the Bilingual Education Act [BEA]), on February 9, 1958, President Dwight D. Eisenhower signed the National Defense Education Act (NDEA) into law. It provided 1 billion dollars over seven years for numerous educational programs, including fellowships and financial aid for the study of foreign languages, math and sciences. Specifically regarding language instruction, it included

> loans to college scholarship funds for students intending to teach in elementary or secondary schools or with defense-related specialties; graduate fellowships for students interested in college teaching; seed money to induce states to establish programs for testing, guidance, and counseling in secondary schools; money to allow colleges to increase provision for advanced foreign language training. (Davies, 2007: 14)

Although it predates the fellowships later funded by Title VII of the Elementary and Secondary Education Act (ESEA), the NDEA model is similar – institutes of higher education were the access points through which individuals obtained the education and training necessary to collectively impact the education workforce on a broad scale. The extent and scope of educator preparation accomplished through the NDEA constituted the first model for pathways into particular content areas and marked the first national investment in education.

> By the summer of 1959, the NDEA had created twelve foreign language institutes to train 925 teachers. By 1963, it had trained 17,400 teachers, and by 1968, there were 106 foreign language and area studies centers receiving $18 million in federal aid. (Skrentny, 2002: 185)

The Language Development Program was designed 'to insure trained manpower of sufficient quality and quantity to meet the national defense needs of the United States' (Public Law 85-864, 1958). Highlights of a report on the first two years of the Language Development Program (NDEA Title VI) include the creation of resources and other supports for foreign language teaching and learning. About $6.5 million was devoted to studies, surveys, research and the development of specialized materials for teaching foreign languages. Instructional curricula were created for 66 world languages, as well as 17 'dialectical variants'. Materials and tests were developed for use in secondary schools for basic skills in the five most commonly taught foreign languages. Research was conducted regarding how best to leverage electromechanical aids for language learning and addressed the effectiveness of methodologies and pedagogical practices for language instruction. Proficiency tests were developed addressing seven competencies in the five most commonly taught foreign languages for both students and educators. NDEA funds were also used to conduct nationwide surveys of foreign language student enrollment.

Although the NDEA may have had little impact on notions around bilingual and/or 'bilingual-bicultural' education, as was initially termed in the first 1968 version of the BEA, it is notable as the first large-scale federal funding to target education and, more specifically, the teaching and learning of languages. The NDEA represents the beginning of the expansion of education programs and supports, which will, in part, later lead to Title VII of the 1965 ESEA. 'NDEA was, as *Congressional Quarterly* later noted, "by far the largest federal commitment to the national general education level" in history, authorizing expenditures of over $1 billion' Davies (2007: 16). As Blanton (2004: 125) notes, between 1959 and 1963, 'NDEA language learning centers increased from nineteen to fifty-five, modern language fellowship awards increased from 171 to 902'.

The NDEA also induced the convening of language educators, which later prompted the founding of both the American Council for the Teaching and Learning of Foreign Languages (ACTFL) and the Teaching of English to Speakers of Other Languages (TESOL) member associations. Both continue to advocate for language education, regularly host national and international convenings and serve crucial roles in facilitating interaction and collaboration around the teaching and learning of languages for educators and other stakeholders around the world. Each has, respectively, earned a pre-eminent position for foreign and English language instructional programs and other areas.

Passage of the NDEA and a new national focus on language also prompted the founding of the Center for Applied Linguistics (CAL) in Washington, DC, which was pivotal in focusing global attention and fostering discussions on the study of languages and linguistics and the role and function of language in society. CAL remains instrumental in the fields of language education and applied linguistics across a wide range of topics. It provides technical assistance regarding federal language education policies and develops and delivers professional development and resources-related language instruction to states and districts across the country. Especially during debates around bilingual education in the 1970s and 1980s, CAL and its leadership, particularly Dr Rudolph Troike, were respected for decisive and well-informed research and resource dissemination regarding language acquisition, its application to schooling and the importance of bilingual education.

1960s Immigration, Politics and Schooling

In order to understand bilingual-bicultural education in the United States and situate the genesis of the BEA, a review of trends in immigration, sociopolitical movements and newfound emphasis on linguistic and cultural maintenance is critical.

Mexican immigration and Mexican-Americans

During World War II, the United States formally invited workers from Mexico to fill employment needs in the agricultural industry through the *bracero* program. Although the system ended in 1964, it brought several immigration waves from Mexico and initiated a long-standing economic relationship between it and the United States, in which the United States relied on migratory farmworkers for its agricultural workforce (Moore *et al.*, 2014). In the portions of Mexico annexed by the United States in 1848, following the Mexican-American War, linguistic and cultural connections were largely maintained well into the 20th century and through the 1950s and 1960s. Especially in communities along the border, Spanish continued to be the primary language used in homes and everyday communication, if not the medium of instruction in schools. Mexican-Americans throughout the Southwest endured a particularly militaristic approach to assimilation, in large part waged through the mechanism of schooling. By the 1960s and 1970s, Mexican-American and Chicano activists' protests were escalating, with substantive focus on issues of equity and schooling. Gutiérrez (2011) described the emphasis on education:

The main Chicano targets for reform in the 1960s were the public schools. The teachers, curriculum, cafeteria food, textbooks, testing, student culture and life, school administration, and governance structure were all Anglocentric. English was the only language allowed spoken in the classroom and schoolyard. Severe punishment awaited the bold who uttered their native Spanish language within earshot of school officials or Anglo students who also reported them. Despite their growing numbers, Chicano students, while physically present for purposes of enrollment counts and audits that led to more state funding, were ignored and bypassed in their academic needs. (Gutiérrez, 2011: 26)

A key movement contributing to Mexican-Americans' civil rights was the expansion and tenets of the United Farm Workers union, led by César Chávez. Chávez fought for migrant farmworkers' rights and 'organized a national boycott of grapes, went on hunger strike to publicize his cause of improving the low wages and poor work conditions of fruit pickers in California' (Skrentny, 2002: 196).

…by the end of sixties, many new Chicano leaders were in favor of ethnically separate institutions. When Chicano students staged mass boycotts of four East Los Angeles high schools in March of 1968, integration was not among the demands they presented to the city school board. Instead, they asked for more bilingual programs, new courses on Chicano history and culture, Mexican food in the cafeterias, more Spanish-speaking faculty and the firing of 'anti-Mexican' teachers (as well as increased student rights, liberalized dress codes and up-grading of facilities). (Wollenberg, 1975: 154)

Similarly, Rodolfo Gonzales launched the Crusade for Justice in Denver in 1966, calling for 'Chicano nationalism' in support of fights against 'school discrimination, police brutality, and other discrimination' (Skrentny, 2002: 196).

Puerto Rican-Americans

The second of two major waves of Puerto Rican immigration to New York occurred after 1945, when access to air travel became more widely available. Charles Abrams (1955) lamented the 'Puerto Rican Problem', describing migrants' participation in the labor force:

The Puerto Rican immigration has been a boon to employers, bringing in a rich supply of cheap labor… Almost 20,000 Puerto Ricans, mainly women have been absorbed by the garment industry and almost 10,000 men by hotels and restaurants, while tens of thousands of others have found factory work or employment in building or domestic service. (Abrams, 1955)

Nieto (2000: 9), citing Rand (1958), noted that 'By 1957, 550,000 or a quarter of all the Puerto Rican people lived in the United States'. From 1953 to 1957, the Puerto Rican Study was conducted to investigate Puerto Ricans in New York City schools. The most comprehensive study of this area up to that time, recommendations included improving English as a second language (ESL) opportunities for Puerto Rican students, which ultimately led to the presence of substantive numbers of Puerto Rican educators. In 1965, an ethnographic study of Puerto Rican students in New York City schools revealed disturbing details demonstrating systemic assimilationist ideologies pervasive across schools (Bucchioni, 1982). In April 1967, the First Citywide Conference of the Puerto Rican Community resulted in a series of recommendations to the mayor of New York City. These included investments in both bilingual education as well as programs and courses in Puerto Rican history and culture.

Findings from an investigative report based on visits to 16 schools in seven cities with significant populations of Puerto Ricans published in 1968, titled *The Losers* (Margolis, 1968), was particularly troubling. Margolis found 'high drop-out and low attendance rates, poor academic achievement, and teachers and administrators who were uninformed and unsympathetic to the plight of Puerto Rican American students' (Nieto, 2000: 16).

Cubans in Miami

In the 1950s and 1960s, Cubans fleeing the Castro regime to the Miami area of Florida constituted the most rapidly growing population of immigrants in the country (Pedraza-Bailey & Sullivan, 1979). Both Presidents Eisenhower and Kennedy routed funds in support of receiving and resettling refugees and, in 1962, the Migration and Refugee Assistance Act codified by Congress created funds for a range of supports, including transportation costs from Cuba, financial assistance to both individuals and state and local agencies, and employment and professional training (Pedraza-Bailey & Sullivan, 1979).

Prior to later support for bilingual programs in Miami-Dade, as early as 1961, a makeshift school was set up in the Florida City refugee center (it was licensed to house 700 unaccompanied minor Cuban refugees) for girls and younger boys. Lawyer Leopoldo Arista was convinced to work as a teacher by Mother María Paz (one of six sisters who helped run the center [Triay, 1998: 61]), who tricked him into visiting a classroom in Florida City. In a book devoted to the Cuban Children's Program, Conde (1999) recounted Arista's experience teaching.

> We once had 1,122 children in Florida City. Imagine the situation we had, sometimes two children per chair... The classes were very informal, as you didn't know how long you would have a child in them. We taught

them a small English vocabulary, tried to explain the differences between American and Cuban cultures, things to help them assimilate. (Conde, 1999: 95)

The sizeable wave of refugees fleeing Cuba and arriving in Florida, particularly Miami, along with the political interests of Kennedy and later President Johnson were ideal circumstances for laying the foundation to creating a bilingual model of schooling. Unlike other immigrant groups of the time, Cubans were provided with substantive federal funds for a wide range of social, economic and education-based supports. Writing in 1979 regarding bilingual education for Cubans, Pedraza-Bailey and Sullivan (1979: 384) recounted, 'Miami had long offered conversational Spanish, even at the elementary level. But beginning in 1960–61 the instructional program for children in grades one to twelve was reorganized so that it became a prototype for current efforts in bilingual education'.

The revision of curricula and instructional materials originally developed in Puerto Rico was among early steps leading to the creation of bilingual schooling in Dade County for Cuban refugees and, in September 1963, Coral Way Elementary opened. It has been identified as the earliest bilingual program in the country (although historically and contemporaneously, bilingual programs already existed). At Coral Way, half of students' days were split between home and target languages (whether English or Spanish). As Pedraza-Bailey and Sullivan (1979: 386) noted, 'Significant efforts were made to institute bilingual education not only at the level of instruction, but also organizationally'.

Sociopolitical Backdrop

History of the BEA is inextricably tied to movements promoting civil rights, which is documented by Kathy Escamilla and extensively by Ofelia García and Kenzo K. Sung to commemorate its 50th anniversary (2018). Escamilla recounts various examples: the *Invisible Minority (Pero no vincibles)* (discussed later in this chapter); leadership of José Angel Gutiérrez and students in Crystal City, Texas; movements among Mexican Americans in the Southwest; the work of Spanish-speaking families and Dr Tony Baez in pursuit of articulated elementary bilingual education programs beyond Head Start in Wisconsin; activist Evelina López Antonetty, who started the United Bronx parents to improve Puerto Rican children's schooling; and 'Chicano leaders like Rodolfo "Corky" Gonzales' who 'connected the Chicano civil rights movements to the notion that bilingual/bicultural education is a language right and something all Spanish-speaking children of the United States deserve' (Escamilla, 2018: 369-370, citing Barbian *et al.*, 2017).

Broader support for the creation and implementation of bilingual education in the United States was in part the result of a series of reports and social movements highlighting inequalities among ethnic groups, as well as addressing the language rights of heritage Spanish speakers by shifts in a range of institutions, including schools.

> ... the public became keenly aware of a number of social injustices taking place on American soil (Guthrie, 1981). Publications such as Michael Harrington's (1962) *The Other America*, James Conant's (1961) *Slums and Suburbs*, and James Coleman and colleagues' (1966) *Equality of Educational Opportunity* (otherwise known as the *Coleman Report*) drew attention to the economic and educational disparities between Whites and racial minorities as well as between the middle class and the poor. (Mavrogordato, 2012: 459)

The Coleman Report

In 1961, President Kennedy took office, and about a year later, he appointed Francis Keppel to be US Commissioner of Education. Keppel had been head of the Harvard Graduate School of Education and enjoyed an acquaintance with John's older brother, Joe Kennedy, with whom he had been a classmate at Harvard (Davies, 2007). As Commissioner of Education in 1965, Keppel approached sociologist James Coleman to conduct a survey of the state of elementary and secondary education in the United States with emphasis on equality in educational opportunity. This marked the first investigation of schooling on a national and quite in-depth scale. Coleman's findings included 'a national sample of student and teacher surveys and inventories of school resources... also to conduct student achievement tests' (Wong & Nicotera, 2004: 126).

Pursuant to Section 402 of the Civil Rights Act of 1964, the findings were published in 1966, titled *Equality of Educational Opportunity*:

> SEC. 402. The Commissioner shall conduct a survey and make a report to the President and the Congress, within two years of the enactment of this title, concerning the lack of availability of equal educational opportunities for individuals by reason of race, color, religion, or national origin in public educational institutions at all levels in the United States, its territories and possessions, and the District of Columbia.

Target populations of the survey were organized around ethnic backgrounds described as 'Negroes, American Indians, Oriental Americans, Puerto Ricans living in the continental United States, Mexican Americans, and whites other than Mexican Americans and Puerto Ricans often called "majority" or simply "white"' (Coleman *et al.*, 1966: 9).

Data were collected from nearly 600,000 students and thousands of school leaders, which were then transferred to electronic format. As time drew near to release the publication, Coleman retreated to a motel room alone, where he spent days surrounded by portions of the nearly

700-page report, insisting on personally revisiting statistical analyses to ensure accuracy.

> Very little was known at the time about America's schools. Funding and resource distribution were a mystery. Test scores of whites and blacks had never been compared because standardized theses, ubiquitous today, did not yet exist nationwide... Coleman's questions were ones that no one had asked, let alone to such a wide degree... Rather than simply looking at the resources and funds going into schools as directed by the government, Coleman wanted to understand outcomes... Several months later, it was time for Coleman to sequester himself in the D.C. motel and analyze the results with the help of a mainframe computer... Coleman, then 41, had one change of clothes. He slept little. Scattered about the room were printouts and analyzing surveys... James McPartland a young graduate student who studied under Coleman and worked on the report. 'He was holed up in that motel—not quite a flophouse, but definitely not elegant—waiting for the pages of analysis that he'd requested to be crunched by the computers in Princeton,' McPartland says. (Dickinson, 2016: 3)

The Coleman study marked a turning point for a number of reasons and in a variety of ways. It impacted not only social sciences research, but also the government's perceived role in educational policymaking, and spearheaded discussions around how to assess equity in education. It was referenced as the basis for future busing systems used for promoting integration (which Coleman later considered unsuccessful due to the resulting 'white flight').

A key finding in the Coleman Report was that schools with fewer resources produced students with poorer achievement rates. And further, students' achievement rates in schools with fewer resources continually decline over time; conversely, students' achievement rates in schools with more resources improve over time. It concluded

> That schools bring little influence to bear on a child's achievement that is independent of his background and general social context; and that this very lack of an independent effect means that the inequalities imposed on children by their home, neighborhood, and peer environment are carried along to become the inequalities with which they confront adult life at the end of school. For equality of educational opportunity through the schools must imply a strong effect of schools that is independent of the child's immediate social environment, and that strong independent effect is not present in American school. (Coleman *et al*. [1966] as cited in Wise [1974]: 8–9)

It was in light of the increases in these populations that, shortly after Lyndon Johnson arrived in the White House in 1963, he embarked on plans for the United States' Great Society programs. Joseph Califano served as Secretary of Health, Education and Welfare, as well as assistant for domestic affairs to President Johnson from 1965 to 1969. Califano (1981: 24) recalled that 'by 1977 these Great Society programs had grown dramatically from the time they started: aid to higher education from $383 million to $5.4 billion; aid to elementary schools, from $538 million to $7.3 billion; Medicaid from $770 million to $14 billion; and Medicare from $3.4 billion to $34 billion'.

Johnson was not personally in favor of bilingual education. As a teacher in rural Texas, he punished students for speaking Spanish at school with ear pinching and spankings (Blanton, 2004: 84). However, bilingual education as a mechanism for improving the social and economic status and educational outcomes of students aligned well with his vision for Great Society programs, which were a key priority in his presidency. Califano's memoir provides accounts of his time working in close proximity to the president and others during the era prior, during and after the passage of the 1968 BEA. Califano (1981: 312) writes that, 'my interest in bilingual education was prompted by... Coleman's 1966 study of educational opportunity which showed that students of Mexican, Puerto Rican, and American-Indian background were completing high school at achievement levels far below the national norm'.

Pre-Bilingual Education Act Programs

Although Miami's' Coral Way program is often referred to as the first bilingual program in the United States, other bilingual and non-English medium education programs were also already in existence prior to the passage of the BEA. These included programs in Texas, Colorado, New Mexico, Arizona and California, among others elsewhere in the country and in Native American and Native Hawaiian communities. The US Senate's 1928 Meriam Report 'was the earliest comprehensive federally sponsored report promoting the use of American Indian languages as languages of instruction in schools, and supporting the continued use and development of those languages in the everyday lives of Indian peoples' (Demmert, 2008: 589). In their seminal text, *A Handbook of Bilingual Education*, Muriel R. Saville and Rudolph C. Troike (1971: 3) noted that 'before the Bilingual Education Act was conceived, several experimental projects, notably those at Coral Way, Florida, San Antonio, Texas, and Rough Rock School on the Navajo Reservation were already under way'.

Navajo

As early as 1940, schools in Navajo country were teaching native language reading and writing as part of core curricula (Spolsky, 1970). Internationally renowned scholar and expert in language policy, planning, and management, Bernard Spolsky believed that utilizing Native languages as media of instruction was insufficient for safeguarding loss and that preservation could not be realized without a central focus on literacy. As was noted by Hinton (2001: 180), 'the bias of bilingual education was often toward the written word, and there was little training available to the teachers in language teaching methods'.

In light of contemporary settler-colonial contexts, it is critical to interrogate the role of traditional 'literacy' and use of 'texts' for language revitalization. Jackson and Whitehorse DeLaune (2018) describe enacting transrhetorical resistance to western hegemonies embedded in traditional notions of 'literacy' through shared storytelling.

> Kiowa stories build relationships by extending cultural knowledge and values through an Indigenous cultural literacy practice aligned with historical resistance to western hegemony. Western literacy practices perpetuate western hegemony. In order to decolonize community writing in this academic context, we must listen—as invited by community members—to the story of Kiowa cultural literacy on Kiowa terms. (Jackson & Whitehorse DeLaune, 2018: 40)

Because schools were the main mechanism for stripping American Indian children of their native languages during the Boarding School Movement, 'teaching of endangered languages was extremely rare until the advent of bilingual education in the United States and elsewhere in the 1970s' (Hinton, 2001: 180). However, several cases in Navajo country were the exception.

Rough Rock Demonstration School

After its inception in 1964, the Office of Economic Opportunity (OEO) was approached by Raymond Nakai, chairman of the Navajo Tribal Council, 'with a proposal for a community-administered Navajo School' (Collier, 1988: 257). Chairman of the Task Force on American Indian Poverty, Robert Roessel, who had taught on the Navajo Reservation, helped to secure $214,300 for a three-year demonstration program led by DINE, Inc. (Demonstration in Navajo Education) (see Collier, 1988) from the OEO, with the initial year beginning July 1, 1965. Rough Rock Demonstration School, which sits at the intersection of Arizona, New Mexico, Colorado and Utah, opened in 1966 (McCarty, 2002: 91). In *A Place to be Navajo: Rough Rock and the Struggle for Self-Determination in Indigenous Schooling*, Teresa McCarty (2002) extensively documented the people and community of Rough Rock, including the sociopolitical maneuvering that led to its opening. Regarding the school's opening, she reported

> Bilingual/bicultural education naturally complemented Rough Rock's community development emphasis. 'Often in the past,' Robert Roessel wrote in the school's first monthly report, 'education has been looked upon by Indian parents as a threat'—an either-or proposition that required a choice between two languages and lifeways (Roessel, 1966, p. 102). In contrast, Rough Rock advocated an additive, 'both-and' approach in which students were exposed 'to important values and customs of *both* Navajo culture *and* the dominant society' (Roessel, 1977, p. 10). (McCarty, 2002: 91)

It was created and overseen exclusively by the Rough Rock people and was the precursor to establishment of several other societal support centers, including the Navajo Curriculum Center, which was 'the first enterprise in the United States to be devoted to the production of Indigenous children's literature' (McCarty, 2002: 94).

Hawaiian

In Hawaii, parents recognized forced English-medium of instruction policies in schools as the source of language shift and loss. As a result, sole use of Hawaiian as the medium for Sunday school programs in churches was instituted and communities 'maintained Hawaiian-language newspapers, controlled electoral politics through their language, and campaigned to restore Hawaiian-medium of instruction' (Wilson & Kamanā, 2001: 148). Efforts to reverse Hawaiian language shift through schooling began as early as the 1920s with 'second-language style courses legislated by the Hawaiian-controlled territorial legislature' (Wilson & Kamanā, 2001: 148). Described Wilson (2014: 221) 'in the 1920s the territorial legislature mandated the teaching of Hawaiian in second language courses for teacher preparation, in the high schools, in the University of Hawai'i, and also in elementary schools in heavily Hawaiian areas' (citing Lucas, 2000).

The Malabar Program

A study conducted by the American Institutes for Research determined that the Malabar Reading Program for Mexican-American children 'significantly improved the educational attainment of the disadvantaged children involved' (Department of Health, Education and Welfare, 1969: 8) and recommended the program be used as a model for other communities working with 'disadvantaged youngsters' with similar 'needs'.

Begun as a pilot program during the 1964/1965 school year, Malabar activities included self-instruction, changes to curricula, individualized instruction, parent participation and cultural activities. Its goal was to improve reading levels among Mexican-American students. Although it was not designed as a bilingual approach to instruction, its characteristics notably represent key areas similar to those present in bilingual-bicultural education.

Personnel for the Malabar Program included a project director, who was an associate professor of education at a local state college with a PhD in education and many years of teaching experience. In addition to general supervision, her responsibilities included oversight of 'research dealing with various aspects of language development' (Department of Health, Education and Welfare, 1969: 10). Two co-directors included the principal, who had completed two years of a doctoral study and a master's degree in administration, and the executive director of the Youth Opportunities Foundation, which was a Mexican-American institution. Their responsibilities principally involved serving on the planning and supervision team and establishing participation and support for the program from the local community. An evaluator, who was a professor at a state college, was responsible for statistical analyses and program evaluation. In addition to teachers (only one-tenth of whom were Mexican-American in 1969), other school staff, parents, volunteers and visitors developed materials and conducted activities to 'develop language and reading skills by talking with them and reading with them at every available opportunity' (Department of Health, Education and Welfare, 1969: 11).

The Malabar Program primarily focused on establishing direct relationships between reading skills and students' self-concept around engaging with reading, becoming readers and recognizing literacy acts in their surroundings both inside and out of school. Parent participation was a critical component; parents were urged to visit the school and mothers were recruited to serve as aides. Teachers described a mother who came to the school for an hour each morning, and as many as five or six mothers visiting one classroom in afternoons; mothers hiring babysitters for younger siblings so they could volunteer for one-on-one and small-group reading and using the pedagogical skills they developed to support older siblings struggling with reading. Families also ran home libraries, which included about 100 books and were created in 15 homes.

An after-school component consisted of lessons presented by a Mexican artist addressing Mexican culture, dance, poetry and song. Although Spanish language materials were largely excluded from the Malabar Program, its teachers created several bilingual books, two of which were stories written by students. Despite the focus on English reading, Spanish was viewed as a resource by teachers and parents. As one Malabar teacher remarked, 'One of our mothers read Spanish as well as English. She was very careful to translate for the non-Spanish-speaking children. The children enjoyed listening to her read and I know she enjoyed reading to them' (Department of Health, Education and Welfare, 1969: 24). The directors of the Malabar Program recommended three components be added:

in-service training to emphasize the school's philosophy and teaching techniques; after-school bilingual activities to allow for more opportunities to learn about Mexican culture and language; and program expansion to higher grades and other groups of Mexican-American students.

Coral Way bilingual program

The development of the Coral Way bilingual program has been extensively documented in *The Coral Way Bilingual Program*, authored by Maria R. Coady (2020). In September 1961, Dade County Public Schools hired Pauline Martz Rojas as a consultant 'to identify a solution to the Cuban refugee situation' (Coady, 2020: 25). Rojas was a 'formidable educator with a national reputation as a highly skilled linguist' (Coady, 2020: 25, citing Mackey & Beebe, 1977).

Rojas spearheaded the start up of Coral Way and was project director for grant monies awarded by the Ford Foundation. She 'had directed the English as a Second Language program in Puerto Rico for twelve years' (Logan, 1967: 50) and was supported by Ralph Robinett, who had also been a director for the English program in Puerto Rico, as well as Paul W. Bell, a local educator who had experience as a bilingual teacher in Guatemala (Jorge *et al.*, 1991). Rojas 'had directed the materials-development project in Puerto Rico which produced [the adapted Fries American English Series]... to provide language-arts instruction in English for students who already could read in Spanish' (Mackey & Beebe, 1977: 56). Because there were few models from which to draw in the United States, she also explored programs offered overseas to the children of US diplomats and wealthy locals in Nicaragua and Guatemala, which used both English and Spanish as media of instruction with the goals of both bilingual fluency and content learning. At the time, Rojas had been a consultant for CAL and was working at the Office of Education in Miami to develop a program to teach English to Cuban refugees who had enlisted in the US armed forces (Coady, 2020).

Rojas' keen capacity for networking played a critical role in laying the foundation for transitioning the existing Coral Way school to one offering bilingual education (Coady, 2020). At the recommendation of Ken Mildenberger, who was then director of the Language Development Program at the US Office of Education, Rojas pursued and secured funding to support the educational needs of Cuban refugee children in Miami through a series of grants from the Ford Foundation (Coady, 2020), with work beginning in January 1963.

Mildenberger would later make remarks as 1963 commencement speaker at Middlebury College in Vermont, in which he warned that when the NDEA was defunded, the only room left for involvement in the teaching and learning of world languages would be in the private sector. Mildenberger not only pointed out the impact on American education that the NDEA had had since its inception, he also noted that people in Washington, DC were fearful that the private sector in our profession 'will be uncritical and will, by silence, desert its proper role of policy leadership'. (Terry, 2016, as cited in Foreign Language Annals, 2016: 642)

Mildenberger later directed the Modern Languages Association of America, which now annually awards the Kenneth W. Mildenberger Prize 'for an outstanding scholarly book in the fields of language, culture, literacy, and literature that has a strong application to the teaching of languages other than English' (Modern Language Association, 2020).

In an interim report to the Ford Foundation, Director Rojas and Assistant Director Robinett described the status of the following projects (Rojas & Robinett, 1963: 1).

(1) The preparation of reading materials for non-English-speaking bilingual pupils entering first grade.
(2) The revision or adaptation of the books of the Fries American English Series for non-English-speaking bilingual pupils who can read and write their vernacular.
(3) The preparation of guides and audio-visual materials for teachers of bilingual pupils.

Starting in November 1963, the Dade school board approved the Project in Bilingual Education of Cuban Refugee Pupils, which 'provided for the revision of instructional materials originally developed in Puerto Rico and the development of beginning reading materials to be developed for bilingual children' (Pedraza-Bailey & Sullivan, 1979: 385). Also in the 1963/1964 school year, the new bilingual program began at Coral Way Elementary. As was reported by Rojas and Robinett (1963), 12 groups were initially included: four groups of first, second and third graders (two native English-speaking and two native Spanish-speaking at each level). In the program 'both English- and Spanish-speaking children were offered an instructional program in both languages in all grades, where half the day was spent in studying the regular curriculum in the native language (English or Spanish), and the other half of the day was devoted to studying in the second language' (Pedraza-Bailey & Sullivan, 1979: 385). A regular (non-bilingual) class also operated at each grade level at inception of the bilingual program. As parents saw its success however, they requested their children transferred out of the traditional English medium program, and within several years, it had been removed because only 11 pupils remained (Logan, 1967). New bilingual grade levels were added each year.

Fries American English Series and Miami Linguistic Readers

Written by Dr Charles Carpenter Fries, a University of Michigan structural linguist considered the creator of the audio-lingual method of language teaching, the Fries American English Series appeared in 1952 as a curriculum for teaching ESL. At the time, it was 'one of the few, if any, ESL reading materials' (Coady, 2020: 28). Revision of the Fries American English Series was among the four initial goals of the Ford Foundation Coral Way grants. Rojas had worked with Ralph Robinett in Puerto Rico, when she adapted the curriculum to be appropriate for teaching ESL to native Spanish speakers and again recruited him as assistant director of the foundation projects. With Dr Rosa G. Inclán (who would later become the first chairlady of a national committee devoted to bilingual education) and Herminia Cantero (both had adapted the materials for Cuban ESL teachers), Rojas led the adaptation of materials to create the Miami Linguistic Readers, which became a central component of the bilingual curriculum.

Voices of the Southwest

In 1966, the National Education Association (NEA) published *The Invisible Minority*, reporting on the survey of models for native Spanish-speaking students led by María Urquides. The foreword provided readers with circumstantial background regarding its genesis:

> Teachers with insight into the problems of Spanish-speaking children have come to realize that two separate but parallel purposes need to be pursued. One is to help the Mexican-American student adjust to the dominant 'Anglo' culture. The other is to foster in him a pride in his Spanish-speaking culture and Mexican origin. These teachers have chosen to recognize the Spanish-speaking ability of Mexican-American students as a distinct asset and to build on it rather than to root it out. They have found that Spanish properly used can be a bridge to the learning of English instead of an obstacle and that Mexican-American students can become truly bilingual and bicultural. (National Education Association, 1966: 1)

Born in 1908 and raised in Tucson, Urquides attended segregated 'Mexican-only' schools. She graduated from Arizona State Teachers College in 1928 as the class valedictorian and first taught at Davis Elementary School, which was 100% Latinx and Yaqui. 'Urquides was remembered both as a strict disciplinarian and as a teacher who encouraged her students to be proud of their Mexican heritage' (Combs, 2008: 870). After finishing a master's degree from the University of Arizona nearly 30 years later in 1956, Urquides taught English and reading at Pueblo High School. At Pueblo, she became committed to ensuring her teaching and the school curriculum reflected students' linguistic and ethnic backgrounds. 'She was particularly troubled that Mexican students fluent in Spanish were nonetheless unable to read and write it' (Combs, 2008: 870).

With Adalberto Guerrero, she co-created a Spanish for Spanish speakers honors class, which was awarded the NEA's Pace Maker School Award. Urquides leveraged the NEA connection to appeal for the need to better understand the challenges facing Latinx students. When the NEA agreed to conduct a survey of Mexican-origin student educators, Urquides served as chair of the Tucson Study Group, which visited schools and surveyed teachers across the Southwest.

Educators and schools in the Southwest and elsewhere had adopted the approach of schooling for native Spanish speakers as building on bilingualism, rather than focusing on English acquisition. The 1965 NEA survey goals were to identify 'constructive approaches' to supporting the needs of native Spanish-speaking students and to facilitate sharing of 'ideas, methods and materials which apply to a bilingual system of teaching' (Bilingual Education: Hearings, 90th Congress, 1967: 159). The report found that although 72% and 75% of the overall male and female populations had spent one or more years in secondary settings, comparatively, only a striking 48.5% and 52% of Latinx males and females had done so (National Education Association, 1966).

It also documented successful bilingual and Spanish language educational programs in several locations in the Southwest: Laredo and El Paso, Texas; Albuquerque and Pecos, New Mexico; Merced, California; Pueblo, Colorado; and Tucson, Arizona. Similar to a case study methodology, each site was described in relative detail in terms of its cultural and linguistic demographics, school setting, materials, instruction and educators.

Biliteracy in Laredo

At the time of the survey, the Laredo Independent School District was larger than the state of Rhode Island, and included the Laredo air force base and suburban homes, as well as farms and ranches 'where many Mexican-American families live' (National Education Association, 1966: 178). It represented a generally balanced blend of Anglo and Mexican-American families and the 'United Consolidated Independent School District has one strong common denominator: Bilingualism' (National Education Association, 1966: 174). Students in the three elementary schools and high school (which, incidentally, was built underground to protect against air strikes, given its proximity to the air force base) were encouraged to become fully bilingual and biliterate. During a visit to one of the elementary schools, a researcher observed a first-grade bilingual class, evenly mixed between native English speakers and native Spanish speakers, whose teacher was a Mexican-American native Spanish speaker. The teacher led the children in navigating discussions in both English and Spanish, illustrated in the following excerpt (National Education Association, 1966: 175):

Then Mrs. Earles asked 'Wouldn't it be fun if we could each be two persons? How many of you think you would like to be two persons?'

Everybody did.

'How can we be two persons? That's right—by speaking two languages. But remember—we have to be careful to speak only one language at a time. Does your teacher mix the two languages?'

'No!' responded the children and she shook her head in affirmation.

'We must always be careful to learn each language well so that we don't have to mix the two. If we learn both languages, we can help each other better. Right? Now I need your help. Can you children help me? I lost my dog and I can't find him.'

All volunteered to help. She asked three 'Anglo' children to go before the class and sing. 'Oh, where, oh where, has my little dog gone?' When they were done, Mrs. Earles said, 'Thank you. But I'm sorry I forgot to say that I didn't lose him here. I lost him in Mexico. Could someone help me find him there?' Again, all volunteered, and three Mexican-American children joined the three 'Anglo' children to sing '¿A dónde, a dónde se fue mi perrito…?'

Prior to its emphasis on bilingualism, the district had attempted an English-only policy, which resulted in 'frustration and failure, a heavy proportion of dropouts among Mexican-Americans, tension between the Anglo- and Mexican-American communities' (National Education Association, 1966: 176). Thus, in September 1964, the school board created 'an experimental biliteracy program', beginning initially with only first grade and expanding to second in year two.

Before discussion of the recommendations for other bilingual programs, the look and tone of the only high school in Laredo are described in the NEA report, illustrating its bicultural richness and the equitably assigned value to students' collective identities.

> …the high school reflects the beneficial effects of the bilingual-bicultural revolution taking place. Picturesquely displayed at the high school's main entrance, on equal terms, are the proud symbols of the two neighbor nations—the American eagle and the Mexican eagle. They are vividly colored, stylized cutouts made by students and suspended from wire supports. Student art work is displayed all throughout the school, and there is stress throughout on the worthiness of each of the two cultures. An unmistakable *esprit de corps* prevails among the students. (National Education Association, 1966: 177)

Superintendent of Instruction for Laredo, Harold C. Brantley presented at the NEA's New Voices of the Southwest Conference, discussing his district's approach to the education of native Spanish-speaking students. He highlighted the importance of the 50-50 model in bilingual education, stating

We have been able to see that the child who comes from the Spanish cultural and language background is definitely happier in school. In addition, we have been able to observe that the native English-speaker and his parents not only have accepted this new program, but are excited about what it can do for the English-speaking child. (National Education Association, 1966: 3)

Spanish for native speakers

Researchers involved in the survey also visited El Paso, Texas; Albuquerque and Pecos, New Mexico; Merced, California; Pueblo, Colorado; and both Tucson and Phoenix, Arizona, where they documented districts and schools implementing Spanish language arts and other coursework designed for native Spanish speakers.

New Mexico is itself unique from the other southwestern states due to its history of Spanish colonization. Visitors to the New Mexico schools noted that the Spanish-speaking person in New Mexico is referred to as 'Hispano' rather than 'Mexican-American'. As remnants of the Spanish colonial period, families in New Mexico ascribed a certain status to Spanish as the higher language in societal bilingualism.

NEA survey recommendations

The NEA-Tucson Survey on the Teaching of Spanish to the Spanish Speaking concluded with a series of recommendations. Among these was increased attention on the need for educational models for teaching native Spanish-speaking students, based on site visits. The NEA authors asserted:

To meet the problem fully, however, further legislation and substantially increased appropriations are needed. An extended series of needs could be listed... But the urgent need is for ACTION and innovation in local school districts almost everywhere. (National Education Association, 1966: 1)

One key outcome of the study publication was a planned symposium to coincide with its release, held in Tucson. It marked the first national convening aimed at addressing the specialized educational needs of language minority students, families and communities across K-12 and higher education settings and the first major step in the development of the BEA.

Las Voces Nuevas del Sudoeste

While social movements were highlighting serious discrepancies between the educational outcomes of wealthy and middle-class white Americans and those from poor and ethnic minority backgrounds, the NEA Commission on Professional Rights and Responsibilities (PR&R)

hosted two conferences focused on issues of civil rights, integration and the education of African-American students. According to the symposium proceedings, the second meeting, in Washington, DC, on May 10–11, 1965, addressed

> The responsibilities of the education profession for advancing civil rights; and [t]he obligation of civil rights movement participants for making practical, constructive proposals to help educators to meet their responsibilities. (National Education Association, 1966: 1)

The third NEA PR&R symposium was held in Tucson, Arizona, on October 30–31, 1966. Its focus was on the education of native Spanish-speaking students and, in particular, those in the Southwest. It was titled The Spanish-Speaking Child in the Schools of the Southwest, *Las Voces Nuevas del Sudoeste* (National Education Association, 1966). Its symposium report highlighted goals:

> To publicize the positive efforts that are currently being undertaken to solve the problems of Spanish-speaking children and to provide a catalyst for the further action that is needed, NEA and its affiliated state organizations in the five Southwestern states held the Third National PR&R Conference on Civil and Human Rights in Education. At this Symposium, we explored the problems from various points of view with two questions in mind: 'What are we doing? What more can be done?'. (National Education Association, 1966: 1)

In reviewing the events leading up to the BEA, Stoller (1977) recounted that participants 'recognized that the educational needs of Mexican-Americans were not being met and called for federal legislation which would fund bilingual schools', citing personal communication with Gilbert Sánchez. Symposium activities began with a review of the existing successful programs involving bilingualism and promoting language maintenance for native Spanish speakers. Bruce Gaarder (1967), citing Bernard Spolsky and Theodore Andersson, scholars of language acquisition and language education, reported on findings from studies demonstrating the benefits of bilingualism and the potential viability of bilingual and Spanish language programs (National Education Association, 1966).

The meeting not only reviewed existing programs, but also highlighted the practical needs associated with the implementation of bilingual programs. At that time, Theodore Andersson was consulting with schools in Laredo. He delineated the requirements for instructors in bilingual programs, noting that Spanish-speaking teachers should 'speak Spanish authentically, naturally, and effectively', 'have an up-to-date understanding of what language is and of the difference between a native language and a second language and a foreign language' and 'understand the inter-relationship of language and culture and be a worthy representative of Hispanic culture' (National Education Association, 1966: 12). Andersson also presented recommendations for educator recruitment for bilingual programs, including the creation of specialized educator pathways through universities. The meeting concluded with presentations by state and federal representatives, including Senators Joseph Montoya of New Mexico and Ralph Yarborough of Texas.

Ralph Yarborough

Ralph Yarborough took his first teaching job in the Delta Common School District, Texas, as the single teacher in a small school, in the fall of 1920. As Cox (2001: 10) wrote, there he 'discovered the challenges and pleasures of working in an underfunded yet relatively independent atmosphere'. He enrolled and completed some courses in Sam Houston State College, and a year later arrived in Le Havre, France, in October 1921. After running out of money due to the cost of living in Paris, he moved to Germany, where he became fluent in German and solicited a local English language magazine, *The Transatlantic Trade*, to hire him as an English language proofreader. By August 1922, he had returned to teaching for the same Delta Common School District in East Texas. However, the short period that Yarborough spent in Europe during this impressionable time assuredly impacted his perspective on cultural interaction, the role of language in society and communities, and the enduring agony of social ills, which were, at that time, acutely present among the poor in Europe.

> He saw the economic, social, and political chaos that gripped Europe and especially Germany in the 1920's. He came to know the bitterness many Europeans felt about the slaughter and political outcome of World War I... Texas had its own poverty, racism, and poor living conditions, but even these conditions sometimes paled in comparison to the problems faced in the aftermath of 'the war to end all wars'. (Cox, 2001: 11)

Yarborough was sworn in as a district judge by Susette Meyer in 1936, the first woman to administer such an oath. Although the cases before him may have had minimal significance outside the district community, Yarborough's views on racism and minority rights were immediately evident based on his rulings. He declared innocence and dismissed cases clearly motivated by racism against falsely accused African Americans. While serving in World War II, he again witnessed the death, destruction and poverty brought about by war in Europe. Later, as military governor of Honshu Province in Japan, he documented the obliteration of cities and towns across the country, including 'atomized Hiroshima' (Cox, 2001: 88).

After several years of tumultuous political ups and downs, Yarborough was sworn into office as Texas Senator on April 29, 1957. A staunch advocate for public schools, that same year, he co-sponsored the NDEA, which marked the first federal engagement in education policymaking. Nearly from its inception, Yarborough's political career was marked by attacks against his advocacy efforts for minorities, including for example supporting the elimination of the poll tax and President Johnson's Civil Rights bill of 1964. Without doubt, his primary priority as a lawmaker was education.

> Yarborough proclaimed that America could avoid a future crisis through better education. He then cosponsored the Elementary and Secondary Education Act of 1965, the president's initial major legislative victory and the first general education measure ever to pass Congress... Yarborough played a critical role throughout passage of the bill...
>
> Senator Yarborough's legislative contributions to education remain unmatched. Bills he sponsored and promoted, radically changed the landscape of American public schools, marked the first steps in breaking down segregation, and opened doors to poor and minority students and communities that had previously been barred. Among dozens of critically impactful laws, his proudest successes were the Bilingual Education Act and the G.I. Bill. (Cox, 2001: 230)

At the conclusion of the NEA's Tucson conference on the education of the Spanish-speaking child, in October 1966, Yarborough declared:

> Politics and government have taught me the value and the joy of a bilingual capability, and my travels in the six inhabited continents have confirmed that opinion. Hopefully, Spanish will furnish a bridge to all the Pan-American cultures. Within about 40 years, according to the state department projections, we expect the population of Latin America to be double that of the United States. Bilingualism can mean a better approach to national and international affairs. It can offer a broader base for understanding among all people. Bilingualism is no longer a luxury in this world; it is a necessity. (National Education Association, 1966: 17)

Said to have been inspired by the symposium to pursue the BEA (Combs, 2008), his assertions were realized just two years later, when President Johnson signed the act into law on January 2, 1968.

3 Early Bilingual Education and the Sociopolitical Backdrop

> Within a couple of months, I was convinced of the wisdom of both bilingual education and parent involvement because I experienced firsthand the tremendous difference that they made in the lives of the children, teachers, and families, and even in the larger community... at P.S. 25, I learned the value of beginning to establish close and caring relationships with my students and their families immediately, from the very first day; I learned the value of bringing my entire self into teaching, and to share my life with my students; and I learned that assimilation can be harmful to students' learning, their feelings about themselves, and their connection with their communities.
>
> Sonia Nieto on teaching in New York City's first bilingual school, P.S. 25, where she was hired by Principal Hernán La Fontaine in 1968 (Nieto, 2011: 23).

An Ill-Defined Program

In signing Title VII of the Elementary and Secondary Education Act (ESEA), the Bilingual Education Act (BEA) on January 2, 1968, President Johnson proclaimed

> Thousands of children of Latin descent, young Indians, and others will get a better start-a better chance-in school. ...What this law means, is that we are now giving every child in America a better chance to touch his outermost limits-to reach the farthest edge of his talents and his dreams. We have begun a campaign to unlock the full potential of every boy and girl--regardless of his race or his region or his father's in-come.

In contradiction to the civil and language rights movements largely responsible for its development, the initial law was designed as remedial and compensatory in nature – to *overcome* the challenges posed by students' native languages. Schools were only eligible to receive funding if they had a high concentration of children from families either with an income below $3000 a year or those deemed as in poverty because they already received aid under the Social Security Act. González (1978: 26) recounted 'that "poverty criteria" be applied in determining the eligibility of children who were to participate in the programs to be funded by the Act... [was] affirmation that bilingual education was seen... as... an educational strategy designed to remediate the effects of poverty and "cultural disadvantagedness"'. Escamilla (2018) asserted that

> passage of the BEA was significant but quite likely never achieved its goals with regard to educational access and equity or social justice. The original BEA never clearly identified what the goals of the program would be. It was never specified if the act was meant to speed the transition to English for those who came to school speaking languages other than English or if the goal was to promote bilingualism/biliteracy and biculturalism. (Escamilla, 2018, citing Crawford, 2004: 369)

Davies (2007) called the initial BEA essentially symbolic, with little real-world impact. Even after the poverty requirement was removed in later amendments, scholars argued its ambiguous explanation for what constituted a bilingual program and omission of details regarding program characteristics, for example, resulted in problematic interpretation and inconsistent implementation among states and in districts and schools across the country (Molina, 1978). Gándara (2015: 113) remarked, 'Although titled the Bilingual Education Act, the law actually skirted any definition of bilingual education'.

The initial bill 'mandated the Commissioner of Education to establish in the Office of Education (OE) an Advisory Committee on the Education of Bilingual Children to provide advice on the implementation of this policy' (San Miguel, 2004: 17). Its first meetings were held on November 25 and 26, 1968, with Dr Theodore Andersson, professor of Spanish and Portuguese and Education at the University of Texas serving as chairman. In a book to honor Andersson's contributions to the teaching and learning of languages and bilingual education, Robert Lado (1993: 13) wrote that he 'defined bilingual education not as a device to impose English but as education to develop educated bilinguals who would use their bilingualism as an asset to themselves and to their country'.

Andersson was born in 1903, in New Haven, Connecticut, to Swedish immigrant parents who interacted with him in the home in English. As a young child, however, due to financial difficulties, he and his mother moved back to rural Sweden for several years, during which time he 'forgot' English and acquired Swedish. He earned a bachelor's and master's degree and a PhD from Yale University, Stanford and Wells, and joined the University of Texas at Austin faculty in 1957. A tireless advocate for promoting multilingualism and heritage language transmission and retention, Andersson was a staunch ally of bilingual education.

When he moved to the University of Texas in 1957, Andersson was appalled to observe that Mexican American children from this state were stigmatized and demeaned for their Spanish instead of valued for their knowledge of a 'foreign' language; and so he began sowing the seeds for bilingual education. (Evans, 2008: 38)

He proposed to the Texas State Department of Education in 1959 that Spanish and English should be the media of instruction for native Spanish-speaking students. He had consulted with local experimental bilingual programs in both Laredo, as discussed earlier, and San Antonio, Texas; Senator Carlos Truán on developing a statewide law promoting bilingual education; and Senator Yarborough on the BEA.

Bilingual Education Program

Johnson appointed Dr Albar Peña as first director of bilingual education programs in mid-1968. Peña was born in Ciudad Mier, Mexico, moving to Falfurrias, Texas, where he graduated from high school and joined the US Air Force, serving in the Korean War. He obtained a bachelor's degree from the University of Texas at Austin in foreign languages in 1957, just one year before the passage of the 1958 National Defense Languages Act (Image 3.1).

Dr Peña had been a Spanish and English teacher in South Texas, where bilingual education was emerging. He attended the University of Texas at Austin on the G.I. Bill and for a time was director of the National Defense Education Summer Institute for Teachers of Spanish-speaking Disadvantaged Children Language Laboratory. Peña was

Image 3.1 Dr Albar Peña, first director of bilingual education programs (Reprinted with permission from Gil Barrera Photographs of the University of Texas at San Antonio, MS 27, University of Texas at San Antonio Libraries Special Collections)

recruited by Tug Andersson into a program created in response to the lack of Mexican-American scholars at the University of Texas and completed his master's and PhD at Texas A&I University with a focus on English as a second language (ESL) and bilingual education. In 1975, Peña helped found and was first president of the National Association of Bilingual Education (NABE), which he initially ran from his office with a small group of volunteers and others (Milk, 2008: 652). He also founded and was director of the University of Texas at San Antonio's Bicultural-Bilingual Studies Division.

In his role as director of bilingual education programs, Peña administered all planning, funding and oversight of new model bilingual education projects. Under his direction, critical groundwork was laid for the implementation and promotion of bilingual programs, including the distribution of funds for research on bilingual education, as well as the creation of professional development and educational pathways established in universities for the preparation of qualified personnel for bilingual programs.

When Johnson left office, Peña remained in his position and continued serving in Washington under the Nixon administration. Despite Peña's commitment to bilingual education, it became politically problematic during the Nixon administration. In a letter written to Senator Edward Kennedy on August 4, 1972, Peña clarified the role of bilingual programs.

> ...bilingual education projects are designed to use the child's first language as the medium of instruction until his competence in English permits the use of both languages in a balanced instructional program. An essential ingredient in all projects is the concurrent effort to develop and maintain the child's self esteem and a legitimate pride in both cultures. (Cited in Skrentny, 2002: 207)

Dr Peña served as director of bilingual programs until 1973, when he moved back to Texas and became director of the Bilingual-Bicultural Studies Division at the University of Texas San Antonio.

The Sociopolitical Backdrop under Johnson

Prior to passage of the BEA, President Johnson had established an interagency committee on Mexican affairs. In a letter dated June 9, 1967, Johnson asserted his commitment to addressing the burdens challenging Mexican-Americans, in part to 'seek out new programs that may be necessary to handle problems that are unique to the Mexican American community' (Inter-agency Committee on Mexican American Affairs, 1968). The passage of the BEA, whether functionally symbolic or not, represented a critical turn in social consciousness regarding the national educational crisis for native Spanish-speaking students. In signing the legislation (although conflating language with ethnicity), Johnson highlighted the sizable educational disparities among ethnic groups in the United States.

> Our educational policies on the teaching of the Spanish speaking have not been among our more enlightened areas of educational endeavor. For instance. take our children who speak only Spanish. If there were only a handful, a few hundred, you couldn't afford to establish separate methods of instruction, but millions of children from Spanish-speaking homes come to schools speaking only Spanish. The tragic results are shown in the dropout rate. Among adults 25 and over, Mexican-Americans in 1960 had an average of 7.1 years of schooling, as compared to the 12.1 years for Anglos, and ' nine for non-whites. The gap between Anglo and Mexican Americans is 5 years, or 41 percent. (Lescott-Leszczynski, 2019: 701)

As established in Chapter 2, a great deal of new sociopolitical attention was directed toward Mexican-American, Puerto Rican, Cuban-American and Spanish-speaking communities during this period. A new era had been initiated in part due to the findings in *Brown v. Board of Education*, the Civil Rights movement and passage of the Civil Rights Act. During this time, social movements against the intrinsically racist power structures embedded in American society were rife. President Johnson's intended legacy was built around his Great Society Programs, which served a critical role in impacting the expansion of federal monies to a range of new areas, not least of which was public education. The first ESEA was passed in 1965, creating waves of funding and a new role for the federal government in oversight of and involvement in education on a national scale. The passage of ESEA meant schools across the country were now in receipt of federal funding and scrutiny regarding federal compliance, especially with Title 601 of the Civil Rights Act of 1964, which states that

> no person in the United States shall, on the basis of race, color, or national origin, be excluded from participation in, be denied the benefits of, or be subjected to discrimination under any program or activity receiving federal financial assistance.

Continued national attention on educational inequity

In 1968, the National Advisory Committee on Mexican-American Education published the report 'The Mexican-American Quest for Equality', which surmised a national 'failure to provide education to hundreds of thousands of people whose cultural heritages is "different" has resulted in shameful waste of human resources' (Cabinet Committee on Opportunities for Spanish Speaking People, 1971: 2). In part resulting from this publication, in December 1968, a series of hearings were held in San Antonio, Texas, by the Commission on Civil Rights, 'an independent, bipartisan, nonpolitical agency of the United States Government established by Congress in 1957' (San Antonio Hearings, 1968/1969: 2). These are described by the Chairman John A. Hannah:

> The purpose of this hearing is to collect information regarding the civil rights problems of Mexican Americans in the five Southwestern States. For the next 5 days we will be concerned with the issues of education, employment, economic security, and the administration of justice as they affect Mexican Americans not only in Texas but in Arizona, California, Colorado, and New Mexico. This hearing, like previous Commission hearings, is designed to explore in one city or area civil rights problems that are representative of problems elsewhere in the Nation. And even though this hearing is in San Antonio, I want to emphasize the fact that it will deal with civil rights problems of Mexican Americans throughout the Southwest. (San Antonio Hearings, 1968/1969: 2)

Ultimately, the commission would produce six reports (two in both 1971 and 1972, one in 1973 and the sixth in 1974) regarding the education of Mexican-Americans in the United States, thereby contributing substantively to the then growing body of evidence demonstrating unequal access to and inequitable education for 'Spanish surnamed' students. As Schneider (1976: 22) recounted, 'a study published in 1972 by the US Commission on Civil Rights [found] sixty-four percent of the Mexican American students in the Southwest were six months behind their expected grade level in reading; yet only nineteen percent were receiving special reading instruction'.

Other reports produced by the Commission on Civil Rights addressed the effectiveness of and positive outcomes associated with bilingual education. These included examples such as a program in San Francisco in which 135 Chinese immigrants and Americans in a bilingual-bicultural program 'for grades one to three... scored 1.5 years ahead of students in the district ESL program in reading and mathematics' (Schneider, 1976: 13). The fifth and final report, issued on February 4, 1974, played an important role in impacting the development of the 1974 BEA reauthorization.

Meanwhile, utilizing schools for linguistic and cultural maintenance remained a priority for some American Indian communities across the country. Havighurst (1978) reminded readers of Mr John Woodenlegs, founder of Chief Dull Knife College and grandson of Wooden Leg, who fought against George Custer at the Battle of Little Big Horn, who in 1970 remarked:

> For over a year I have spent most of my time working on education... Our goals have been: 1. To educate our schools and the local communities to the idea of community schools, serving the needs of the local people over and above daily education of children. 2. To encourage parents to be more concerned and involved with the schools, including active member- ship on school boards. 3. To help teachers get more knowledge of the Cheyennes, their past history and culture and present life. 4. To encourage Cheyenne resource people to go into classrooms to talk on history and culture. We feel our children need education which gives the best of both cultures. We feel that many of the values of our past Cheyenne society can still serve us well in this modern world. We feel we need this to give us understanding. (Havighurst, 1978: 16)

Nixon's Approach to Bilingual Education

Nixon's perspective on the native Spanish-speaking community varied from other Republicans at the time because, coming from California, he recognized the political gravity support from this community could carry. In remarks made to Gustavo Nat Ordat, then president of Mexico, Nixon expressed his respect and appreciation for US-Mexico relations and Mexican-Americans on September 3, 1970:

> As I think of Mexico and the United States, I think of the present, of the great contributions that Mexican Americans (and all Spanish speaking people) have made to our country and are making. I think of the contribution and of the debt we owe to the main obligation that we have not adequately fulfilled in the past and that we hope that we can more adequately fulfill in the future so that all Mexican Americans (and all Spanish-speaking people) can play their equal part in the progress of this Nation. (Conde, 1970: iv)

Although the Nixon administration funded more community programs for Latinx communities than had Presidents Kennedy and Johnson and appointed the first Latina Cabinet-level member (Romana Bañuelos as US Treasurer Secretary), high-ranking official Henry Quevedo described the 'sad and often humorous clashes between the "tactical" Chicano Republicans and "ideological" ones' (Burt, 2007: 1).

Office of Civil Rights (OCR)

Leon Pannetta was appointed director of the OCR for a brief period from 1969 to 1970. During this time, he led staff to pursue compliance issues primarily related to the Equal Educational Opportunities Act, almost entirely related to the education of African-American students. Panetta was also generally concerned with ensuring interaction among regional stakeholders and communities across the United States and would travel to meet with individuals representing various constituencies. He describes one such visit to San Francisco, during which he met with 'a group of California Mexican Americans' (Panetta & Gall, 1971: 335) on December 4, 1969:

> Don Morales, who was taking very seriously his job as my chief gadfly to include Spanish-speaking minorities in more of our considerations, had worked out the meeting. Some of the men I knew from Kuchel days, but most were new faces. They came on hard. They were cynical about this Administration, but they were cynical about most. Nobody in Washington had done anything about the fact that Mexican American children were being assigned to classes for the mentally retarded because they could not speak English, that Mexican American youths were dropping out of school at an alarming rate, that the same language barrier destroying the children was also hindering adults who were trying to get health care or welfare assistance.
>
> As a first step, I made a commitment to them that I would prepare a memorandum to all school district with a high concentration of Mexican American students, requesting that they inform us of their actions to assist children in meeting their language problems. The group was still skeptical, but they were kind and we parted on good terms after one of the most intense lobbying sessions I had been through in Kuchel's office or any place. Obviously, others had not been sitting down much with this group, or more would have been accomplished by this time. (Panetta & Gall, 1971: 335–336)

Department of Health, Education and Welfare (DHEW)

Elliot Lee Richardson was named Secretary of DHEW in 1970.[1] During his brief time at DHEW, its annual report notes a range of activities designed to better support the needs of language minority students, in addition to those defined specifically as bilingual education. Under his leadership, the Office for Spanish-Speaking American Affairs identified research and development priorities, created Spanish language materials, established a task force on Mexican-American educational leadership and engaged several media-related initiatives, including for example, the production of the film, *You and Mañana*.

On August 3, 1970, Richardson submitted a letter to Senator Walter F. Mondale of the Subcommittee on Education, regarding the education of language minority students in US schools, referencing the 'ethnic isolation' of Mexican, Puerto Rican and American Indian children. In the letter, Richardson argued that ethnic isolation perpetuates homogeneity by limiting interactions with Anglo peers, aggravates educational motivation and achievement and deprives students of opportunities to acquire English. He wrote:

In summary, some of the most important needs of Mexican-American, Puerto Rican and American Indian children related to ethnic isolation are: (1) The need for ethnic or cultural diversity in the educational environment: Heterogeneity. (2) The need for total institutional reposturing (including culturally sensitizing teachers, instructional materials and educational approaches) in order to incorporate, affirmatively recognize and value the cultural environment of ethnic minority children so that the development of positive self-concept can be accelerated: Bi-Cultural Approaches: with, as an important corollary. (3) The need for language programs that introduce and develop English language skills without demeaning or otherwise deprecating the language of a child's home environment and thus without presenting English as a more valued language: Bi-Lingual Component. To meet the needs of ethnically isolated children described in numbers 2 & 3 above, participation of Anglo children in the Bi-Cultural/Bi-Lingual program is essential. (Education of the Spanish Speaking, 1972: 44)

Committee on Mexican-American Affairs

On December 31, 1970, President Nixon demonstrated increased attention toward the needs, opportunities and inequities faced by native Spanish speakers in the United States when he signed a bill transforming what had previously been the Inter-Agency Committee into the Cabinet Committee on Opportunities for Spanish-Speaking People (CCOSS). The president asserted, 'In signing this bill, I reaffirm the concern of this government for providing equal opportunity to all Spanish-speaking Americans' (Conde, 1970: 8). Authorized for five years, CCOSS was an independent body located within the executive branch. Major program areas included economic affairs, housing and community development, legislative concerns, government placement services and communications. Its staff reported directly to the president, who relayed findings and activities to Congress. It was composed of various cabinet members whose programmatic areas were relevant to Spanish-speaking communities, including the Secretary of DHEW. In the area of education, the then expanded CCOSS activities also directly addressed bilingual and other programs at the elementary, secondary and postsecondary levels. It 'evaluated and advocated the funding of 14 bilingual education programs, several Teacher Corps programs, both urban and rural, and other programs or projects related to the education problems of the Spanish speaking' (Conde, 1970: 19). The committee's first priority was investigating compliance with both *Brown v. Board of Education* and Title VI of the Civil Rights Act of 1964. Among its activities, foci included:

- Interceding directly with the Secretary of DHEW to save and fund an exemplary program for Spanish-speaking children known as the Malabar project. (see Chapter 2)

- Co-sponsoring with DHEW and the Department of Justice, the first Title VI conference for Spanish-speaking children to which were brought legal staff from DHEW Civil Rights Office, Department of Justice Civil Rights Division, the Mexican-American Legal Defense Fund, the California Rural Legal Assistance League and leading Spanish-speaking constitutional experts to develop the principles for Title VI actions on behalf of Spanish-speaking schoolchildren.
- Participating in the issuance by the Secretary of DHEW of a memorandum to school districts having more than 5% Spanish-speaking children to inform those districts that discrimination against Spanish-speaking children will cease as of this fall and to require Title VI compliance in programs for Spanish-speaking children.
- Participating in DHEW's National Conference on Title VI guidelines for Spanish-speaking children at which DHEW policy personnel met to develop guidelines for the fall of 1970 compliance with desegregation plans in school districts serving Spanish-speaking children.

Ultimately, the most impactful action emerging from the Nixon administration in terms of program oversight for language minority learners came from the director of the OCR.

The Office of Civil Rights under Pottinger

Stanley Pottinger was appointed director of the OCR within the DHEW in 1970 and remained in the role until 1973. Pottinger earned his undergraduate degree in 1962 and law degree in 1965, both from Harvard. After his tenure at OCR, he was assistant attorney general in the Civil Rights Division at the Department of Justice and in 1977 served as special assistant to the attorney general. Describing his time running the Civil Rights Division at Department of Justice, Pottinger recalled 'It was such a bizarre balancing act, trying to do liberal work in a conservative administration' (Span, 1995). Reflecting on Washington politics, 'There's a perverse relationship between being in Washington and the state of the nation. It's more fun being there when the country's in trouble' (Span, 1995). (After civil service, Pottinger moved to New York, where he entered into finance with fruitful gains and socialized with the elite, dating celebrities including Gloria Steinam, Kathie Lee Gifford and Connie Chung. He next forayed into the arts, first in movie-making and later fiction writing, ultimately authoring several mystery novels.)

May 25, 1970 OCR Memo

Pottinger, as director of OCR, was in part motivated by the Commission on Civil Rights investigations and resulting reports, to review Civil Rights Act compliance in school districts in various parts of the country. Testifying before subcommittee hearings regarding the education of the 'Spanish-speaking child', he described efforts he directed to 'review civil rights and educational literature addressed to the question of discrimination against national origin minority group children' (Education of the Spanish Speaking, 1972: 38). The result of these investigations was the now somewhat well-known May 25, 1970 Memo, which essentially gave teeth to the OCR for pursuing violations under Title VI of the Civil Rights Act on the basis of national origin or language background. It addressed a range of issues, including not only equitable access to schooling and bilingual education as an available program option for language minority learners, but also the widespread issue of children placed in classes for the 'mentally retarded' due to language background. Its four key points were:

(1) Where inability to speak and understand the English language excludes national origin minority group children from effective participation in the educational program offered by a school district, the district must take affirmative steps to rectify the language deficiency in order to open its instructional program to these students.
(2) School districts must not assign national origin minority group students to classes for the mentally retarded on the basis of criteria which essentially measure or evaluate English language skills; nor may school districts deny national origin minority group children access to college preparatory courses on a basis directly related to the failure of the school system to inculcate English language skills.
(3) Any ability grouping or tracking system employed by the school system to deal with the special language skill needs of national origin minority group children must be designed to meet such language skill needs as soon as possible and must not operate as an educational dead end or permanent track.
(4) School districts have the responsibility to adequately notify national origin minority group parents of school activities which are called to the attention of other parents. Such notice in order to be adequate may have to be provided in a language other than English.

In congressional testimony regarding the 1974 BEA reauthorizations, Pottinger described the genesis and purpose of the 1970 memo:

In conducting Title VI compliance reviews pursuant to 45 CFR 80.7, the DHEW Office for Civil Rights found in 1970 that certain common practices by school districts were effectively denying equality of educational opportunity to national origin-minority-group children with English language deficiencies. It accordingly issued on May 25, 1970, a memorandum of guidelines designed to clarify its policy concerning the responsibility of school districts to provide equal educational opportunity to such children. The memorandum provides in part: Where inability to speak and understand the English language excludes national origin-minority group children from effective participation in the educational program offered by a school district, the district must take affirmative steps to rectify the language deficiency in order to open its instructional program to these students (35 Fed. Reg. 11595; July 10, 1970). (Bilingual Education Act Hearings, 1974: 8)

Division of Bilingual Education's 1971 guidelines

In 1971, the Division of Bilingual Education issued guidelines to provide support for schools and districts in complying with the May 25 Memo and Title VI of the Civil Rights Act by 'outlining steps in program development, amplifying procedures for planning and submitting applications for implementation and continuation of bilingual education programs' (Molina, 1978: 17).

> The 1971 guidelines and the philosophical position of Title VII suggested a maintenance approach to bilingual education. The guidelines emphasized the intent that students in bilingual education programs would 'develop greater competence in English, and become more proficient in their dominant language'. (Molina, 1978: 17)

The 1971 guidelines were later revised by William Bennett during the Reagan administration through a new OCR memo established in 1985, which eased language and created more broad interpretation of the 1970 Memo.

Task force on education

From June 21 to June 25, 1971, the Task Force on Education, within the Cabinet Committee on Opportunities for Spanish-Speaking People convened on Capitol Hill. In earlier testimony, Dick W. Hays, assistant commissioner for special concerns, of the OE, described appropriations intended for 'Spanish-speaking' students:

> Language difficulties are one of the most serious educational handicaps experienced by Spanish-speaking children. To help them, as well as all non-English-speaking children, develop their full potential for learning, a program based on the concept of bilingualism was established in OE. The amount budgeted for bilingual education grants under title VII, ESEA, has increased from $25 million in fiscal 1971 and $35 million in fiscal 1972, to $41 million requested in fiscal 1973. (Education of the Spanish Speaking, 1972: 75)

Findings from a survey conducted by the US Civil Rights Commission (1971) indicated that 66% of schools in Texas discouraged the use of Spanish in classrooms and 33% did so on playgrounds. 'No Spanish' rules at this time were commonplace, as described by Stoller (1975):

> Each teacher, principal, and superintendent employed in the free schools of this state shall use the English language exclusively in the classroom and on the campus in conducting the work of the school. The recitations and exercise of the school shall be conducted in the English language except where other provisions are made in compliance with school law. (Stoller, 1975: 46, citing US Civil Rights Commission, 1972: 15)

Center for Applied Linguistics (CAL)

In 1972, Dr Rudolph C. Troike, Jr was appointed director of CAL, then based in Rosslyn, Virginia. Born in Brownsville, Texas, and trained in anthropology and linguistics, Troike spent two years as a graduate student at the University of Texas abroad 'in Mexico City, on the E.D. Famer International Fellowship, at the *Escuela Nacional de Antropología e Historia* (National Anthropology and History School)' (González, 2008: 860). He was an ESL teacher in Ankara, Turkey, working in a Georgetown University program and was later hired by the English Department at the University of Texas, Austin. During his time there, scholarship focused not only 'on Indigenous languages (Tonkawa, Coahuilteco, Nahuatl, Uto-Aztecan) but also the beginnings of the application of linguistics to language teaching and eventually to bilingual education' (González, 2008: 860).

Under Troike's leadership, CAL's priorities shifted to serving as an advocacy organization for preserving minority language maintenance and language rights, particularly through bilingual education programs under the BEA. His leadership and policy recommendations decisively impacted elements added to the 1974 BEA reauthorization. CAL began publishing its Linguistic Reporter series in 1959, following its founding, to track and disseminate information pertinent to the teaching and learning of languages, applied linguistics and global language issues. Its September 1973 volume added a recurrent section: Bilingual Education News..., in an 'attempt to keep the readers of the *Linguistic Reporter* apprised of what is happening in bilingual/bicultural education so that they will be aware of factors which might influence their programs and their decisions' (Center for Applied Linguistics, 1973).

Indian Education Act, 1972

The Indian Education Act, passed in 1972, specifically supported '*Indian* bilingual-bicultural programs' (McCarty, 1992: 6) and was also part of the ESEA. It 'created an Office of Indian Education, established a National Advisory Council on Indian Education, provided funding to local education agencies', awarded grants for special projects and gave fellowship awards for graduate studies (Whiteman, 1986: 30). For example, in 1976, the Indian Education Act provided $18 million to 'school and tribal education projects in the form of 210 separate grants, aimed to supplement existing education programs and to train Indian personnel for work in the schools' (Whiteman, 1986: 22).

Lau v Nichols, 1974

The *Lau v Nichols* case was brought by parents of Chinese ancestry children in San Francisco in 1970 and impacted 1800 students (Ujifusa, 2016). Plaintiffs claimed that a lack of educational support services violated their children's right to equal educational opportunities. After several rulings by lower courts (including one in which the future first Secretary of Education, Shirley Hufstedler, wrote the dissenting opinion), the Supreme Court found on January 21, 1974, that under Title VI of the Civil Rights Act, the students' rights were in fact, violated by a lack of supports. However, the court did not identify particular program models for language minority learners.

The *Lau* decision affirmed the May 25 Memo, which is referenced in nearly all contemporary investigations of OCR compliance with Title VI of the Civil Rights Act (Moore, 2008). The landmark *Lau* decision has arguably played the most instrumental role in impacting language minority students' right to additional educational supports. In remarks before the Senate Conference on Mexican American Education in Texas, Senator Joseph Montoya of New Mexico, who had been a strong advocate for bilingual education and the initial BEA, compared *Lau* to the *Brown v Board of Education* decision, declaring

> In 1954 the Supreme Court said that a black child had the right to an equal education in the United States of America. Amazingly, in this country, in this century, it was necessary for a court to point out that the color of a child's skin had nothing at all to do with his rights to equality under the constitution... A few weeks ago the Supreme Court handed down another such decision... which will cause just as great an upheaval in education at the local level as the 1954 decision did... This time the Court said that a child whose language was different from that of the majority was still entitled to equal educational opportunity under our laws. (Montoya, 1974, as cited in Schneider, 1976: 55).

It also came at a particularly important time – while Congress was negotiating changes and provisions under the 1974 reauthorization of the BEA. The day after the court's decision, Senator Edward Kennedy made the following statement before the Senate floor:

> The decision for the first time states unequivocally the right under the Civil Rights Act of 1964 for non-English-speaking students to receive special educational instruction to meet their language deficiencies... The evidence seems clear that bilingual education programs containing respect for the recognition of the cultural background of the limited English-speaking students is the best way to meet this problem. Although the Court did not recommend a specific remedy to the language deficiency of the non-English-speaking students, it is clear that bilingual education will in most cases provide the fullest educational opportunity for those children. (Remarks by Senator Kennedy, as cited by Schneider, 1976: 44)

The *Lau* Remedies were published in 1975 under the title, Task Force Findings Specifying Remedies Available for Eliminating Past Educational Practices Ruled Unlawful Under *Lau v Nichols*. It provided districts with guidance regarding the identification of students in need of educational supports based on language background, the types of programs that should be made available for language minority learners and existing criteria and standards for the qualifications and preparation of educators in these programs. The Remedies address areas delineated as follows:

(1) Identification of student's primary or home language.
(2) Diagnostic/prescriptive approach – districts must identify the nature and extent of each student's educational needs and prescribe an educational program utilizing the most effective teaching style.
(3) Educational program selection.
(4) Required and elective courses – districts must show that these are not designed as discriminatory.
(5) Instructional personnel requirements, indicating that educational personnel in programs must be linguistically and culturally familiar with students' backgrounds.
(6) Racial/ethnic isolation or identifiability of schools and classes – it is not legally permissible to create racially or ethnically identifiable schools based on language background.
(7) Notification to parents of students whose primary or home language is other than English – districts must notify caregivers if students are identified as English learners.
(8) Evaluation – plans must include both a product and a result and conduct periodic evaluation throughout program implementation.
(9) Bilingual/bicultural program – programs that serve English learners must utilize the students' native languages and cultural background in instructing, maintaining and further developing necessary skills in both the students' native languages and English.

The *Lau* decision was instrumental in myriad future cases, including the outcome of the *ASPIRA of New York, Inc. v Board of Education*, which impacted native Spanish-speaking students in New York City schools. In this case, parents of Puerto Rican students filed a lawsuit in 1972 to address 'the deficient education of Spanish-speaking children in the city' (Reyes, 2000: 39). Signed on August 29, 1974, the Aspira Consent Decree mandated that schools provide core content instruction in Spanish in language arts, math, science and social studies for Puerto Rican language minority students, in addition to ESL supports.

CAL prepared a Directory of Bilingual Education Programs in the United States 1972/1973, listing 425 bilingual demonstration projects in 38 states, the District of Columbia, Pacific Trust Territories, Puerto Rico and the Virgin Islands. These reportedly included 32 languages, 18 of which were Indigenous (Center for Applied Linguistics, 1973).

As noted by Macías:

> By 1980 the Office of Civil Rights...had over five hundred agreements with school districts in compliance with Lau v. Nichols, providing affirmative language and educational action to meet the needs of nearly 80 percent of the national enrollment of LEP language minority students. (2015: 64)

Note

(1) Later appointed attorney general, Richardson would receive national attention for resigning from this position in October 1973, when he refused to obey presidential demands to fire the special prosecutor assigned to the Watergate investigation. His actions helped precipitate the resignation of Richard Nixon from the presidency.

4 Capacity Building

> There is little doubt that joining the bilingual education movement that began in the mid-1960s had a dramatic impact on my relationship to, and with, my two languages. Previously, I had taken them both for granted as sources of education and enjoyment. Now they became the direct objects of professional concern, headaches, achievements, and disappointments…I realized that there was another side to languages: that they could be used to oppress or liberate.
>
> Josué M. González (2011) in Words were all we had: Reflections on becoming biliterate (de la Luz Reyes, 2011: 35).

Congressional compromises resulted in changes to the Bilingual Education Act (BEA) in the 1974 reauthorization that fundamentally undermined its emphasis on bilingual-bicultural education. The revised legislation no longer labeled programs bilingual-bicultural; 'bicultural' was dropped. Whereas the 1968 text read 'That the use of a child's language and cultural heritage is *the means* by which a child learns' was changed to *a primary means* by which a child learns is through the use of such child's language and cultural heritage' (Schneider, 1976: 53). In addition, *where appropriate* was added to alter 'using bilingual educational practices, techniques, and methods'. The 1974 iteration removed the poverty requirement and allowed English-speaking students to enroll in programs funded under the BEA. These and other changes 'set the tone for two decades, defining bilingual instruction as *transitional*, use of the first language being only a temporary means to another end' (Gándara, 2015: 114).

Appropriations for Capacity Building

After gradual increases in funding for, and activities conducted under, the BEA and its two amendments (1969 and 1972), by the 1974 reauthorization, a surge in investments were instated. Interpretation of the BEA, Title VI of the Civil Rights Act and the *Lau* Remedies, which emerged from the landmark *Lau v Nichols* case coalesced, creating an environment rich with dialogue around the government's responsibility for educating language minority students. On the eve of the passage of the 1974 reauthorization, Senator Kennedy spoke on the Senate floor:

Perhaps most distressing when one reviews the past 7 years has been the inertia, the lack of direction and the absence of leadership evident in the U.S. Office of Education in the area of bilingual education. For the first several years of this administration, the original budget request from the President actually was less than the Congress had authorized the previous year. In addition, in 1973 some $9.75 million was impounded. Once again, this year's original budget request was some $15 million less than the $50.35 million level Congress appropriated in the original fiscal year 1974 Labor-DHEW Appropriations bill.

When the United States is the fifth largest Spanish-speaking country in the world and when a near majority of people in this hemisphere speak Spanish, surely our educational system should not be designed so that it destroys the language and the culture of children from Spanish-speaking backgrounds.

Despite the diminished priority placed on bilingual education (BLE) in the 1974 iteration of the BEA, it set forth considerable efforts toward the expansion of programming and the creation of systemic supports and infrastructure. As was reported following an evaluation of Title VII programs published in 1973, existing programs prior to 1974 suffered in particular due to lack of institutional supports, resources, tools and, notably, qualified educators.

Thirty-two of the thirty-four Title VII projects sampled had developed an evaluation design. All but one attempted to carry out the objectives of their evaluation plan. Several basic problems, however, delayed or hampered the evaluation process. For example, the necessity of translating some tests into Spanish, the development of new instruments appropriate for the target population, and the absence of clearly defined evaluation goals prevented projects from carrying out their objectives. In addition, only a few projects collected useful baseline data related to bilingual education. Though most projects attempted to assess the language dominance of pupils, the language competence in both English and Spanish was not measured. (Development Associates, 1973: 50)

A series of funding streams were initiated in 1974 to address bilingual program needs and issues of consistency – for resource creation and distribution, evaluation and assessment regarding quality of programs and curricula, and funds for the provision of educator preparation for bilingual trainers, staff and leadership at the school and district levels.

Table 4.1 illustrates appropriations under the BEA from 1974 through 1980. This chapter delves more deeply into what this money looked like in implementation – the systemic supports it allowed for, as well as activities that transpired closer to 'the ground' for BLE prior to the onset of its later dismantling during the 1980s.

Table 4.1 BEA appropriations 1974–1980

Fiscal year	Appropriation ($)
1974	68,308,000
1975	91,252,000
1976	104,770,000
1977	123,600,000
1978	143,600,000
1979	158,600,000
1980	173,600,000

Other key provisions in the 1974 version were

- graduate fellowship program for study in the field of training teachers for BLE programs;
- programs to support the development of materials to be used in bilingual programs;
- grants for research or demonstration projects in BLE;
- grants for supplementary educational centers and services;
- contracts with state education agencies (SEAs) for the development, in such agencies, of leadership capabilities in the field of BLE;
- a national Office of Bilingual Education (OBE);
- a National Advisory Council on Bilingual Education;
- a National Clearinghouse for Bilingual Education (NCBE);
- Native American children also became eligible program participants;
- funded Bilingual Resource Centers.

In concert, these constituted early steps in laying the groundwork leading to a national infrastructure for the expansion and enhancement of BLE in the United States.

Native American language programs

It is important to note that although in the first year of the BEA, only five programs funded Native American languages bilingual education, it was quickly recognized and leveraged by tribal language communities across the country, and a decade later, the number had grown to nearly 70, representing 10% of projects (McCarty, 1992, citing Leap, 1983). As Hinton (2001: 42) noted, 'bilingual education was seen from the beginning as a tool for language maintenance and the development of cultural pride'. More pertinent and impactful for federal Native American programs was the 1972 Indian Education Act, 'which supported specifically *Indian* bilingual-bicultural programs' (McCarty, 1992: 6) and the Indian Education Assistance and Self-Determination Act, 'which channeled funds for those instructional services directly to Indian tribes and communities' (McCarty, 1992: 6).

However, the BEA remained instrumental because under Title VII, in addition to funding school programs, it formed a Native American Materials Development Center, which produced hundreds of materials for programs, university courses in literacy, and helped facilitate certification for teachers (McCarty, 1992). Other crucial supports involved a focus on local capacity building, which included educator training and professional development activities (McCarty, 1992).

Peach Springs: The Hualapai Bilingual Academic Excellence Program

The Hualapai Bilingual Academic Excellence Program (HBAEP) was "nationally recognized for its achievements in curriculum development, native language and literacy, and...interactive instructional technology" (Watahomigie and McCarty, 1994: 27). Also Peach Springs School, HBAEP opened in 1975, is located in land now identified as northwestern Arizona, and was funded by the BEA. Prior to inception of the bilingual/bicultural approach, the school "centered its curriculum around English and conventional subject area study" (Watahomigie and McCarty, 1994: 30). During early program development, the all Hualapai staff "generated a list of community and student characteristics and resources, and identified distinctive Hualapai ways of teaching and learning" (Watahomigie and McCarty, 1994: 34). Formerly not a written language, in its first three-year grant cycle, Peach Springs School educators studied linguistics, developed Hualapai orthography, created a 500-word dictionary, and a series of instructional materials. Early on, community concerns were raised regarding the imposition of formal education on Hualapai people, but ultimately community members played central roles in development and refinement of curriculum. For example, recounted Watahomigie and McCarty (1994: 38):

> One elder, the daughter of a medicine man, offered to assist with materials development. She wanted, she said, to pass on her cultural knowledge to future generations. She was especially knowledgeable of native plants and their uses, and provided classroom demonstrations and accompanied the staff and students on field trips to collect native plant species.

Office of Bilingual Education

The 1974 reauthorization of the BEA created the OBE, whose responsibilities included conducting:

> (1) a national assessment of the educational needs of people in the U.S. with limited English-speaking ability, and (2) an assessment of the number of teachers and other kinds of trained personnel needed to meet the goals of bilingual education set forth in the original legislation. (Stoller, 1976: 51)

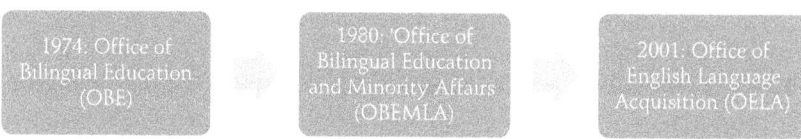

Figure 4.1 Evolution of the OBE

OBE activities were conducted by three major divisions: elementary and secondary programs, postsecondary programs and program development. The Division of Elementary and Secondary Programs was responsible for managing demonstration programs in local education agencies (LEAs), determining bilingual needs and initiating and supervising the development of techniques, standards and procedures for bilingual programs. The Division of Postsecondary Programs administered graduate fellowships and grants to institutes of higher education (IHEs) and SEAs for bilingual educator preparation, training and development. The Division of Program Development directed and coordinated activities related to SEA assistance and the supports provided by Title VII resource centers (see Chapter 5). Despite erosion to the nature of *bilingual* education, throughout the 1970s, the OBE remained committed to 'promoting bilingual innovation and improvement through technical assistance and the support of demonstration projects' (Development Associates, 1978: 35).

When the Department of Education (ED) was created in 1980, OBE 'was restructured and expanded to become the Office of Bilingual and Minority Languages Affairs (OBEMLA)' (ED Facts, 1990: 6). At the time, it was 1 of 13 offices within ED. During this period, OBE (which would later become OBEMLA) oversaw three core areas: those related to state and local bilingual programs; those associated with staff development and training for bilingual educators; and research and evaluation efforts regarding BLE. Research and evaluation activities included three centers: multifunctional resource centers, the NCBE, and evaluation assistance centers (ED Facts, 1990). In 1976, Stoller (1976: 52) reported OBE's oversight of 356 BLE programs and special programs, five resource centers and 12 teacher training programs.

After the 2001 reauthorization of the Elementary and Secondary Education Act (ESEA), OBEMLA was renamed the Office of English Language Acquisition (OELA) and the clearinghouse it oversaw was renamed the National Center for English Language Acquisition (NCELA). Figure 4.1 illustrates the evolution of the OBE from 1974 to its current OELA title.

Bilingual Education Advisory Committee

A nine-member National Advisory Committee on the Education of Bilingual Children was stipulated in the 1968 BEA, which

Shall advise the Commissioner in the preparation of general regulations and with respect to policy matters arising in the administration of this title, including the development of criteria for approval of applications thereunder. The Commissioner may appoint such special advisory and technical experts and consultants as may be useful and necessary in carrying out the functions of the Advisory Committee. (P.L. 90-247, Sec. 707, 1968: 819)

The original committee consisted of nine commissioner-appointed members, including a chairperson, at least four of whom were acquainted with 'dealing with the educational problems of children whose native tongue is a language other than English' (P.L. 90-247, Sec. 707, (a), 1968: 819). Although the National Advisory Council was codified in the original 1968 BEA, the committee was not chartered until January 4, sworn in on January 10 and first met on January 11, 1973 (Bilingual Education Act Hearings, 1974: 79). At that meeting, members were tasked with reviewing proposed rules and amendments to the BEA, as revised on October 31 [1972] congressional hearings (Bilingual Education Act Hearings, 1974: 79). The first chairlady was Rosa Guas de Inclán, who had worked as a consultant for BLE in Dade County Public Schools in Miami, Florida, and played a leading and instrumental role in creation of the Coral Way School (see Chapter 2). In testimony before Congress, de Inclán later reported that the committee collectively determined themselves inadequately acquainted with and thus unprepared to develop such recommendations. De Inclán described the predicament:

> Most of the Committee members had either received the copy of the regulations only the day before coming to Washington or not at all. Some concern was therefore expressed by all as to the difficulty, near impossibility, of achieving the task at hand. It was only at the risk of not being able to make any recommendations at all prior to approaching deadlines that the Committee went through an overview of the proposed regulations and a discussion of some of the points that had been subject to revision at the October hearing, and others that some members of the Committee had singled out as needing clarification, editing, or discussion. (Bilingual Education Act Hearings, 1974: 79)

In continuing her account, the chairlady further described the ill-equipped members, noting help solicited from La Raza and Rudolph Troike of the Center for Applied Linguistics (CAL), who gave 'us some statements from a linguistic point of view' (Bilingual Education Act Hearings, 1974: 79). De Inclán lamented the grave exclusion of scholarship in the areas of linguistics and anthropology 'in connection with bilingual education, which deals with language and culture primarily' (Bilingual Education Act Hearings, 1974: 79). De Inclán vehemently argued before Congress that English as a second language, while perhaps a complementary type of approach to BLE, in and of itself, was insufficient for the instruction of language minority learners (Bilingual Education Act Hearings, 1974: 84).

> ...bilingual education could mean almost anything to anybody. Well, bilingual education does not mean English as a second language, as we have seen it proposed in various position papers that are circulating around and have no business circulating around. Again, I will repeat, these papers have not come to the Committee on the Education of Bilingual Children, whose function it is to review all policy and philosophy concerning those children. English as a second language is a component of bilingual education. But English as a second language alone is not bilingual education.

Recommendations of the Advisory Committee on the Education of Bilingual Children to the Commissioner of Education were to involve the following:

(1) To increase the coordination of activities conducted by all offices involved with bilingual education.
(2) To improve the capacity of bilingual educational personnel through increased employment opportunities and improvement in training and education programs for teachers, administrators, researchers and other professionals, as well as paraprofessionals in the field of BLE.
(3) To improve consideration for and provision of technical assistance to all language minority learners in light of the universal application of BLE across languages.

The 1974 BEA reauthorization identified required backgrounds for members of the NACBE. Eight 'shall be persons experienced in dealing with the educational problems of children and other persons who are of limited English-speaking ability' (Section 732 (a) of Public Law 93-380, 1974). Of the eight, at least one had to have experience on a board of education serving bilingual programs. At least three members were to have had experience training bilingual teachers. Two were to have had experience working in general education settings and at least two had to be classroom teachers with demonstrated teaching abilities for bilingual instruction. A key responsibility of the NACBE was producing an annual report to the director of the United States Office of Education (USOE) Congress regarding BLE programs in the United States.

Figure 4.2 illustrates the varying composition of the National Advisory Committee for BLE across the various reauthorizations of the BEA until its removal from Title VII. Notable prior to its dismantling is the addition of members with expertise in *alternative approaches* to BLE for language minority students.

In its first annual report, published November 1, 1975, and titled *Bilingual Education: Quality Education for All Children* (J.A. Reyes

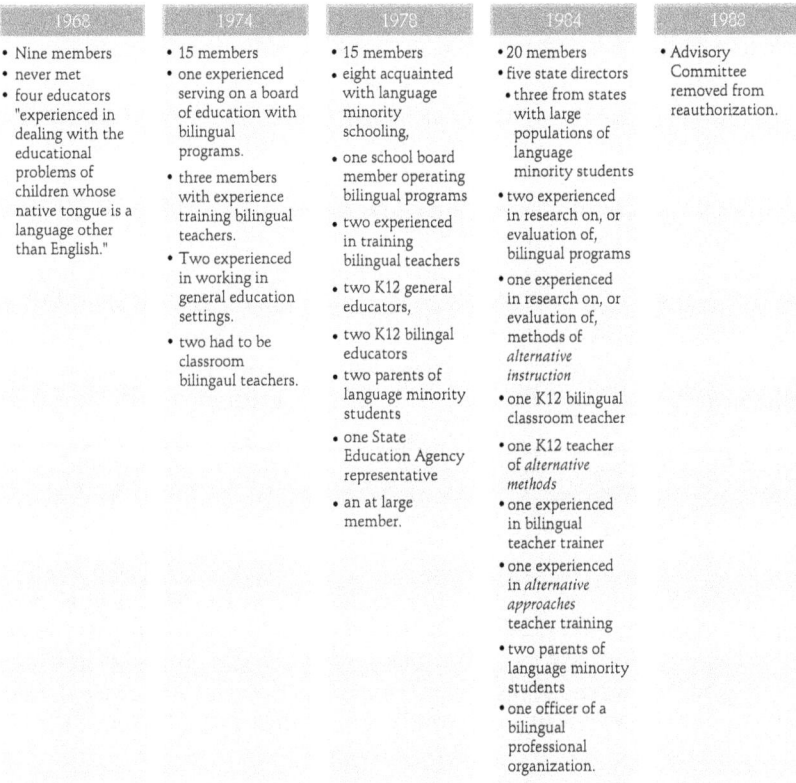

Figure 4.2 National Advisory Committee members

Associates, Inc., 1978), the subsequent chairperson, Rosita E. Cota penned:

> It has always been my heartfelt notion that any endeavor must, with deference to the past, develop and expand to insure success and progress. With this premise in mind, and in an attempt to insure the continued success of bilingual-multicultural education, school and community personnel must view cultural and linguistic differences between children as positive attributes on which to build.
>
> Although the bilingual-multicultural education movement has focused thus far on linguistically different children, because of their educational priorities, from this point forward emphasis must be placed on promoting bilingual-multicultural education both as quality education and as a viable approach for all children. (J.A. Reyes Associates, 1978: 1)

In Section 732(a) of the BEA reauthorization in November 1978, the National Advisory Council on Bilingual Education remained composed of 15 members, including 8 acquainted with language minority schooling,

1 member serving on a school board operating bilingual programs, 2 experienced in training bilingual teachers, 2 with experience in elementary and secondary education, 2 bilingual classroom teachers, 2 parents of language minority students, 1 SEA representative and 1 member at large.

Under Section 752(a) of the BEA, amended in 1984, the council was expanded from 15 to 20 members and its title changed to National Advisory and Coordinating Council on Bilingual Education (1985). The composition of its members shifted away from expertise in BLE to also include 'alternative approaches' to teaching language minority learners.

Ultimately, the advisory committee was removed from the BEA in the 1988 reauthorization. Then chairman, Dr Anthony Torres, Superintendent of the Community Consolidated School District in Chicago appointed by Ronald Reagan, had earlier charged that the superior approach to instructing non-English-speaking students was through English, also citing shortages of educators proficient in Spanish and other languages. In a *Chicago Tribune* article (November 16, 1985), he declared

> The objective of bilingual education is to teach English to non-English-speaking students. It is not intended as a home language maintenance program, nor is it intended as a method of teaching ethnic pride or home culture. Unfortunately, in too many cases the basic mission has been forgotten. I question how recruiting teachers from Spain, Mexico, Puerto Rico or wherever will accomplish the basic objective. (Torres, 1985)

Bilingual program models

In its final version, the 1974 reauthorization remained vague in its definition of a 'bilingual' program. This neglected explication would later provide impetus for claims made by English-only advocates that bilingual programs were poorly implemented, inconsistent and not more effective than English immersion settings. As OBE Director John Molina recounted:

> During the first few years the newly Federally funded bilingual education programs experienced many difficulties due to the inexperience of educators in this country as well as the vagueness inherent in the Act itself... The lack of appropriate materials in non-English languages, and need for trained bilingual teachers made difficult the starting of new programs with appropriate emphasis on native languages. (Molina, 1978: 16–17)

Fiscal year activities in 1975 included 319 basic programs; in FY 1978, 558 basic programs were funded. These included programs offered in a wide range of languages, not only approximately 76% of programs in Spanish, but also 5.47% in Native American languages, 5% in French, 2.7% in 'Asian' language(s), as well as programs in Filipino, Micronesian and Pennsylvania Dutch, to name a few. Table 4.2 displays all languages funded under the BEA in FY 1978 (National Clearinghouse for Bilingual Education, 1979: 5).

Table 4.2 BEA program language representation

Language group	Percentage of funds
Spanish	75.95
Native American (0.81% in Alaska)	5.47
French	5.15
Asian	2.71
Italian	1.97
Portuguese	1.66
Filipino	1.35
Micronesian	1.25
Yiddish	0.55
Greek	0.52
Arabic	0.23
Pennsylvania Dutch	0.19
Russian	0.16
Armenian	0.12
Hungarian	0.08
Other	2.64

A key 265-page report produced by the US Commission on Civil Rights (1975), *A Better Chance to Learn*, investigated existing bilingual programs, documenting findings demonstrating successful programs and shared characteristics. It noted that 'although they differ greatly in scope and structure, successful programs share a conscious consideration of student needs in setting educational goals and in designing the instructional program' (US Commission on Civil Rights, 1975: 85).

The four programs reviewed for the report were in Philadelphia, PA (Spanish/Puerto Rican); Johnstown, CO (Spanish/Mexican American); Rock Point, AZ (Navajo); and San Francisco, CA (Chinese). The report described bilingual programs as typically beginning in the early grades, such as pre-kindergarten or first grade, with programs at the middle and high school levels more rare, although both the Philadelphia and San Francisco sites articulated fully from kindergarten through high school. Two of the locations offered either monolingual English or bilingual settings (San Francisco and Johnstown), and two were whole-school programs, in which all students were enrolled in the bilingual program (Philadelphia and Rock Point). The commission reported that students in bilingual-bicultural classes received the same instruction as in monolingual settings, with the addition of curricula that also included 'consideration for the cultural heritage of both groups of students' (US Commission on Civil Rights, 1975: 86). Each group of native language speakers was taught to develop expression in both their native language and their respective target language (TL) and 'both groups receive subject matter instruction in their native languages until they have sufficient second language skills to receive subject matter in that language' (US Commission on Civil Rights, 1975: 86).

Students learned language arts in both languages. The media of instruction varied across programs, depending on contextual factors, such as degree of exposure to the languages and rate of language development and acquisition. For the most part, media were used separately for different content areas, but native languages may have been used for clarification or for complementary purposes; repetition (concurrent translation) was avoided. Following detailed descriptions of the four existing programs, including a chapter dedicated to the issue of program assessment and evaluation, the commission reported that its 'basic conclusion is that bilingual bicultural education is the program of instruction which currently offers the best vehicle for large members of language minority students who experience language difficulty in our schools' (US Commission on Civil Rights, 1975: 137).

Bilingual Teacher Training

In the 1974 BEA reauthorization, 'increased emphasis was placed on both preservice and inservice training. Included were funds to increase the capacity of postsecondary institutions to prepare people to work in bilingual education programs and a fellowship program to develop teacher trainers' (National Clearinghouse for Bilingual Education, 1979: 4). Newly allocated funding intended to improve supports for bilingual programs through several new systems 'to increase the capacity of postsecondary institutions to train personnel to work in bilingual programs; for a national network of training, materials development, and dissemination and assessment centers; and for fellowship programs for bilingual teacher trainers' (Coballes-Vega *et al.*, 1979: 1). Specifically, fellowship programs were for full-time graduate students in IHE programs approved by the Commissioner of Education. A critical consideration for the fellowship program was its focus on *teacher trainers* – these were meant to produce graduates equipped to function in professional development and leadership roles using expertise attained through the programs.

In 1975, $3 million was allocated to 30 IHEs and 474 fellows. By 1978, fellowships had grown to 778 students in 47 IHEs. Table 4.3 displays fellowship enrollment (Coballes-Vega *et al.*, 1979: 2).

Table 4.3 Fellowship funding

Fiscal year	Funds ($M)	Number of fellowships awarded
1975	3	474
1976	4	708
1977	4	672
1978	5	778

Findings from an evaluation of the fellowship program between the 1975/1976 and 1977/1978 academic years were published in 1979, based on data collected through surveys distributed to IHEs (Coballes-Vega *et al.*, 1979). The following areas were addressed by the six-item survey (Coballes-Vega *et al.*, 1979: 5):

(1) The total number of students in the programs.
(2) The disciplinary concentrations of the students in the programs.
(3) The number of students who dropped out of the programs.
(4) The current employment status of the graduates.
(5) An estimate of the number of teacher trainers needed in the region served by the program.
(6) Significant achievements of the graduates of the programs.

In total, 49 surveys were distributed and 44 responses received, a 90% response rate (though three of the non-respondents were new programs, meaning a more realistic rate was 95%).

Evaluation data showed that over the three academic years of 1975/76 through 1977/78, 1675 students were enrolled in fellowship programs. An additional 1194 students were enrolled in programs without fellowship funding. Data from survey results are displayed in Table 4.4 (Coballes-Vega *et al.*, 1979: 7). In their introduction to the report, researchers indicated that an estimated 10,000 teacher trainers were needed in 1978, based on the National Center for Education Statistics (NCES) data, to train 100,000 teachers, who in turn, could serve as educators in bilingual programs, supporting the estimated 3.6 million 'limited-English-speaking' students. Programs were making reasonable progress toward fulfilling the educational goals needed to, by extension, provide professional development and support services to the 100,000 needed bilingual teachers.

Findings showed that 959 of the Other students were in master's-level programs, while 235 were in doctoral programs. Based on the numbers of students reported to be receiving both Title VII fellowship funding and the Other category, the authors asserted 'figures indicate that the bilingual teacher trainers programs are reasonably well institutionalized,

Table 4.4 Enrollment data

Fiscal year	Title VII students (actual)	Title VII students (reported)	Other students (reported)
1975	474	408	205
1976	708	611	349
1977	672	656	640
Total	1854	1675	1194

judging by the high number of students (over 1,000) who attend the programs without Title VII support' (Coballes-Vega et al., 1979: 8).

Most of the Other students (959) were enrolled at the master's level, 235 were in doctoral programs. In the San Francisco region, there were 283 Other master's students and only 218 fellows in master's programs. Conversely, there were 176 doctoral fellows and only 41 Other students. The report authors cite this as evidence of the critical need for Title VII fellowship funds for supporting doctoral studies. The three regions with the most enrolled students were Dallas (466), San Francisco (394) and New York (343), which were also the regions with the highest populations of language minority learners, as per NCES statistics of the same time period. The survey included an item regarding disciplinary areas, but authors cautioned:

> …at this time…there is quite a lot of controversy in the field of bilingual education surrounding the establishment of 'bilingual education' as a disciplinary concentration *per se*. The prevalent thinking of OBE is that bilingual education is *not* a discipline, but an interdisciplinary *approach* to special educational needs. (Coballes-Vega et al., 1979: 9)

The largest number of doctoral students (87) were in BLE, with sizeable numbers also in reading (49), administration (48), curriculum (47) and research (36) (it is also notable that 87 doctoral and 43 master's-level respondents did not respond to the discipline question). Table 4.5 illustrates employment information regarding the students in master's-level programs surveyed (Coballes-Vega et al., 1979: 11). The vast majority of graduates were employed at LEAs.

Of the 78 respondents in doctoral programs, 33 worked in IHEs, 24 in LEAs, 12 in SEAs, 2 cited other employment, 5 were post-doctoral students and 2 were unemployed (see Table 4.6).

Over four times the number of master's degrees than doctoral degrees were awarded between 1975 and 1978. While 442 were at the master's level, only 82 were for doctoral studies. Survey findings suggested that Title VII fellowship support may not have been sufficient to cover the costs of programs, given that 368 master's and 14 doctoral students cited

Table 4.5 Master's-level employment

Master's-level employer/employment status	Number
Local education agency	274
State education agency	22
Doctoral student	7
Institute of higher education	43
Other employment	42
Unknown	19
Unemployed	35

Table 4.6 Doctoral fellows' employment status and employers

Doctoral-level employer/employment status	Number
Institute of higher education	33
Local education agency	24
State education agency	12
Post-doctoral student	5
Other employment	2
Unemployed	2

'Other' supports. Coballes-Vega *et al.* (1979) found that although 316 doctoral degrees were anticipated, survey respondents indicated only 82 doctoral degrees were earned. Funding sources for master's and doctoral students are shown in Table 4.7.

The researchers concluded that 'the Title VII Fellowship Program would appear to have met its objectives only to a small extent' (Coballes-Vega *et al.*, 1979: 13). They warned that data are incomplete and insufficient to merit thorough assessment of the fellowship programs, calling for maintained attention toward and funding provided for these and other programs, and noted 'the obvious inability of these [doctoral] students to obtain financial support outside of Title VII fellowship assistance' (Coballes-Vega *et al.*, 1979: 14). Further, they recommended

> There needs to be more attention given to the employment of masters graduates. If most of these graduates find employment in LEA's, it is unlikely that more than a few of these individuals are employed either as trainers of other bilingual education personnel or in leadership positions. If this is the case, then certainly these graduates have not met the intent of the legislation establishing the fellowship program as a program to educate teacher trainers. Most of the masters graduates appear to have returned to LEA's as classroom teachers. (Coballes-Vega *et al.*, 1979: 14–15)

In a paper presented at the 7th International Bilingual Bicultural Education Conference in April 1978, Maria Estela Brisk (1978) discussed bilingual higher education programs. She noted that 'It has been estimated that more than 130,000 bilingual teachers are needed throughout the nation to provide appropriate education for some 68 language

Table 4.7 Fellowship funding sources

Total Title VII funded		Total 'Other' support	
Masters	Doctoral	Masters	Doctoral
442	82	368	14

groups' (Brisk, 1978: 1–2). She asserted the challenges faced, and insufficiencies provided by, IHEs:

> It seems that many bilingual children in IHEs are offered standard teacher-training curricula embellished with a smattering of language and culture courses, or conversely, are isolated from monolingual colleagues in special programs that emphasize culture and language to the exclusion of rigorous educational courses. (Brisk, 1978: 2)

According to the *Guide to Title VII ESEA Bilingual Bicultural Programs 1977–78* (Author, 1978), Title VII funded 515 school programs, 101 training programs and 48 fellowship programs at 16 different universities (Table 4.8).

Training programs served 27 language groups and fellowship programs served 18 language groups; however, Brisk (1978: 5) noted that 'of the languages served by Title VII basic programs (i.e., K-12), 22 are not included in any of the teacher training or fellowship programs'.

Findings from a survey designed to identify the needs of directors and educators in bilingual programs funded under Title VII, published in Spring 1978 (Reifle & Goldsmith, 1978), showed agreement among both directors and teachers regarding the need for teacher training. Roughly 91% of responding teachers had five or fewer years of bilingual teaching experience and over half (287 of 560) had fewer than two years' experience in bilingual programs (Reifle & Goldsmith, 1978: 71). Most-needed areas indicated by respondents were curriculum and teaching methodology specific to BLE. The authors surmised that 'the nature of the training most needed by teachers may, therefore, require the duration and intensity of college-level coursework for adequate results' (Reifle & Goldsmith, 1978: 71). Further, they asserted

Table 4.8 Types of degrees by training and fellowships

Type of degree	Training	Fellowship	Total
Certification, credential or endorsement	27		27
AA	12		12
Associate of Fine Arts	1		1
BA or BS	73		73
MA, EdM or MAT	56	29	85
EdD or PhD	3	24	27
Graduate credit	3		3
Total degree programs	175	53	228
Total universities	101	48	116

Colleges and universities could make an important contribution to bilingual education by offering programs designed to provide area specialization in bilingual education to currently employed teachers, perhaps in the evenings and summers. Our data suggests that the success of such programs would depend largely on local project willingness to provide a quid pro quo to participating teachers in the form of release time, compensation, or other incentive. (Reifle & Goldsmith, 1978: 71–72)

Additional Needs

Changes to the 1974 BEA reauthorization weakened emphasis on bilingual-bicultural education and undermined the positionality of language as a right. However, other shifts functioned as systemic, national-level mechanisms for the expansion and enhancement of bilingual education in the United States. The OBE elevated the status of bilingual education as a field and facilitated critical activities that impacted on-the-ground programs, including oversight of demonstration projects to explore the effectiveness of various program types, characteristics and settings. The convening of a national advisory committee devoted to bilingual education produced an advocacy body of authority to direct comprehensive oversight of the state of BLE, importantly in part due to its responsibility for producing annual reports to the president and Congress regarding the national state of BLE. Among the most impactful investments in the 1974 reauthorization were the fellowship programs, which injected a new senior-level career pathway into the field by focusing on postgraduate studies with the goal of yielding a new cadre of bilingual educator trainers. Graduates from fellowship programs spanned the country and across various systems and levels of BLE, from placement in universities, to LEAs, SEAs, schools, advocacy organizations and other agencies to foster new developments in bilingual education and its implementation.

The groundwork laid through the establishment of the OBE, the advisory committee and fellowships to feed a BLE educator pipeline would not have been sustainable however, without additional systemic supports – particularly for the creation, distribution and dissemination of resources for use as curricula and for the instruction, assessment and evaluation of bilingual programs. Whereas the advisory committee was tasked with advocating for, and painting its vision of BLE in the United States, a national clearinghouse was also instituted for the logistical management and oversight of resource development and a national network of centers was created for the development of BLE resources. These are described in Chapter 5.

5 Systemic Infrastructure

...there were half a dozen district administrators anxiously awaiting my reaction to the bilingual program.

'What do you think?' the assistant superintendent asked.

'I think it is an admirable effort in responding to the language needs of children', I replied. 'But let me ask an important question. Why don't you have the English speaking teacher present the English language activity and the Spanish speaking aide present the Spanish activity?'

'It's interesting you bring this up, because that's the way we used to do it. However, on our last monitoring visit from the state education agency, the program officer noted that the teacher is being paid from a Title VII bilingual grant and therefore has to teach the Spanish lesson, and the teacher aide is being paid from our Title I grant and therefore cannot be allowed to teach in the Spanish language'.

Stunned as I was, I had the presence of mind to ask, 'Did you get this criticism in writing?'

'Yes sir, we sure did'.

Before I left the district I had a copy of the monitoring visit report from the State Department of Education specifying which language each of the two instructors could use in keeping with their source of pay, rather than their language proficiency.

As I was leaving, I was asked one more question, 'What do you think we should do?'

Without hesitation I responded, 'Have the English speaking teacher teach in English, the Spanish speaking aide teach in Spanish, and lie like hell to the State Department of Education'.

José A. Cárdenas (1994: 58) on observation of a school district in West Texas in the late 1970s.

As is illustrated in the scenario Cárdenas recounted, implementation of educational policies can lead to compromised fidelity of intended goals. Although the Office of Bilingual Education (OBE), the National Advisory Council on Bilingual Education (NACBE) and fellowship programs played important roles in the large-scale expansion of bilingual programs, the administration of demonstration projects and organizational needs for the maintenance and development of bilingual programs also remained key to realizing the Bilingual Education Act (BEA). To address needs on a national scale, a clearinghouse was instituted, to be overseen by the OBE. In addition, OBE directed activities, operating as a national infrastructure for bilingual education, including notably, large-scale networks of support centers.

The signing of the August 1974 BEA coincided with the advent of John Molina serving as director of the first Division of Bilingual Education. Molina played an instrumental role in overseeing the implementation of improvements made to the BEA through its later reauthorization, which took effect in February 1975. Table 5.1 illustrates the extent to which key programs repositioned the viability of bilingual accessibility on a national scale between 1973 and the 1978 BEA reauthorization.

> While the new legislation did include a definition of a bilingual education program, it was not the service or maintenance approach that many advocates wanted. Nonetheless it was a big step. Training became mandatory with 15% of basic grants set-aside for such activities. As Director, I encouraged degree oriented training rather than strictly inservice. A network of centers set up to develop and assess bilingual education curriculum materials became an integral part of the program… my administration joined with many professionals in the field in taking a leadership role to establish the network. (Molina & Chavez, 1978: 23)

The Clearinghouse

Among the provisions added in 1974 was the addition of a national clearinghouse 'on information for bilingual education, which shall collect, analyze, and disseminate information about bilingual education and such related programs' (Predaris, 1983: 29). During October and November 1976, six Bilingual Clearinghouse Conferences were held to solicit feedback from stakeholders in the field of bilingual education regarding the creation, role and function of a National Clearinghouse for Bilingual Education (NCBE) (Arawak Consulting Corporation, 1977). Hosted by the National Institute of Education (NIE) and the US Office of Education (USOE), the conferences were held in San Diego, Seattle, Chicago, New York, San Antonio and Miami. The goal of the meetings was to 'receive guidance from potential users of the clearinghouse as to what such services should provide' (Arawak Consulting Corporation, 1977: 12).

The assemblies constituted part two of a six-phase process established to implement the creation of the NCBE. The phases are outlined as follows (see Arawak Consulting Corporation, 1977: 83):

Phase I: A recently completed preliminary design study sponsored by the USOE to explore technical alternatives for the clearinghouse.
Phase II: The conferences and synopsis of comments and results.

Table 5.1 Funding history of Title VII programs, 1973–1977

	1973 ($m)	1974 ($m)	1975 ($m)	1976 ($m)	1977 ($m)	1978 estimate ($m)
Total authorization	135	135	135	140	150	160
Total appropriation	45	68.32	81.2	96.7	115.2	135
Total obligation	33.25	67.6	81.2	96.17	115.1	135
Presidential request	41.13	35	70	70	115.2	135
Total for basic projects	33.25	66.6	64.6	69.5	85.725	93.975
Total number of students served	129,280	339.595	162,124	190.000	235,000	255,000
Total for program development			3.79	9.275	9.275	11
Total for graduate fellowship			3.0	4	4	5
Total for centers			9.83	12	12	18
Total of SEA awards				1.2	3.9	4.375
Total for research (Part C)				100,000	200,000	2.5

Phase III: Immediately following Phase II, implementation of some of the near-term recommendations.
Phase IV: A more systematic design of the clearinghouse relying on the results of the first three stages.
Phase V: A full implementation of the clearinghouse.
Phase VI: Establishment of the clearinghouse.

In total, 424 people attended one of the six conferences and each followed the same day-long agenda. Prior to meetings, each participant received 'Information Needs in Bilingual Education', which posited challenges associated with the implementation of bilingual education. The document was designed to foster reflection prior to attendance at the events. Its closing line read 'Rather than try to "crystal ball" what kinds of information you need, we encourage you to reflect on your own experiences and interpret them during the Conference' (Arawak Consulting Corporation, 1977: 86).

During the morning plenary session, federal representatives addressed conferees, including Division Director Molina and chief of the Multicultural/Bilingual Division of NIE, Jose Vazquez. Next, they engaged in two two-hour working groups (averaging fewer than 15 people each) led by facilitators who were 'encouraged to draw divergent opinions' (Arawak Consulting Corporation, 1977: 10) rather than consensus. The goal of these break-out meetings was to produce major recommendations, which were reported during afternoon plenary periods (Image 5.1).

In all, over 300 recommendations were made regarding the formation of the bilingual clearinghouse. These are summarized in Table 5.2 (Arawak Consulting Corporation, 1977: 13–14).

Image 5.1 Conference meeting regarding the new NCBE

Table 5.2 Bilingual clearinghouse national recommendations

Summary of National Recommendations
A national advisory board must be established to formulate policy for all aspects of the clearinghouse.
The clearinghouse should be national in scope, and should be supportive of all bilingual efforts in the nation.
The clearinghouse must have a clearly written 'statement of mission'. The statement must have wide distribution.
The clearinghouse must not duplicate or bypass existing bilingual projects.
The clearinghouse must aggressively seek information, nationally and internationally.
The clearinghouse must not do any screening. It must collect, categorize and prepare all available information and materials for quick retrieval.
The clearinghouse should directly reach individuals, professionals, parents, teachers, bilingual protagonists and antagonists, industrial and commercial users.
An aggressive public relations function must be a part of the clearinghouse. Efforts to create positive bilingual education policies must be vigorously undertaken.
The clearinghouse must have as a minimum a periodic newsletter, and must consider a journal and other periodic specialized reports.
The clearinghouse must play a strong role in research, having its own research program and stimulating other centers to perform research.
The clearinghouse must not be involved in direct interpersonal assistance.
Clearinghouse services should be free of charge, particularly in the first years. Subsequently, sliding fee scales may be incorporated.
The following topic areas must be included in the clearinghouse: • Curriculum materials • Tests and their evaluations • Data collected on research projects, surveys and census • Information sources in bilingual education • Training material for bilingual education • Federal legislation and guidelines • Funding sources for research and training • Effective classroom practices and unpublished ideas • Human resource file with names, addresses, telephone numbers of people with specific experience or knowledge • Court cases and decisions • Parental and community development • Bilingual education for the handicapped, special and gifted persons • International data, research and reports • Demographic data and studies
Personnel of the clearinghouse must be professional, multi-lingual and multi-ethnic, and should come from the education field.

Based on the recommendations collected through conference events, the potential for a bilingual education clearinghouse was framed with five major objectives (Image 5.2). First, as a means for transferring information and materials regarding bilingual education; second, for problem-solving assistance to classrooms, administrators and communities; third, for national coordination of bilingual education-related activities; fourth, for aggregation and analysis of information regarding bilingual education; and fifth, to facilitate communication among researchers and policymakers regarding needs for knowledge, techniques and materials.

Image 5.2 Attendees at a bilingual clearinghouse meeting

The first contract for the NCBE was awarded to InterAmerica Research Associates (1979) of Arlington, Virginia, and its activities began on October 1, 1977 (Predaris, 1983: 29). Its basic functions were to provide research, reference and referral services to bilingual educators; establish a computerized database to ensure effective retrieval and processing of bilingual education resources; develop and make available timely information products to consumers interested in bilingual education; and coordinate information gathering and processing among bilingual education programs.

Within the Title VII network, the NCBE's role was to provide information to support regional and local activities 'to distinguish between NCBE's and similar services provided by the existing network of centers' (Gorena, 2008: 575). Renamed the National Clearinghouse for English Language Acquisition (NCELA) in the 2001 reauthorization of the Elementary and Secondary Education Act (No Child Left Behind), the clearinghouse remains in operation (a solicitation for vendors to contract with the Department of Education (ED) is posted to re-compete for the project approximately every five years). Its functions over the years have remained comparable throughout various presidential administrations. As Gorena (2008) writes, its role in language minority schooling is

> to serve as a national conduit of information to support regional and local activities... NCBE was primarily responsible for responding to the information needs that the Title VII centers found difficult to address given their regional focus. (Gorena, 2008: 575)

Resource Centers

The 1974 BEA reauthorization also added funding for three types of assistance centers: Materials Development Centers (MDCs),

Dissemination and Assessment Centers (DACs) and Training Resource Centers (TRCs). These were created to develop, test and disseminate bilingual materials. Prior to the establishment of the centers, materials were primarily developed by several regional adaptation centers and local education agencies (LEAs) (see Development Associates, 1978). Definitions of the three centers are as follows:

Training resource centers: In designated service areas of the country, to serve personnel participating in bilingual programs in LEAs or teacher training programs in Institutes of Higher Education (IHEs).
Materials development centers: For the development of instructional and assessment materials in various languages for use by teachers and students in bilingual programs.
Dissemination and assessment centers: For the publication, dissemination and evaluation of the materials produced by the MDCs.

Table 5.3 depicts Title VII center funding over the period of the centers' inception in 1975 through 1978. From 1975 to 1978, 60% of funding was allocated for materials development and dissemination ($20.3 million) and 40% for educator training ($13.8 million). After the 1975/1976 fiscal year (FY), the number of MDCs decreased from 19 to 14, which remained consistent through 1977/1978. The number of TRCs increased from 7 to 15 in FY 1976/1977, and again to 16 in FY 1977/1978. Materials and dissemination centers were allocated 67% and training centers only 33% in FY 1975/1976; the following year the distribution shifted from 59% and 41% in 1976/1977; and further to 57% and 43%, respectively, the next year (1977/1978).

Despite three separate sets of responsibilities and assignments, the participants in Development Associates' (1978) field interviews to assess the effectiveness of materials development showed the inter-relation between each type of center and suggested inconsistencies with centers' intended roles vis-á-vis one another. As one TRC staff person shared, 'DACs have too much to do just publishing. They can't handle assessment forms, so we wind up doing needs assessment work ourselves' (Development Associates, 1978: 58).

Table 5.3 Title VII center expenditures, 1975–1978

Fiscal year	OBE expenditure on Title VII centers ($)
1975/1976	9,900,685
1976/1977	12,000,000
1977/1978	12,286,260
Total	34,186,945

The Network

Together, these centers and others administered by the OBE comprised The National Network of Centers for Bilingual Education (The Network), to develop new instructional materials, pilot and assess their utility and disseminate them to bilingual programs. As of 1978, the OBE was overseeing activities conducted by a total of 33 centers serving more than 500 districts in 39 states, the District of Columbia, Puerto Rico, the Virgin Islands, American Samoa and the Trust Territories. Each of the three centers previously defined (training resource, materials development and dissemination and assessment) was assigned to a particular regional territory and language background and provided products, services, information and other supports to districts, state education agencies (SEAs), IHEs and bilingual educators. Each of the materials and dissemination centers was partnered and designed to work in tandem on the creation and distribution of curricula, materials and assessments in assigned languages; each pair functioned essentially as a publishing operation.

To assess the effectiveness of The Network, the OBE contracted with Development Associates (1978: 2) on July 1, 1976, to conduct 'A Study of the State of Bilingual Materials Development and the Transition of Materials to the Classroom'. The study involved conducting an inventory of existing bilingual instructional materials in a range of languages; site visits to centers, commercial publishers and distributors to assess the development and distribution of materials; and a survey mailed to LEAs regarding the needs and uses for bilingual materials. The objectives of the study were to compile a list of available bilingual materials; identify gaps in the available materials and needs; identify materials development and dissemination methods; and summarize the state of materials development, including their transition to and application in classrooms.

Report findings illustrated the scope and scale of The Network for creating, disseminating and providing training regarding new materials. The functions and tasks of the bilingual centers are shown in Table 5.4. Despite each type of center's distinct roles and responsibilities, they shared a range of similar attributes, in that they were experimental programs funded expressly by the OBE and designed to expire at a future time. Although federally funded, each center was bound by local protocols and regulations and as such, responsiveness necessitated sensitivity to communities' needs. Materials were developed in a wide range of languages. In addition to Spanish (55%), French (9%), Portuguese (6%), Greek (2%), Italian (2%), Russian (0.75%), Yiddish (0.75%) and Vietnamese (0.5%), 13% were devoted to 'Asian' (including Korean, Japanese, Chinese, Filipino), 5% for Native American, 3% for both 'Pacific' and Alaskan languages (Eastern Aleut, Western Aleut, Dana'ima Athapaskan, Swich'in Athapaskan, Whidh'in Athapaskan,

Table 5.4 Resource center functions and tasks

Function	Task	Responsible Center
Assessment of needs	Survey directors of centers on priorities	DAC
	Assess needs for instructional materials	DAC
Creation of instructional materials	Develop materials	MDC
Evaluation of materials	Pilot test instructional materials, teacher training materials and testing materials	MDC/TRC
	Assess applicability of materials	DAC
	Assess effectiveness of materials	DAC
	Develop assessment instruments	DAC
	Conduct pilot tests	TRC
	Analyze, compile, report and interpret pilot test data	DAC
	Provide technical data on finished products	DAC
	Make publication decisions	DAC
	Develop procedures for evaluating impact of BL/BC programs	TRC
Assembly and distribution of materials	Collect and compile materials from Title VII programs	DAC
	Publish instructional and testing materials	DAC
	House materials	TRC
	Disseminate information on bilingual education	DAC
	Disseminate products	DAC
	Assist LEAs and IHEs on materials selection	TRC
Other functions	Train professional staff	TRC
	Train community members	TRC
	Provide feedback information on effective training models to MDCs	TRC
	Provide means for involving parents and community organizations in programs	TRC

Upper Kuskokwim Athapaskan, Upper Tanana Athapaskan, Inupiat Eskimo, Siberian Yup'ik, Eskimo and Sugpiaq Eskimo) language materials were included. In total, 14 materials centers and 3 dissemination centers were found to be engaged in 109 publishing programs in 32 languages for K-12 bilingual education settings.

Spanish materials were created for third to twelfth grades and adults in language arts, social science, science/health, fine arts, Spanish as a second language, math, social studies, career education and teacher training by centers across the country.

Figure 5.1 illustrates the relationships, activities and functions among the three types of bilingual centers.

French materials were developed for reading, French language structure, contemporary stories, social studies readers, song books,

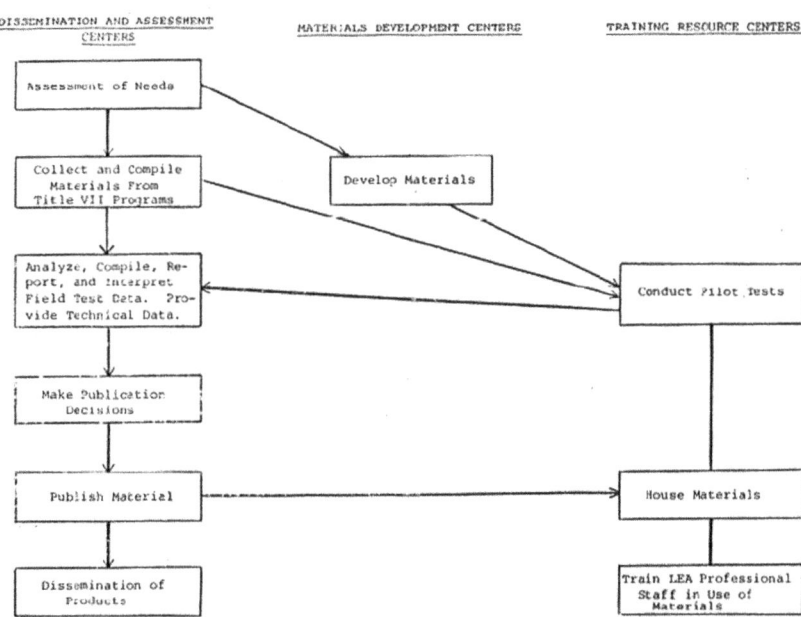

Figure 5.1 Resource center relationships, activities and functions

social-cultural awareness, language communication, career education, social studies and teacher training for Grades K-9 in New Hampshire, Fort Worth and Dallas. Greek and Italian materials were created in language arts, social studies and fine arts, as well as for language assessments in Grades K-6 by the New York City board of education. Materials for reading/language arts and career education were developed for Grades K-12 by the New Hampshire College and University Council. Materials were developed for reading/language arts, math, environmental studies, fine arts, social studies, history and culture, US history, world geography, world history, government, economics and sociology in Korean, Japanese and Chinese for Grades K-12. Filipino materials were developed in reading/language arts, math, environmental studies, fine arts and social studies for Grades K-3.

Among Pacific languages, materials for language arts for Grades 4–6 were developed in Ilocano; for readers in Grades 1–3 in Samoan; social studies in Marshallese for Grades 1–4; reading for third grade in Kusaiean; language arts and social studies for Grades 1–3 in Chamorro; language arts for Grades 1–3 in Carolinian; reading and social studies for Grades 6–10 and 1–5, respectively in Palauan; reading, science and social studies in Ponapean for Grades 4–6; reading for first grade in Yapese; and social studies for Grades 3–4 in Turkese. Language arts materials were

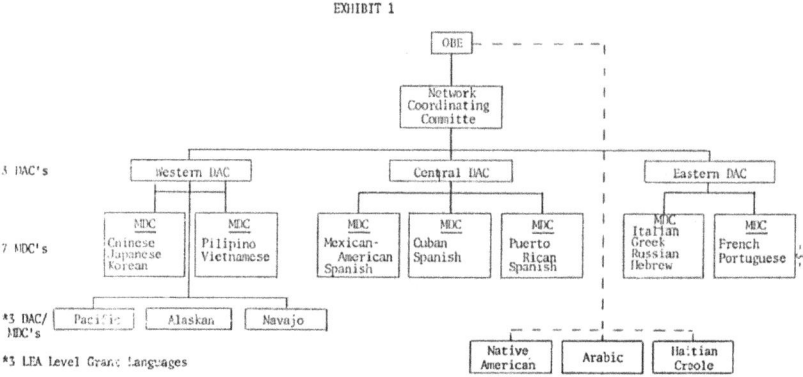

Figure 5.2 Relationship between the OBE and The Network

created for Grades K-12 in Vietnamese. Finally, for grades prekindergarten through adult education, materials were created for math, science, language arts, reading readiness, Navajo literacy materials, Navajo children's magazine and educational games in Navajo. Materials for Alaska Native language programs were developed for Grades K-12 and teacher preparation, including dictionaries, for grammars, language handbooks, cultural studies and teacher training.

Figure 5.2 illustrates the relationships between the OBE and the Network centers, including the respective language foci.

The maps in Figure 5.3 show the Title VII network of centers by region. In concert, these served as core infrastructure for supporting the needs of bilingual programs.

Materials development centers

The MDCs were established and created instructional materials for use by LEAs, IHEs and other bilingual instructional programs. The OBE assigned MDCs the following responsibilities (Development Associates, 1978: 50):

- To develop and revise materials according to research, needs assessments and pilot testing data.
- To develop multimedia materials for classroom use by teachers and students.
- To produce materials for teacher training.
- To design criterion-referenced tests and other assessment instruments to accompany developed materials.
- To plan, formulate and conduct design testing.

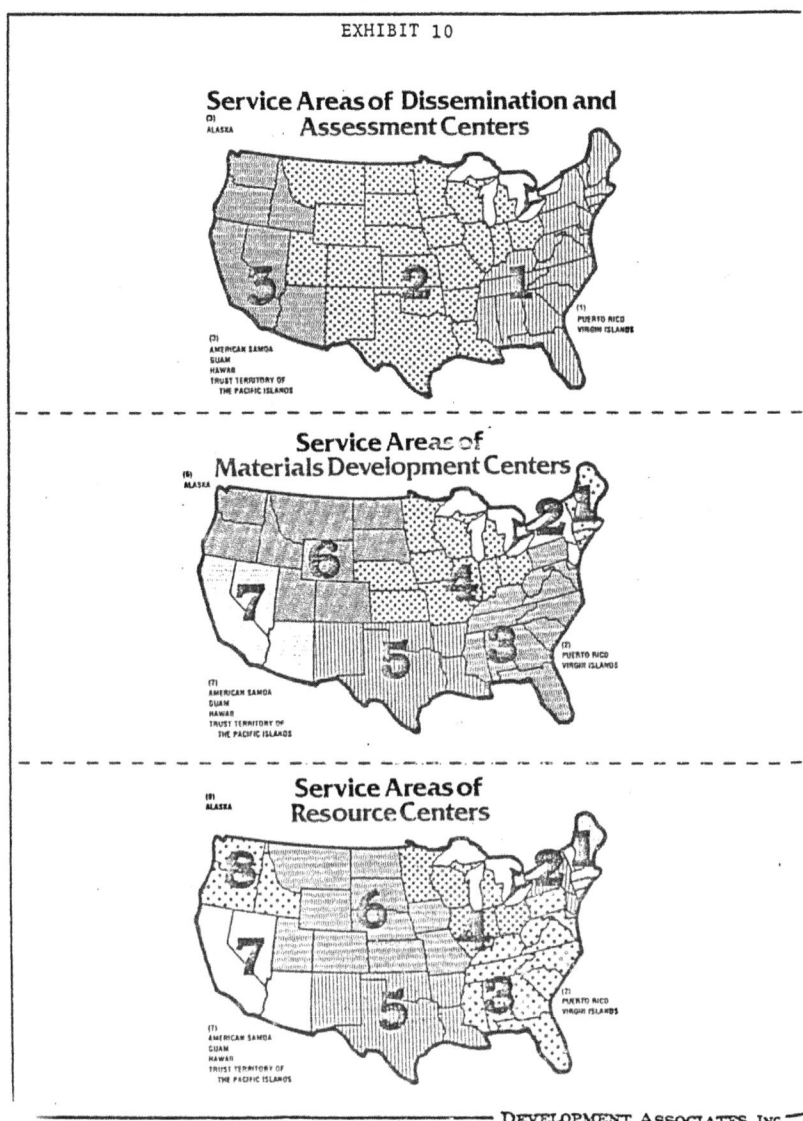

Figure 5.3 Service center regions

- To cooperate with DACs in the development and implementation of pilot test designs.
- To train TRCs' teacher-training staff involved in pilot testing.

Other responsibilities for MDCs included the provision of input regarding needs assessments to the DACs and TRCs and conducting research related to materials development and implementation. Table 5.5 shows

94 A History of Bilingual Education in the US

Table 5.5 Exhibit 6: Materials development centers – grants by center and language group

Language	MDC	1975–1976 ($)	1976–1977 ($)	1977–1978 ($)	Center total ($)	Language total ($)
Alaskan	Fairbanks, AK		300,000	300,000	600,000	600,000
Asian	Berkeley, CA	593,283	500,000	432,000	1,525,281	2,375,283
	Los Angeles, CA		175,000	175,000	350,000	
	Seton Hall, NJ		250,000	250,000	500,000	
Native American	Albuquerque, NM	300,000	350,000	350,000	1,000,000	1,000,000
Pacific	Honolulu, HI			325,000	325,000	325,000
Vietnamese	Urbana, IL		83,333	83,333	166,666	166,666
French	Berlin, NH	200,000	190,000	190,000	580,000	1,246,667
	Urbana, IL		83,334	83,333	166,667	
	Fort Worth, TX		250,000	250,000	500,000	
Portuguese	Berlin, NH	200,000	190,000	190,000	580,000	580,000
Greek	Bronx, NY	161,000	110,000	110,000	381,000	301,000
Italian	Bronx, NY	151,000	110,000	110,000	381,000	381,000
Russian	Bronx, NY		110,000	110,000	220,000	220,000
Yiddish	Bronx, NY		110,000	110,000	220,000	220,000
Spanish	Miami, PL	800,000	620,000	620,000	2,040,000	8,156,486
	Bronx, NY	161,000	110,000	110,000	381,000	
	Tucson, AZ	499,499	450,000	450,000	1,399,499	
	Pomona, CA	717,320	600,000	600,000	1,917,320	
	Fort Worth, TX	707,000	250,000	250,000	1,207,000	
	Milwaukee, WI	245,000	200,000		445,000	
	Urbana, IL		83,333	83,334	166,667	
	Dallas, TX		300,000	300,000	600,000	
Totals		4,735,102	5,425,000	5,482,000	15,652,102	15,652,102

each MDC's funding for 1975–1978, including language, allocated dollar amount and location.

Dissemination and assessment centers

The primary role for DACs was to publish the bilingual/bicultural materials created by MDCs, as well as those produced by LEAs, IHEs or other sources. The DACs' primary role was to solicit, review and assess Title VII developed materials and establish quality standards for products and materials. Their responsibilities were organized into four areas (Development Associates, 1978: 51–52): (1) publication and dissemination; (2) needs assessment; (3) pilot testing; and (4) technical assistance.

Publication and dissemination involved selecting appropriate Title VII project-developed products; national marketing for all products published; production and distribution of review pieces regarding products; and collection, publication and dissemination of information regarding bilingual education. Needs assessment involved the development of instruments for data collection regarding needs in the field, and all steps involved in conducting the assessment, such as data analysis and interpretation. Pilot testing included all areas related to piloting products, including study design, site selection, data collection, analysis and interpretation. Technical assistance from DACs was provided for program implementation and evaluation, educator training for program evaluation, guidance regarding assessing the viability of data collection instruments and the selection of instruments. DACs provided materials to network centers and surveyed center directors to identify areas in need of additional materials.

Although the DACs oversaw national needs assessments, findings of which informed materials development and training activities, and despite the establishment of The Network in 1975, the first national needs assessment was not conducted until 1977 and focused on Spanish, neglecting less commonly taught languages. Table 5.6 shows each DAC's funding for 1975–1978, including language, allocated dollar amount and location (Development Associates, 1978: 300).

Training resource centers

TRCs functioned as the link between the LEAs, IHEs and other educational organizations conducting bilingual programs and the network centers. Their responsibilities were the delivery of services to Title VII LEAs, IHEs and other institutions for the implementation of bilingual education programs. The services provided by the TRCs ranged considerably on a national level and they commonly provided supports for programs external to their assigned region, depending on areas of need, language background and/or expertise. The responsibilities of TRCs involved participation in MDC piloting of new materials

Table 5.6 Exhibit 7: Dissemination and assessment centers – grants by center and language group

Language	DAC	1975–1976 ($)	1976–1977 ($)	1977–1978 ($)	Center total ($)	Language total ($)
Spanish	Fall River, MA	200,000	208,333	208,333	616,666	2,874,998
	San Antonio, TX	375,000			375,000	
	Austin, TX	550,000	525,000	525,000	1,600,000	
	Los Angeles, CA		141,666	141,666	283,332	
French	Fall River, MA	200,000	208,333	208,334	616,667	616,667
Portuguese	Fall River, MA	200,000	208,334	208,334	616,668	616,668
Pacific	Los Angeles, CA		141,667	141,667	283,334	283,334
Asian	Los Angeles, CA		141,667	141,666	283,333	283,333
Totals		1,525,000	1,575,000	1,575,000	4,675,000	4,675,000

Table 5.7 Exhibit 8: Training resource centers funding 1975–1978

TRC	1975–1976 ($)	1976–1977 ($)	1977–1978 ($)
Berkeley, CA	601,461	600,000	600,000
Fullerton, CA		250,000	250,000
Sacramento, CA		150,000	150,000
San Diego, CA	861,629	700,000	700,000
Prospect Park, IL	637,493		
Arlington, IL		500,000	500,000
Lafayette, LA	375,000	385,000	385,000
Boston, MA		250,000	250,000
Albuquerque, NM	470,000	470,000	470,000
Brooklyn, NY	300,000	350,000	350,000
Philadelphia, PA		250,000	250,000
Providence, RI	135,000	300,000	300,000
Austin, TX	250,000	250,000	279,260
Dallas, TX			200,000
Salt Lake City, UT		200,000	200,000
Tacoma, WA		200,000	200,000
Seattle, WA		145,000	145,000
Totals	3,630,583	5,000,000	5,229,260

and the provision of assistance and supports to LEAs, IHEs, SEAs, other centers and organizations, as necessary and appropriate. Virtually all exchanges with on-the-ground stakeholders in bilingual programs occurred through the TRCs, including materials piloting, identification of needs, selection and provision of materials and professional development for educational personnel. Table 5.7 shows each TRC's funding for 1975–1978, including allocated dollar amount and location. Despite the expansion of bilingual programs and supports for their implementation, educational equity for language minority students remained bleak. In addition to the evaluations commissioned United State Office of Education and other bodies to investigate the implementation of the BEA in the 1970s, other studies emerged. These were generated in part as a result of ideological and political shifts, which evoked English-only expectations in a range of societal areas, including schooling. Unwarranted findings in publications produced in the late 1970s and 1980s contributed to erosion of the country's infrastructural supports for bilingual education. These and the English-only movement are discussed in Chapter 6. Some have referred to the subsequent 'historical' period as 'the sunsetting of the Bilingual Education Act' and 'a grand erasure' of bilingual education (Wiley, 2014).

6 Language Ideologies, Politics and Policymaking

> Parents did not teach the [Native] language because they loved us and they didn't want us to suffer, to be abused, or to have a tough life... they tried to protect us from the humiliation and suffering that they went through.
>
> Darrell R. Kipp (2000: 7), Blackfeet language educator and activist; quoted by McCarty (2013: 156)

> I just want to learn [my Native language] real bad... because I think it is a big important part of my life if I am going to be a Native.
>
> 'Damen', youth interview, June 1, 2004; quoted by McCarty (2013: 156)

Sociopolitical Underpinnings

If the Bilingual Education Act (BEA) had emerged in part from positioning language as a human and civil right, by the mid-1980s, that critical precept was effectively null and void as per the US Department of Education (ED). After accomplishments resulting from various changes to the 1974 reauthorization of the BEA, bilingual education entered a troubling and perilous era beginning in the late 1970s, during which it suffered, in part, as a mechanism for political gameplay. Although there had not been a single congressional objection to the original 1968 version of the BEA, throughout the 1980s, sociopolitical shifts made bilingual education the subject of new scrutiny and increased claims against its effectiveness, which were particularly acute under the Reagan administration.

The Epstein Report (1977)

Among the most outspoken adversarial voices countering bilingual programs was *Washington Post* journalist, Noel Epstein. The Institute for Educational Leadership (IEL) invited Epstein to join it as a journalist-in-residence to conduct research and analysis regarding bilingual education programs, findings of which were published in a 'study' titled *Language, Ethnicity, and the Schools: Policy Alternatives for Bilingual-Bicultural Education*. His assigned task was

To synthesize information from many arms of government and many scholarly disciplines—to bring together legislative, regulatory and legal history, to examine the works of linguists, educators, anthropologists, sociolinguists, political scientists, historians and others, to interview policymakers, advocates, and critics… to contribute to the growth of national understanding about bilingual and bicultural education. (Halperin, 1978: v–vi)

Prior to the publication of his report, a first draft of the paper was 'presented and debated at a meeting of key federal education officials conducted by IEL's Educational Staff Seminar on April 20, 1977' (Halperin, 1978: vi). Due to contentious discussion, an additional meeting was scheduled for further deliberations and held on June 2, 1977. The conclusions Epstein established were clear – bilingual education is not only ineffective, but is also an attempt at maintaining ethnic connections for heritage minority language speakers and thus threatens American assimilation. The opening paragraph to Epstein's (1977) critique of bilingual education reads:

A good deal of American social policy is based on what might be called the Columbus Complex. This is the urge to sail off in a new direction in the belief that, at some point we are bound to bump into *something*. The exploring spirit is, of course, a critical element of the human drama, always to be encouraged. But problems arise when we are unsure about which way we are headed or why. (Epstein, 1977: 1)

A portion of Epstein's assertions against bilingual education was based on what he termed *affirmative ethnicity*. He cited Bruce Gaarder's (1977) argument that minority languages should be legally protected or otherwise risk inter-generational language loss, referencing the decline in Franco American language maintenance. 'The impulse of the bilingual-bicultural movement, then', Epstein (1977: 37) wrote, 'is by no means unique—except in its contention that government is responsible for financing and promoting ethnic languages and cultures'.

Epstein's attacks against bilingual education were among the more mainstream. He claimed connections to two member associations – the National Association of State School Boards and the United Auto Workers Union.

The National Association of School Boards suggested that the legislation could be read as promoting a divisive, Canadian-style biculturalism. The United Auto Workers union was concerned that the bicultural component might lead to separation rather than integration in schools. Neither group, however, pressed these issues publicly. (Epstein, 1977: 21–22)

In 2018, Epstein co-authored his wife's memoir, describing her escape from Nazi-run Poland as an infant. Born Anita Kuenstler on November 18, 1942, *Miracle Child: The Journey of a Young Holocaust Survivor* chronicles her birth in the Krakow ghetto, her infancy, childhood and accomplishments later in life. These include as a teacher before moving to Washington, DC. The memoir recalls

> I landed a job as Director of Government Affairs **for the nation's state boards of education**, whose offices were near the Congress. As my husband drove me to my new office, I saw the dome of the U.S. Capitol ahead. It suddenly hit me: They were going to let a *greenah* (an immigrant) like me lobby members of Congress. I broke into tears. (Epstein, 2018: 128)

It seems that of the two organizations Epstein referenced as aligned with his anti-bilingual education stance, one may have been where his wife was employed as a lobbyist.

The AIR Report (1977/1978)

In 1977, the American Institutes for Research (AIR) produced preliminary findings of a report later published in 1978, *Evaluation of the Impact of 38 ESEA Title VII Spanish/English Bilingual Education Programs* (Danoff et al., 1977/1978). In the study, researchers compared English reading and math test performance of elementary students in 38 districts receiving Title VII funds (presumably 'bilingual' programs) with a sample of students not in bilingual instructional settings. Students were observed for periods ranging from five months to two years. 'The AIR Report is bulky and technical. It consists of three volumes filled with tables and statistical analyses plus an appendix—a large amount of technical information that few people would care to lift, let alone read' (Hakuta, 1986: 220). The final report is so colossal (and unwieldy) that today it can only be accessed via microfiche. Initially produced preliminarily, it met with intense critique from researchers representing various areas of expertise, including bilingual pedagogy, linguistics and language policy.

Broadly, the report's findings were that the Title VII 'bilingual' programs in the study were not producing educational outcomes superior to those of students in the sample group to which they were compared (students not in bilingual programs). Researchers' responses cited numerous fundamental methodological flaws, ranging from the appropriateness of staff (few were bilingual) to errors in statistical modeling. One of the more detailed retorts was authored by José A. Cárdenas, founder of the Intercultural Development Research Association (IDRA), whose counter was based on secondary analyses of data detailed in the report's three volumes, much of which contradicted results of the AIR study. Generally, challengers established that findings were essentially unwarranted, in large part due to methodological inadequacies.

Responses to the AIR Report

Defenders of bilingual education raised the issue that regardless of the accuracy of the evaluation findings, they should be viewed as baseless, given the lack of federal support for research regarding the development, implementation and necessary key elements for successful bilingual programs. Two other studies were conducted regarding the effectiveness of bilingual programs around the same time period, one by the General Accountability Office, prompted by Senator Edward Kennedy, and another by the comptroller-general (San Miguel, 2004), with mixed reviews. 'When national evaluations by the Congressional General Accounting Office (GAO) or the AIR find grave shortcomings in bilingual programs, the almost total lack of funding for the research needed to improve them should be kept in mind' (Troike, 1978: 2). Combined with the plain-speech claims by Epstein published in *The Washington Post* and disseminated through more generally accessible channels, the AIR Report contributed considerably to the genesis of mainstream attacks against bilingual education.

Intercultural Development Research Association

Unlike many other responses, the IDRA delved deeply into the three-volume AIR Report. Its analyses of the AIR Report revealed 'critical weaknesses surrounding the theoretical basis on which the design is premised, and serious questions concerning the evaluation methodology which is utilized' (Cárdenas, 1977: 1). Cárdenas (Image 6.1) identified the following 'major issues' with associated details and conclusions.

Image 6.1 José A. Cárdenas

(1) Identification of language groups – teachers are unreliable indicators of students' language abilities, particularly those who are non-bilingual; language speaker classifications were ill-defined.
(2) Comparability of treatment and control groups – Title VII personnel were asked to 'nominate' comparison classes with comparable student demographics; district variables were unaccounted for; nearly half of the projects reviewed did not identify a comparison group.
(3) Instrumentation – the source of data for determining English proficiency were the Comprehensive Tests of Basic Skills (CTBS), Forms S and T and the CTBS Reading Test, Level C for students identified as Spanish monolingual; a substantial number of students' overall scores were missing reading total scores; researchers did not follow the publisher's guidelines for determining overall scores.
(4) Pre- and post-testing – dates ranged from November 4 to December 12, 1975, for pre-tests and April 6 to June 9, 1976, for post-tests; 18 of the 37 projects were pre/post-tested within less than five months, highly compromising the validity of findings.
(5) Variability of instructional treatment – although AIR described 'most' programs as being maintenance bilingual, that program definition was not provided; in fact, there were variations among project descriptions in terms of curriculum ('one project offers 1½ hours per week in English oral language development; another offers 9 hours per week' [p. 10]); variations in time for reading, culture and math were evident in project descriptions; the study, therefore, did not account for inter-program differences.
(6) Variability of teacher characteristics:
   (a) Educator credentials: The study conflated teachers' 'regular' and 'bilingual' credentials as analogous; in fact, 47% of Title VII teachers in the study did not have a bilingual credential and 23% did report having a bilingual credential; AIR neglected to use 'bilingual credential as an independent variable in assessing differential impact of Title VII programs' (p. 15).
   (b) Educator professional development: Although the AIR Report claimed 93.8% of teachers had attended professional development, this was over a five-year period; the actual range among teachers in the study was from 1 to more than 30 days over the five-year period; quality assessment of training was neglected in the study.
   (c) AIR 'Bilinguality Scale': Although 67% of Title VII teachers reported using Spanish and English at home and 69% reported using both languages with their children, only 50% reported proficiency in both languages; 49% reported not being proficient in Spanish, raising 'serious questions concerning the validity of the findings' (p. 17).

(7) Costing of bilingual education – rather than reviewing specific cost records, AIR interviewed 'cognizant local personnel' regarding per pupil costs for bilingual programs; the study organized costs into the following categories: (1) Title VII funds, (2) other bilingual funds, (3) other additional funds for the school, (4) basic district funds; by lumping together the first and second categories, the study contradicts its purpose; the study did not distinguish between costs of programs in start-up versus ongoing phases of existence.

In a brief summary publication produced by the IDRA, Cárdenas (1977: 3) suggested that 'It is unfortunate and perhaps irresponsible for the US Office of Education to release and give such wide dissemination to findings of such questionable validity just prior to the congressional deliberations on the refunding of the Bilingual Education Act'.

Former AIR staff

In June 1977, former AIR staff submitted written testimony prepared for the Congressional Record, to be presented during the Hearings of the Subcommittee on Elementary, Secondary and Vocational Education to 'express our concern with several issues raised by the AIR Interim Report' (Arias *et al.*, 1977: 1).

Finding: 'Less than one-third of the students enrolled in the Title VII classrooms in grades 2 through 6 were of limited English-speaking ability'. (pg. 3)
Comment: Limited English speaking ability was never assessed. Rather, AIR took the information given by the teachers as the only measure of children's linguistic ability... the reported lower number of students classified as having 'limited English speaking' ability is questionable...'
Finding: 'Approximately 85% of the project directors indicated that Spanish-dominant students remain in the bilingual project once they are able to function in school in English' (pg. 4).
Comment: Interpretation of statements to mean that project directors are implementing language 'maintenance' programs. This conclusion is totally unfounded for two reasons: a) Project Directors were not specifically asked to identify their projects as transitional or maintenance and b) no criteria were designed for evaluating projects as transitional or maintenance. (Arias *et al.*, 1977: 2)

Based on the challenges raised regarding the feasibility of the findings presented by the AIR study, staff asserted that 'We seriously question whether one of the major study objectives has been thoroughly addressed – "to identify those educational practices which result in greater gains in student achievement"' (Arias *et al.*, 1977: 7).

Michael O'Malley, senior research associate, National Institute of Education

Michael O'Malley was at the time senior research associate for the National Institute of Education, within the Department of Health, Education and Welfare. His review of the interim AIR Report focused in part on methodological shortcomings. In written testimony before the House Subcommittee on Elementary, Secondary and Vocational Education of the Committee on Education and Labor (Arias *et al.*, 1977: 4, see Bilingual Education Hearings, 1978), O'Malley stated that 'Analysis of the procedures on which these conclusions are based reveals a number of methodological and statistical problems which render the conclusions as merely tentative'. An excerpt of O'Malley's more lengthy response asserted:

> In our technical review, we performed a number of independent checks to determine the initial comparability of the groups. Evidence from these checks strongly suggests that the non-Title VII group was either initially superior to the Title VII group or at least different in some important respects. AIR performed some of these independent checks but assumed that the initial differences found are unimportant. A more cautious interpretation of these data would lead to probing the nature of the differences, as is suggested in our review.

Center for Applied Linguistics

As the director of language and public policy at the Center for Applied Linguistics, Tracy Gray vigorously defended bilingual education against the unfounded claims put forth in the AIR Report. In response to the interim report, Gray (1977) wrote 'Response to AIR Study "Evaluation of the Impact of ESEA Title VII Spanish/English Bilingual Education Program"'. In it, she delineated criticism on a series of grounds, and asserted that the AIR Report 'gives the illusion that certain types of inferences can be made about the program, when, in fact, they are not justified'. She argued that it 'does serious disservice by failing to distinguish between the effects of good programs and weak programs, and treats bilingual education as an undifferentiated uniform whole, which it is not' (Gray, 1977: 1).

First, Gray noted that the five-month interval between pre- and post-testing conducted by researchers was insufficient time for claiming statistical impact by psychometricians. Second, she discussed the lack of random assignments, rendering it 'possible that differences that may be observed in the post test score are the result of pre-existing group differences rather than treatment effects' (Gray, 1977: 2). Third, monolingual English teachers were the mechanism through which students' language proficiency levels were identified, which she termed 'notoriously unreliable' (Gray, 1977: 3). Fourth, the study neglected to account for in-group variation, despite the fact that not all students had participated in the program for the same period of time (some had recently begun participating).

Fifth, although some programs were in their fourth or fifth year of implementation, tests were conducted in fall 1975 and spring 1976. Although the BEA passed in 1968, bilingual materials development and teacher preparation were not federally funded until 1974, meaning extreme variation among programs' curricula, class-hours devoted to language instruction, teacher expertise, community involvement and students' language abilities; therefore, 'To compare Title VII projects as a unit is highly misleading' (Gray, 1977: 3). Gray (1977: 4) concluded that 'the stated conclusions in this interim report are not warranted by the method of analysis used in the report'.

Development Associates: *Consafic Chingatropic*

One of the primary organizations conducting research and other contracted activities related to bilingual education during this period was Development Associates, which remained active in the field into the 1990s. Bob Cervantes, who went on to lead a lengthy career in the California Department of Education (CDE) was on staff at Development Associates during the 1970s. He published a response to the AIR study in March 1979, after moving to the CDE. Although by this time numerous challenges had been raised and published, Cervantes sought to document additional contextual information also at play during this contentious time.

The picture Cervantes painted is how the contract to conduct the study undertaken by AIR was itself rooted in corrupt politics, ultimately serving to undermine bilingual education. Research such as the AIR study is initially generated through the creation of a Request for Proposals (RFP) put out by the federal government, in this case the US Department of Health, Education and Welfare. Parties interested in conducting activities delineated in the RFP respond with proposals, which are judged based on a series of items, including quality of the proposal, qualifications of staff, timeline, management plan and cost, among other areas. It is through this process that many non-profit organizations and 'think tanks' operate across the country, particularly in Washington. The AIR Report was associated with RFP 74-61 and was initially issued on April 1, 1974, in the *Commerce Business Daily*. Six criteria for scoring proposals were spelled out in the RFP (Cervantes, 1979: 3):

(1) Technical approach and promise in meeting objectives.
(2) Data collection, analysis and reporting.
(3) Scope and comprehensiveness of overall evaluation plan.
(4) Qualifications of proposed project director.
(5) Management plan, staff assignments and relationship of assignments to staff expertise.
(6) Staff capabilities and corporate experience.

Proposals were reviewed from May 21, 1974 to June 25, 1974, after which six submissions were narrowed to two: Development Associates, a minority-owned small business in Washington, DC, and AIR, based in Palo Alto, California. The 'best and final' award to AIR was made on June 28, 1974, raising mammoth concerns and questions from staff involved in proposal development and review at Development Associates, as well as the US Office of Education (USOE). USOE's review panel *Summary List of Items for Negotiations* for AIR June 17, 1974, as cited by Cervantes, clearly demonstrated a sorely lacking proposal, plan and proposed personnel.

(1) AIR's unfamiliarity with the substantive issues in bilingual education.
(2) A weak data collection system.
(3) Inadequately described 'training plan for testers, site-visit procedure, and test logistics'.
(4) A focus on a literature search to the detriment of other scheduled tasks.
(5) Skimpy discussion of achievement and questionnaire development and no discussion of affective tests.
(6) Vague discussion of racial and ethnic outcomes.
(7) Inadequate discussion of issues involved in the non-Spanish study and inexperienced staff assignments.
(8) Weak cost-benefit analysis plan.
(9) Problematic matching of treatment and comparison schools and [lack of] control(s) of significant variables.
(10) Questions concerning instrument 'tryout' prior to 'full-scale' use.

Cervantes (1979) listed four areas in point of comparison between Development Associates' and AIR's proposals, piquing curiosity along the way in their descriptions. Evidence makes it abundantly clear that the contract should have gone to Development Associates. Although Development Associates' staff had been 'orally advised as being the lead bidder', they did not win the contract. A highly unusual practice, the final review panel meeting was held on a Saturday (Cervantes, 1979: 6). Cervantes' (1979) proposed explanation is retribution by the Nixon administration for the president of Development Associates declining to contribute to its re-election campaign.

> Beginning in March, 1972 and continuing for several years, representatives of President Nixon's staff had placed pressures on DA to contribute time, money, and clerical services to the President's re-election campaign. On March 17, 1972, a White House special assistant wrote a memorandum to the Chief of Staff, outlining a 'responsiveness program' by which the White House would seek to direct the distribution of discretionary funds in such a way as to maximize the President's chances of re-election. In early spring of 1972, the DA president was contacted by representatives of the re-election campaign for President Nixon and asked for a minimum contribution of $1,000 because DA had 'done so well under the

Nixon Administration'. The president of DA refused to make a contribution. He was advised that the White House was upset with his unwillingness to contribute to the President's re-election campaign. Subsequently, the DA president was invited to the White House for lunch and an invitation was again extended to DA to contribute to the re-election campaign. Again, the DA president declined. At the conclusion of the luncheon, he was informed that 'his uncooperativeness could lead to consequences adversely affecting Development Associates'. (Cervantes, 1979: 8)

Cervantes' (1979) documentation of the genesis of the AIR Report provided further evidence that from the outset, it was at best highly compromised, and at worst, entirely illegitimate.

1978 Reauthorization

Despite uproar from the bilingual education community regarding findings in the AIR Report and its numerous, in some cases, highly detailed critiques, which ultimately provided ample evidence of fundamental flaws and baseless judgements of Title VII programs, its utility was groundbreaking amid growing anti-bilingual education rhetoric. It provided footing for growing claims about a lack of effectiveness of bilingual education programs for language minority students. As Sinclair (2018) noted, it was central to Congress shifting focus in the 1978 reauthorization away from bilingual education.

> The committee report states, 'The author of the [AIR] study testified that "there is no compelling evidence in the current data of the Impact Study that Title VII bilingual education as presently implemented is the most appropriate approach for these students"'. (US House of Representatives, 1978: 84)

Although much of the infrastructural supports remained in the new iteration, as has been discussed in previous chapters, 'In the 1978 reauthorization, support for bilingual education began to evaporate' (Gándara, 2015: 114). Changes to this iteration irrevocably tipped the teetering balance between bilingual and English-oriented settings for language minority learners – bilingual-bicultural education as envisioned as part of the development of the 1968 BEA vanished. This disappearance made possible by the clearly erroneous AIR Report – an historical snapshot quintessentially capturing the politics of policymaking.

In the 1978 reauthorization, bilingual education was framed only as *transitional* in nature for the purpose of facilitating students' acquisition of English. Native language supports were limited to 'for the *extent necessary*'; funding for late-exit, maintenance programs (the goals of which involved full bilingualism and biliteracy) was removed. Other changes in 1978 included changing the label referring to language minority learners from 'Limited English-speaking ability' to 'limited English proficient' and restrictions on funding to programs for a period of only one to three years.

Office of Bilingual Education activities

Dr Josué González was director of the Office of Bilingual Education (OBE) from 1978 to 1981, during which time the commissioner ordered an audit of the bilingual program. It 'examined aspects of the Title VII program including program purpose, program regulations, grants management, research and program assessment, internal management, and external relations' (US Office of Education, 1979: 192). The AIR Report claimed a lack of coherence and consistency across the various training and support services. Director González oversaw a wide range of activities to better structure and improve activities conducted under the BEA. These are documented in *Strengthening Bilingual Education*, the 1980 report on The Condition of Bilingual Education in the Nation. The purpose of the publication was to serve as 'a blueprint for change to improve the performance of the U.S. Office of Education in meeting the needs of children with limited proficiency in English' (US Office of Education, 1980: 1).

To strengthen educational programs for language minority students, a series of actions were initiated by González (see US Office of Education, 1980: 2–3). These included

- Adoption and implementation of an initiative to ensure that scarce federal resources are targeted at children with limited English proficiency.
- Initiation of an internal study to identify the key objectives against which overall program performance should be measured.
- Revision of funding criteria for the basic program to help ensure that school districts and children most in need are served.
- Creation and application of tighter review guidelines for both program (OBE) and grants management (GPMD) staff to ensure greater cost-effectiveness in funded projects and more uniformity in the review of project budgets proposed by potential grantees.
- Revision of application requirements to reduce paperwork for local education agencies (LEAs).
- Establishment of a standard to describe the skills that teachers and other staff members must have to be considered bilingual.
- Development of a demonstration program to encourage the provision of services to special populations of children with limited English proficiency such as the handicapped, the gifted and talented, and preschool children.
- Adoption of regulations to ensure increased parental and community involvement in the planning and operation of Title VII projects at the local level.
- Reorganization of training and support services to focus effort more clearly and effectively on the needs of local educational agencies.

- Implementation of a phased plan to increase the coordination between Title VII and other educational programs that serve children with limited proficiency in English.
- Development of a comprehensive research plan for the years 1979–1983.
- Appointment of a new director and acting deputy director.
- Development of principles to guide the reorganization of the Office of Bilingual Education on a functional basis including the possible use of rotation and/or transfer of staff to meet an urgent need for renewal within the organization.
- Addition of six positions within the Office of Bilingual Education.
- Adoption of a series of steps to improve performance in pre-application technical assistance, responsiveness to applicants and monitoring of approved projects. Included is a new effort to provide intensive technical assistance to grantees with weak projects and to base decisions for continued funding on their willingness and ability to improve performance.

The first of numerous problems referenced in response to the audit was findings from the AIR study, notably, that an 'excessive' number of English-speaking students were participating in bilingual programs. In response, the commissioner dictated that by October 1, 1979, 75% of students in bilingual programs be of 'limited English-speaking ability'. Actions conducted to achieve this goal included direct telephone calls and mailers sent to all grantees regarding the initiative; a National Management Institute convened in October 1979 for all Title VII basic programs involving State Education Agency staff; and direct instructions regarding the 75% representation goal provided during annual budget discussions. The OBE then conducted 173 site visits to investigate the percentage of students in programs qualifying as limited English-speaking ability and procedures for identifying students' eligibility criteria for inclusion in Title VII programs. Findings were presented in April, indicating that 71% of students in Title VII programs currently qualified as non-native English speakers and, therefore, the target of achieving 75% by October could be reasonably accomplished. The initiative was to be expanded for fiscal year 1980, to also ensure that no less than 60% of all students in Title VII settings were non-native English speakers.

González (Image 6.2) also directed the streamlining of the existing resource centers into bilingual education service centers (BESCs) and evaluation, dissemination and assessment centers (EDACs). In the revised system, EDACs developed evaluation plans for use by districts to assess Title VII program effectiveness. Staff from the EDACs would train BESC staff and state education agency (SEA) assistance units, who would, in turn, train districts to select instruments and mechanisms for assessing the effectiveness of Title VII programs.

Image 6.2 Josúe M. González, director of the Office of Bilingual Education

Perhaps most notably, González also created 'a special grant program to schools of education' for which 'the college would be expected to appoint a full-time faculty member to undertake' oversight of the Bilingual Education Fellowship Program (US Office of Education, 1980: 13). In the first year of appointment, the federal government would reimburse institutions 100% of a director's salaries, followed by two-thirds in the second year and one-third in the third year. To further strengthen the fellowship program, additional new provisions included limiting program eligibility for students already in possession of a master's degree; additional stipulations for employment conditions necessary for graduates' repayment of federal tuition assistance; procedures for the commissioner to defer repayment; and delineation of a repayment schedule for fellowship program graduates.

Commissioner González developed a comprehensive plan to be implemented between 1979 and 1983 for research activities related to bilingual education. Planned studies were organized into three types: Assessment of the National Need for Bilingual Education (seven studies); Improvement in the Effectiveness of Services for Bilingual Students (seven studies); and Improvement in Title VII Program Management and Operations (six studies). González also committed the OBE to a staff increase (from 48 to 54), improving pre-application technical assistance and responsiveness to LEAs.

A new US Department of Education (ED)

In February 1978, Carter instructed the Office of Management and Budget, the Department of Health, Education and Welfare and Congress to collaboratively devise a plan to institute a new federal Department of Education (Stephens, 1983/1984). After much tribulation among congressional leaders, teachers' union lobbyists and others, a bill to create the new agency was signed by the president on October 17, 1979. Carter's presidential campaign benefited greatly from its contact with, and support from, the National Education Association (NEA), the country's largest teachers' union. Partnership between the two was solidified when Walter F. Mondale was selected as vice presidential candidate, whose brother led a Midwest chapter of the NEA (Stephens, 1983/1984). Although its new secretary was sworn in on December 6, 1979 (Image 6.3), the new department did not open until May 1980.

Shirley Hufstedler was appointed as the first secretary of the new Department of Education. She said that the new agency, which was composed of $14 million worth of programs previously overseen by the Department of Health, Education and Welfare, would 'strive unceasingly the very highest possible quality at every level of the educational process... (and) seek out models of success and hold them aloft for all to see' (Connell, 1980). She 'called upon the president's 12-year-old daughter, Amy, as "a symbol of all the children of America" to unveil the fledgling department's new flag, a bright banner in vivid color depicting an acorn and an oak tree with the sun behind them' (Connell, 1980).

The opening of ED was celebrated by a visit to James F. Oyster Bilingual Demonstration School, where Hufstedler and Rosalynn Carter 'began the day by touring a red brick public schoolhouse where children are taught in both English and Spanish' (Connell, 1980). In a report for *The Washington Post*, Christopher Connell (1980) wrote that 'In a colorful assembly in a weathered auditorium, youngsters from grades 1 to 6... pledged allegiance to the flag and sang in both languages and performed folk dances. Mrs. Carter and Mrs. Hufstedler each spoke in both languages to thank the youngsters and extol bilingual instruction'. Hufstedler pronounced that

Image 6.3 Swearing in of Shirley Hufstedler as ED Secretary (Courtesy: Jimmy Carter Presidential Library)

> One could not have a better way to begin the celebration of today as 'Salute to Learning Day'. I think every youngster in the United States should have an opportunity to speak at least two languages. (Connell, 1980)

Carter and Hufstedler also attended 'a geography lesson on Mexico, listened to a poem on slavery recited in Spanish and viewed a presentation on Latin American music and dance' (Valente, 1980).

Lau Notice of Proposed Rulemaking

Hufstedler had previously been the judge who authored the dissenting opinion in the *Lau v Nichols* case, prior to its overturning by the Supreme Court. As such, she was keenly familiar with the history, purpose and goals of bilingual education and viewed bilingualism as a resource and a right of language minority students. In a statement for the congressional hearings on labor and human resources before which Hufstedler was sworn in, Al Perez, associate counsel for the Mexican-American Legal Defense and Educational Fund, recounted Hufstedler's involvement in *Lau* as evidence of her familiarity with the negative impact of English in schooling for language minority learners.

> Judge Hufstedler has demonstrated an understanding of two factors which contribute to our high dropout rate: English-only instruction and segregated schools. When the Ninth Circuit denied a petition for rehearing *Lau v. Nichols*, Judge Hufstedler dissented, demonstrating that she was acutely aware of and sensitive to the predicament of so many of our children: that of not understanding the language in which they are being instructed.

Several months after ED's opening, Hufstedler published a Notice of Proposed Rulemaking (NPRM), 'Nondiscrimination Under Programs Receiving Federal Assistance Through the Department of Education' (Moore, 2008: 511), which stipulated bilingual education as a required program for state and district compliance with the *Lau* Remedies. 'These regulations mandated the use of bilingual education under certain circumstances for correcting the problems identified by the Supreme Court in *Lau*' (González, 2008: 836). Hearings were held and the NPRM was published in the *Federal Register* in August 1980. A decade earlier, when Pottinger had penned the May 25, 1970, memorandum of understanding, his office had failed to publish the memo in *The Federal Register*, which contributed to its undoing through politically oriented policymaking.

> Hufstedler had been involved with the *Lau* litigation starting in the early 1970s, when she served on the U.S. Appellate Court for the Ninth Circuit in California. This was the panel of judges who had reviewed and upheld the original district court ruling in *Lau*. Hufstedler had been the

only judge on the panel who had voted to reverse the ruling, but two other judges had refused. Later, Hufstedler's position was vindicated by the Supreme Court in its reversal of the lower court in 1974. (González, 2008: 832)

As was noted in a brief biographical article about Hufstedler (Ujifusa, 2016) after her death at the age of 90, 'the opinion she wrote that she was particularly proud of was a dissent in *Lau v Nichols*'. In an earlier interview, Hufstedler stated

> By the time I became Secretary of Education, we then had in place the so-called Lau Regulations, which was a reflection of that decision and about equal protection for youngsters whose initial language was not English. So I thought that was an achievement that I've always enjoyed a lot.

Hufstedler described the *Lau* NPRM as 'setting broad parameters in order to meet the civil requirements of equal opportunity' (Williams, 1980: 1). Describing the regulations, Hufstedler stated 'The object of the proposed rules is to teach... English as quickly as possible and to teach them other subjects in a language they can understand' (Williams, 1980: 1).

Specifically, the NPRM provided comprehensive guidance to SEAs and LEAs regarding the provision of bilingual programs for emergent bilingual learners. Essentially, the NPRM that Hustedler developed realized the true intent of the *Lau* decision. Three services were explicated in the 1980 NPRM:

(a) Equal access to compensatory education.
(b) Improving English language skills.
(c) Bilingual instruction.

When the *Lau* NPRM was published in *The Federal Register* in August 1980, then candidate Ronald Reagan was running on a platform in part based on the deregulation of government.

Reagan rescinds Hufstedler's NPRM

The Reagan administration's first Secretary of Education, Terrell Bell, swiftly rescinded the *Lau* NPRM regulations within weeks of the presidential inauguration, in February 1981. Bell and Reagan railed against bilingual education, instead proposing instructional models for non-native English-speaking students that prioritized English acquisition, such as English as a second language. Echoing arguments raised by Epstein several years earlier, before the National League of Cities in early March 1981, Reagan declared that 'it is absolutely wrong and against [the] American concept to have a bilingual education program that is now openly, admittedly dedicated to preserving their native language' (Feinberg, 1981: 2).

During the Carter administration, lawyer and bilingual advocate, James J. Lyons had been appointed as senior adviser to the assistant secretary for legislation. He led the responses from the department to the strong sociopolitical opposition to Hufstedler's 1980 NPRM. Lyons' shrewdness and legal knowledge meant he was 'able to contain the damage' (González, 2008: 536) after Bell withdrew the NPRM. Reagan's new Secretary of Education retained Lyons to navigate revoking the NPRM and develop a new policy for enforcing *Lau* Remedies. As is recounted in Lyons' biography in *The Encyclopedia of Bilingual Education*:

> Conservatives within and outside the Reagan administration pushed for a total renunciation of *Lau v. Nichols*; Lyons countered their ideological arguments with cogent legal analysis, and in the end, Secretary Bell promulgated the result-oriented set of *Lau* enforcement guidelines Lyons had developed. (Martínez, 2008: 537)

Bell's removal of the 1980 NPRM marked the first key policymaking aimed at crippling bilingual education's ascension from the 1970s. Its imprint was emboldened by a series of publications that emerged during the Reagan administration claiming the ineffectiveness of bilingual programs. Perhaps most deleterious to the field, several of these suggested a new program alternative for the instruction of language minority students: structured immersion, which would later become fundamental to the English-only movements in California (1998), Arizona (2000) and Massachusetts (2002).

Casteñeda v. Pickard

In *Casteñeda v. Pickard* (1981) a school district in Raymondville, Texas was charged with discrimination on several bases: because the district 'used ability grouping in a way that segregated and created learning obstacles for LEP students' (Singh, 2008: 114); that educators' backgrounds were not representative of school demographics (about 90% of students were of Mexican heritage); the district's provision of bilingual education for overcoming linguistic barriers to core content learning was inadequate; and administration of English-only standardized assessments to identify academic growth was inappropriate. Plaintiffs claimed the district was violating both Title VI of the Civil Rights Act and the Equal Educational Opportunities Act, as determined in the *Lau v. Nichols* decision. *Casteñeda*, extended beyond *Lau* however, because it aimed 'to describe in broad terms the qualities of an appropriate program that would satisfy *Lau*' – through establishment of a 'three-pronged test' (Singh, 2008: 114):

(1) The instructional program implemented must be based on sound theory.
(2) The program should be implemented with appropriate practices, staffing, and resources.

(3) There should be evaluation and evidence of effectiveness.

The 'three-pronged test' has been used in myriad subsequent cases. These include, under the first prong – *Guadalupe Organization v. Tempe Elementary School District* (1972), which found maintaining a bilingual program was not necessary for compliance and *Teresa P. v. Berkeley Unified School District* (1989), which determined monolingual English teachers sufficiently comply and credentialed and non-credentialed educators are comparable. Under the second prong – in *Serna v. Portales* (1974), which found 'that students should be able to keep up with non-LEP peers, participate successfully in the curriculum without simplified materials, and have retention and drop-out rates similar to non-LEP students' (Singh, 2008: 115); in *Cintrón v. Brentwood Union Free School District* (1978) substitution of ESL support due to limited bilingual staff was determined unacceptable; in *Ríos v. Read* (1978) teachers with insufficient bilingual aptitude and a dearth of textbooks were in violation; and, in *Keyes v. School District No. 1, Denver* (1983) schools' use of interviews, rather than language assessments to ascertain language proficiency among bilingual educators was found deficient.

The Baker de Kanter Report

Working for ED, Keith Baker (a sociologist) and Adriana de Kanter (an intern at the time and later political scientist) produced the first of a series of reports investigating the effectiveness of various program models for the instruction of language minority students. Not one of the three models that Baker and de Kanter compared for teaching language minority students involved long-term native language maintenance. By this time, the 1978 reauthorization was driving program implementation – bilingual education advocates were in the distressed position of no longer fighting *for* native language maintenance, but rather fighting *against* submersion approaches contingent on the imposition of English.

Baker and de Kanter reviewed 28 programs, comparing three program models for the instruction of language minority learners: transitional bilingual education (TBE), English as a second language and structured immersion. It is notable that the Baker de Kanter Report marks the first significant mention and explication of 'structured immersion' as a model for the instruction of language minority learners. It later became the basis for the English-only movement's Sheltered English Immersion and Structured English Immersion (SEI), which were often used interchangeably.

In their introduction to a book published subsequent to the Baker de Kanter Report, Birman and Ginsberg (1983) define structured immersion as a model in which

> Almost all instruction is given in English. There are, however, important differences between immersion and submersion. First, immersion teachers are fully bilingual. Second, although students can ask questions of the teacher in

the home language, an immersion teacher generally replies only in English. Further, the curriculum is structured so that no prior knowledge of English is assumed when subject areas are taught. No content is introduced except in a way that can be understood by the student. The student in effect learns English and content simultaneously. Structured Immersion programs may include home language arts classes. (Birman & Ginsberg, 1983: xii)

The Baker de Kanter Report responded to two research questions: (1) Is there a sufficiently strong case for the effectiveness of TBE for learning English and non-language subjects to justify a legal mandate for TBE?; (2) Are there any effective alternatives to TBE? That is, should one particular method be exclusively required if other methods are also effective? (Baker & de Kanter, 1983: 33).

Baker and de Kanter claimed that structured immersion was a superior model to TBE based on three case: two cases in Québec, Canada (Barik & Swain, 1975; Lambert & Tucker, 1972) and one case in McAllen, Texas (Peña-Hughes & Solis, 1980). (McAllen, Texas, is a border town and largely regarded as bilingual and bicultural in nature.) Considerable debate over whether implementation of the effectiveness of the French model into contexts in the United States has been extensively documented (Becker & Gersten, 1992; Collier, 1992; Collier & Thomas, 1989; Gersten & Woodward, 1985; Ramírez *et al.*, 1991; Thomas, 1992; Verhoeven, 1991). Regarding the projection of the French model into US contexts, Secada (1987: 379) wrote, 'Baker relies heavily on the success of the Canadian French-immersion programs for his arguments concerning structured immersion, [but] there is a fundamental difference between the two. Baker's immersion goes from limited initial use to no use of the native language; Canadian immersion goes from no use to extensive use of the native language'. Baker and de Kanter claimed that

> TBE has had mixed success. Although it has worked in some settings, it has proved ineffective in others and has had negative effects in some places. Furthermore, alternative instructional methods have been found to succeed—even to be superior to TBE—in some schools. (Baker & de Kanter, 1983: 46)

Cazden (1992: 1) noted that 'evidence supporting structured immersion within the U.S. context has been weak. Baker and de Kanter could only find one U.S. study of structured immersion involving Spanish-speaking children (Peña-Hughes & Solis, 1980), and that was a program that existed only in kindergarten' (which also integrated Spanish language arts lessons).

Orientations in language planning

It was during this political and policy assault on bilingual education that Richard Ruíz' (1984) seminal *Orientations in Language Planning* was published. It proposed three approaches to positioning language for planning purposes – language-as-problem, language-as-resource and language-as-right. Despite acknowledgement and belief among bilingual advocates of the language-as-right orientation, Ruíz argued that the more practical and likely successful tact to employ in promoting equity for language minority learners was to engage the language-as-resource orientation to promote cooperation among divisive factions. Ruíz (1984: 16) defined 'orientations' as 'A complex of dispositions toward language and its role, and toward languages and their role in society'.

His contributions to the field are innumerable. A text in reverence to Ruíz' work, *Honoring Richard Ruíz*, included reprints of classic publications, other stories and contributions by colleagues and friends, and he was commemorated in a special issue of the *Bilingual Research Journal*. He 'spoke of cooperation, consultation, healing, and a new social consensus with a positive view of non-English languages, of multilingualism, as societal *resources* for everyone' (Macías, 2016: 174). However, he neglected to define 'resource', and may have overlooked highly complex, supra-dimensional issues amid debates surrounding English-only and bilingual education. Macías asserted that

> The impact, in general, I surmise, is on two fronts: (a) it gave the field a shorthand political vocabulary for the valuation of language diversity—if it was valued as good then it was a resource; if valued as bad then it was a problem—without engaging in evidence, research, or having to 'prove the point'; (b) it also made a complex situation with many nuances (especially related to research and methodology) more referentially simple, allowing the bilingual teacher, parent, and students to engage in the language politics and to position themselves and others ethically (morally in support or opposition) to bilingual education. (Macías, 2016: 190)

The three orientations could be viewed as oversimplified – ultimately downplaying critical discussions around issues of power structures, English hegemonies and ethnolinguistics inherent to bilingual educational settings (discussed in Chapter 7). At the time that Ruíz' (1984) piece was published, the *Bilingual Research Journal* 'was... in 8" by 10" format, with a magazine feel and carried advertisements for companies involved in curricular materials and other commercial products of interest to the bilingual education profession and community' (Macías, 2016: 189–190).

1984 and 1988 reauthorizations

By the 1984 reauthorization of the BEA, its focus on English over bilingualism was immediately evident. It referenced 'structured English-language instruction, and, to the extent necessary to allow a child to achieve competence in the English language, instruction in the child's native language' (Sec. 703 [a] [4] [A]). Perhaps most harmful to the spirit of the original legislation, the 1984 iteration added 'Special Alternative Instructional Programs' (SAIPs). Whereas funds were initially allocated for SAIPs at 4% in 1984, the 1988 reauthorization expanded the percentage to 25%.

OCR Title VI Language Minority Compliance Guidance

In 1985, during Reagan's second term in office, his newly appointed Secretary of Education William Bennett, who was a vocal opponent of bilingual education, further curtailed bilingual programs in favor of instructional approaches using English as the medium of instruction by producing new guidelines for compliance with the *Lau* Remedies. These alleviated the requirements for the integration of non-English language instruction and supports for language minority learners. Later, Bennett also created constraints impacting the Office of Civil Rights' capacity to enforce compliance with the *Lau* Remedies by reducing both its budget and staff. The implications were significant, writes San Miguel (2004: 67), 'These actions served to effectively dismantle the civil rights component of this program and to weaken the mandatory provisions of federal bilingual education'.

Later, a statement was posted by OCR in September 1991 to supplement the May 1970 and 1985 memoranda regarding appropriate instructional programs for language minority students. It articulated, based on findings in both *Casteñeda* and subsequent cases, in instances where bilingual education is implemented (1991: n.p.):

> If a recipient selects a bilingual program for its LEP students, at a minimum, teachers of bilingual classes should be able to speak, read, and write both languages, and should have received adequate instruction in the methods of bilingual education. In addition, the recipient should be able to show that it has determined that its bilingual teachers have these skills.

Responses to Baker de Kanter

As with the AIR Report, researchers in the field of bilingual education immediately challenged Baker and de Kanter's findings (see, for example, Collier, 1992; Salazar, 1998; Willig, 1985). Many advocates countered by conducting meta-analyses of their own. In particular, Willig (1985) conducted a study in which she reviewed 21 of the 28 programs evaluated in the report by Baker and de Kanter (1981, 1983). Describing her findings, she reported:

> A major result of the current synthesis has been the revelation that bilingual education has been badly served by a predominance of research that is inadequate in design and that makes inappropriate comparisons of children in bilingual programs to children who are dissimilar in many

crucial respects. In every instance where there did not appear to be crucial inequalities between experimental and comparison groups, children in the bilingual programs averaged higher than the comparison children on criterion instruments. (Willig, 1985: 312)

The Ramírez Report

Due to the limited evidence shown by the Baker de Kanter Report, 'the decision was made by the US Department of Education to initiate and finance a study of educational programs for language minority children' (Cazden, 1992: 1). Generally referred to as the Ramírez Report, an eight-year study commissioned by ED again compared educational outcomes of students in various language instruction programs, and was published in 1991 (Ramírez *et al.*, 1991). Its 'primary study objective [was] to assess the relative effectiveness of structured English immersion strategy, early-exit, and late-exit transitional bilingual education programs' (Ramírez *et al.*, 1991: 1). The first project officer overseeing research activities for ED was Keith Baker (Cummins, 1992).

Findings in the Ramírez Report showed that late-exit programs that provided 40% or more instruction in students' home languages 'had significantly higher mathematics skills than students in the late-exit site who were abruptly transitioned into English instruction' (Ramírez *et al.*, 1991: 648). Students in the same late-exit program also showed 'the highest level of reading scores at the end of first grade [and] posted higher scores at the end of sixth grade' (Ramírez *et al.*, 1991: 648). Generally speaking, 'by the end of grade six, students in the two late-exit sites that used the most Spanish for instruction... posted higher growth than the site which abruptly transitioned into almost all English instruction' (Ramírez *et al.*, 1991: 649). In addition to math skills, students in the two late-exit sites, for whom 40% of instruction was conducted in the home language, outperformed the other groups in English skills and development, whereas students who transitioned quickly to English 'appeared to exhibit a decrease in their rate of growth in English language skills' (Ramírez *et al.*, 1991: 653). The Ramírez Report concluded that

> Providing LEP students with substantial amounts of instruction in their primary language does not impede their acquisition of English language skills, but that it is as effective as being provided with large amounts of English... students who are provided with substantial amounts of primary language instruction are also able to learn and improve their skills in other content areas as fast or faster than the norming population, in contrast to students who are transitioned quickly into English-only instruction. (Ramírez *et al.*, 1991: 654)

Despite clear evidence showing the superiority of late-exit bilingual programs provided in the full, two-volume Ramírez Report, challengers to bilingual education remained vocal, and it grew to become a

120 A History of Bilingual Education in the US

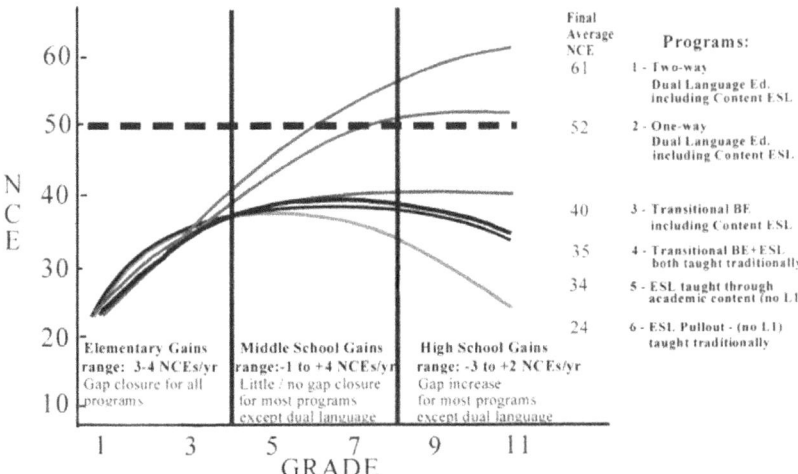

Figure 6.1 Thomas and Collier model comparison (Reprinted with author permission)

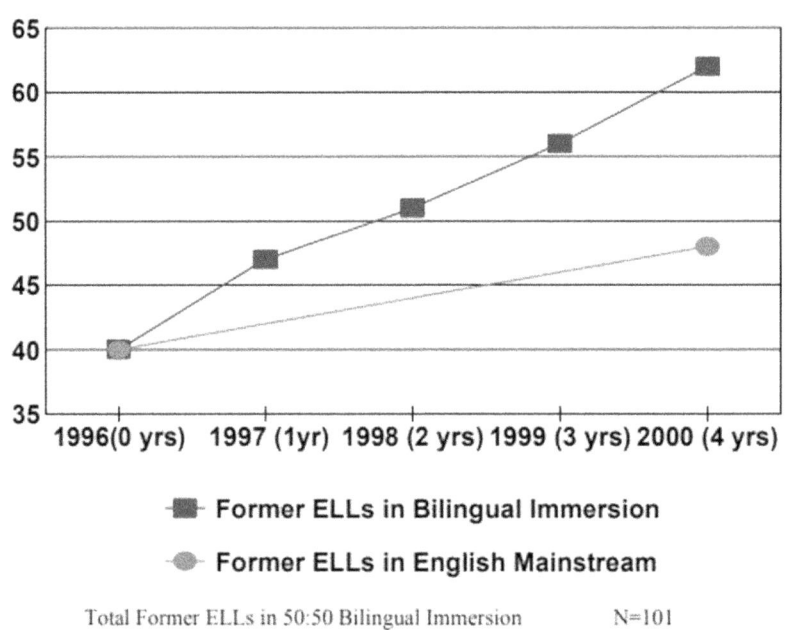

Figure 6.2 Comparison of outcomes in bilingual immersion and English mainstream settings (Reprinted with author permission)

fundamentally politicized issue, unresolved through the late 1990s and 2000s, when the English-only movement emerged.

1994 reauthorization

During the Clinton administration, the 1994 reauthorization attempted to rectify past ills from earlier iterations, but the BEA essentially never recovered from its 1978 reauthorization. In 1994, new grants were included, preference was given to programs promoting bilingualism and the inclusion of Native American, Alaska Native, and Native Hawaiian languages for receipt of funds was introduced. As Gándara (2015: 115) recounted, 'With support to build a cadre of well-prepared teachers, instructional materials, and pedagogical strategies that could equalize education for English learners, it appeared that support for bilingual education was back'.

Thomas and Collier

Still cited as among the most indisputable evidence of the effectiveness of bilingual education were meta-analyses conducted by Wayne Thomas and Virginia Collier, professors at George Mason University. The first of a series of longitudinal study findings was published in 2002, *A National Study of School Effectiveness for Language Minority Students' Long-Term Academic Achievement*. The language minority program model outcomes chart remains among the more persuasive and distilled illustrations comparing student outcomes in various program models for teaching emergent bilingual learners (see Figure 6.1).

Thomas and Collier (2004: 10) have since produced numerous follow-up studies, including *The Astounding Effectiveness of Dual Language Education*, which included a comparable chart comparing educational outcomes of language minority learners in various language instructional programs (Figure 6.2).

In addition to the work done by Collier and Thomas (2002), research and scholarship have continued in opposition to the English-only movement and in support of the effectiveness of bilingual education. Advocates have responded to the sociopolitical and policymaking attacks against bilingual education by growing new factions of educators, stakeholders, researchers and scholars to continue the battle for language rights in US schools.

The English-only movement

The short success of the English-only education movement occurred roughly from 1998 to 2002, during which time a series of voter-generated initiatives were passed at the state level in California, Arizona and Massachusetts (see McField, 2014). A similar initiative was proposed, but failed to win enough votes to pass in Colorado in 2002. Its opposition, the 'No on 31' campaign, had 'a well-run campaign, an effective message, and grassroots support that extended across the state' (Escamilla & Hopewell, 2008: 27) and, ultimately, it was defeated by 56% of voters.

California's journey

Despite clear evidence regarding the effectiveness of bilingual education for language minority students' educational outcomes, the English-only education movement emerged first in California in 1998, which passed Proposition 227, called 'English for the Children', with 61% of the vote (McField, 2008). It required that students who identified as English learners be placed in Sheltered or Structured English Immersion (SEI) settings (these terms were used interchangeably in reference to the program) for one year. Despite the SEI requirement, the initiative allowed parents to appeal for three different types of waivers to exempt their children from the SEI requirement. One estimate proposed that bilingual programs in California districts fell from 25% to 8% of overall models (McField, 2008: 695). It would be difficult to quantify the deleterious impact of Proposition 227 on the state's language minority learners. Scholars have investigated its impact in myriad areas (see McField, 2006; Parrish *et al.*, 2002). In 2016, Californians essentially overturned Proposition 227, when Proposition 58 was passed, which no longer required English-only as the primary instructional model for emergent bilingual students.

Arizona's restrictionist policies

In 2000, a similar ballot initiative emerged in Arizona, led by the same California English-only proponent, Ron Unz (who was seeking political notoriety for an anticipated run for state governor). It was Proposition 203, revised to create additional restrictions to the waiver options available under Proposition 227 in California and also required SEI as the primary instructional model for language minority learners. Unlike in California, Arizona's legislature was much more conservative and led by a Republican majority. In addition, shortly after its passage, a new Republican Superintendent of Public Instruction was elected – Tom Horne, whose campaign platform centered on anti-bilingual education (Wright, 2008). Under Horne's leadership, SEI was strictly enforced by the Arizona Department of Education.

An unrelated case, *Flores v. Arizona*, claiming inequitable funding for language minority learners in the Nogales and Douglas Unified School Districts was filed in 1992. It alleged that the state was in violation of the 1974 Equal Educational Opportunities Act (EEOA) by providing insufficient funds for the instruction of English learners (see Lillie *et al.*, 2010). The case resulted in the 2000 Flores Consent Order, which delineated various sanctions to create more equitable access and supports for language minority learners, but the state remained largely out of compliance with its requirements. Ultimately, an appeal to *Flores* was heard by the US Supreme Court, which did not find in the plaintiffs' favor.

The Arizona legislature passed House Bill 2064 in 2006, which attempted to develop a statewide definition of SEI – what implementation of the model should look like had been generally unclear and left to decision-making among districts and schools since the passage of Proposition 203 in 2000. It required English learners be in 'English language development' (ELD) settings for a minimum of four hours a day and created an English language learner (ELL) task force to 'develop and adopt research-based models of SEI programs for use by school districts and charter schools' (Lillie *et al.*, 2010: 5). Task force members heard testimony from both SEI and bilingual advocates, including professors and district leaders. Among those promoting SEI was Kevin Clark, a staunch English-only advocate with no experience in the fields of education, language minority schooling or applied linguistics. In his presentation, Clark attempted to provide an explanation for a 'discrete skills inventory' to comprise the state's required four-hour block of ELD as part of the SEI model. Clark described the following areas of language, recommending these be the basis for the four-hour block ELD curriculum: phonology, morphology, syntax, lexicon and semantics. Based on task force recommendations, instruction of English learners in the ELD four-hour block began in the 2008/2009 academic year. Implementation of ELD and the four-hour block was catastrophic, causing mass confusion among educators, school and district leaders across the state. In educator professional development regarding the ELD and discrete skills inventory, the Arizona ELD materials described students' placement in the setting as 'segregated' (Markos, 2013, personal communication). (See Moore [2014] for additional details regarding Arizona's implementation of SEI, the four-hour block, ELD and the discrete skills inventory.)

In February 2019, Arizona's Governor Doug Ducey signed Senate Bill (SB) 1014, which "passed the Legislature with unanimous support" (Targeted News Service, 2019: 1). It eliminated the required four-hour ELD block and "allows public schools and teachers to develop their own research-based models based on the needs of their individual students" (Targeted News Service, 2019: 1). Either SEI or alternative models approved by the Arizona Department of Education may be implemented under the new law for instruction of emergent bilingual learners, but it still "requires that students spend 120 minutes per day in…English instructional models" (Butvilofsky and Gumina, 2020: 207) and "continues to allow for segregation" (Martínez, 2020: 262).

Massachusetts' shifting ideologies

Massachusetts passed Question 2 in 2002, which also required SEI and English-only as the primary model for instruction of language minority learners. As a program model, it was initially defined by the state through the development and delivery of required educator professional development for compliance with the SEI mandate. Although it passed with two-thirds of voters approving, the governor had earlier attempted to undermine Question 2 and prior to its implementation in the 2003/2004 school year, 'the legislature exempted K-12 Two-Way Immersion programs from the waiver provisions in the law' (de Jong *et al.*, 2005: 599). This made it permissible for 'two very different program types: maintenance and developmental bilingual education through TWI [Two-Way Immersion] and English-only through SEI' (de Jong *et al.*, 2005: 599–600). Fifteen years later, on November 22, 2017, Governor Baker signed the Language Opportunity for Our Kids (LOOK) Act into law, which reinstated bilingual programs, created a new dual language endorsement for educators and ELL parent advisory councils and established a state Seal of Biliteracy.

Conclusion and Implications

The purpose of this volume is to leverage the accomplishments of innumerable advocates for language minoritized learners who, despite flawed educational language policy implementation, endured in their support of and involvement in bilingual settings around the country. Educators have shown commitment to ensuring that children's education remains viable, providing any and all opportunities for emergent bilingual learners' home and heritage language maintenance, promotion and, ultimately, development of full biliteracy and rich ethnic and cultural family and community connections. In the spirit of practicality and utility, rather than further rehashing the bilingual education wars, a more productive turn is to what from past infrastructure can be gleaned for future expansion and fine-tuning of bilingual programs. In many ways, the imminence of bilingual education is in dual language education programming, but a new era must properly frame and account for the complexity and power inherent to dual language settings, which by definition are composed of majority English-speaking and language minoritized learners. Future groundwork must be approached from an equity-driven and bilingual-bicultural perspective, as was initially espoused in the BEA. The next and concluding chapter revisits the status of the field of language minority schooling in 2020 and beyond and discusses shaping a sociopolitical consciousness for dual language education.

7 Current Endeavors and Future Possibilities

Ga mi yu je. Hank va yu:m kyu bay vak d̄igav'k baj hma:ny ga va wik ba d̄inyud ba u:wjo gwaw vim hankyu. Haygu i:yil, Ba i:yil d̄anyudk ba u:wjoy wi. Ga yum yih d̄op yīd̄ Ba hmasnych gwe spok han jay me. Dadaha:dk ha:n yo:k, gwe ga ha:n nyu jivda:d nyu yum nyu va wi:j wi.

Greetings. We are here to discuss bilingual education and how indigenous schools and communities are implementing bilingual/bicultural education programs. The purpose of these programs is to help children capitalize on the varied cultural and linguistic resources in their environment, and to strive to improve the quality of life for indigenous people.

Lucille J. Watahomigie and Teresa L. McCarty, introduction to Bilingual/Bicultural Education at Peach Springs: A Hualapai Way of Schooling (1994: 27)

Hegemonic Backdrop

The recent expansion of dual language education programs in the United States has, in many cases, been born out of appeal by white, middle- and upper-class monolingual families who see multilingualism as a beneficial attribute for their children. Scholars have intensely challenged the appropriation and gentrification of dual language education (Freire *et al.*, 2017; Heiman & Murakami, 2019; Heiman & Yanes, 2018) by the monolingual white majority. Flores (2016: 28) described *monolingual hegemonic Whiteness*, arguing that 'as bilingual education became institutionalized, it became reincorporated into hegemonic Whiteness'. García and Sung (2018: 328) concern that contemporary approaches to 'dual language' education shift foci from the initial purpose of bilingual education under the Bilingual Education Act (BEA):

> Instead of the prior bilingual education lens of educational equity and cultural affirmations, regardless of whether they were connected to a broader agenda of self-determination or not, an ideology in which neoliberal marketization of everything, including the ideas of multiculturalism

and culture itself, now forms the new basis undergirding social consciousness and formations.

Guadalupe Valdés shared a 'cautionary note' regarding the remaking of bilingual programs into dual language education long before the more recent surges in dual language programs. Valdés (1997) recounted the story of an entrenched Mexican-origin educator whose strong opinion against dual language education grew from centuries of fighting for the rights of Mexican heritage students and families.

> She has been a champion of bilingual education for children of Mexican origin, and is opposed to the concept of dual-immersion. 'Dual language immersion education is not a good idea', she says, rising to her feet. Then, switching to graphic Spanish, she adds, 'Si se aprovechan de nosotros en inglés, van a aprovechar de nostoros también en español'. Translated freely, she said, 'If they take advantage of us in English, they will take advantage of us in Spanish as well'. For Maria, what is at issue here is not an educational approach but intergroup relations, and the place of the powerful and the powerless. (Valdés, 1997: 19)

Martínez *et al.* (2015: 39) described examples of teachers' perspectives 'informed by ideologies that privilege Spanish and bilingualism… [that] can be seen as fundamentally counterhegemonic'. To combat hegemonies inherent to the very nature of dual language education, which by definition involves a balance between majority and minority learners, Flores (2016: 34) suggested 'we must resituate the battle for bilingual education within contemporary struggles that seek to develop new subjectivities outside of hegemonic Whiteness'. In discussion of global Indigenous languages, McCarty *et al.* (2019) revisited the 'four Rs' – resurgence, reclamation, revitalization and resilience. They described 'clear evidence of the generative ways in which Indigenous peoples are challenging hegemonic metaphors of language death and extinction and reconfiguring power relations to wedge open new spaces for language reclamation in and out of schools' (McCarty *et al.*, 2019: 14).

This chapter reviews contemporaneous progress in the development of dual language programs, interwoven with scholarship stressing the requisite central positionality of language minoritized learners in educational endeavors toward bilingualism, biliteracy and/or multilingualism. It discusses the prospect of again orchestrating the systemic infrastructural supports created by the Bilingual Education Act (BEA) and what it might take to foster federally mediated future expansion on a national scale.

Language Education in the United States

The BEA, which later became Title VII, faded in its prominence in the Elementary and Secondary Education Act (ESEA). In 2001, under No Child Left Behind, the title 'Bilingual Education Act' was removed, leaving only 'Title VII'. The description of language minority schooling was again moved to fall under Title III in the 2017 Every Student Succeeds Act version of the ESEA. During growth periods in the late 1970s and 1980s, bilingual programs were traditionally identified as either 'maintenance' (late-exit) or 'transitional' (early-exit) (see Baker & Wright, 2017; Wright, 2019), as discussed in Chapter 6.

Throughout the existence of the BEA and Title VII, the issue of distinguishing between and prioritizing the two were central to deliberations. The key distinction and reason for contentious debate surrounding which should be preferable for emergent bilingual learners involved divergent educational goals. In maintenance (late-exit) programs, priorities involved both students' native language maintenance, with the goal of achieving lifelong biliteracy, and the preservation of cultural connections, while also learning English. In transitional (early-exit) programs, the purpose was to utilize students' home language(s) for the sole purpose of transitioning to full English-only instruction. In today's systems of schooling, bilingual programs are primarily referred to as 'dual language' or 'two-way immersion' (an umbrella intended to encompass both one-way and two-way immersion, despite the label's obvious reference 'two').

The Seal of Biliteracy

Perhaps most emblematic of the significant increase in dual language programs in the United States in recent years is the widespread adoption of Seals of Biliteracy among states across the country. As of 2020, 40 states and the District of Columbia have approved a statewide Seal of Biliteracy, which is conveyed to students who (in most states) demonstrate proficiency in a language in addition to English (in some cases, course completion is sufficient). The concept of the Seal emerged from the grassroots efforts of Californians Together, intended to off-set California's restrictive English-only policies, which were generated by the passage of Proposition 227, 'English for the Children', in 1998. Developed in 2008, a Seal of Biliteracy 'takes the form of a gold seal that appears on the transcript or diploma of the graduating senior and is a statement of accomplishment for future employers and for college admissions' (Seal of Biliteracy, n.d.).

California legislation adopted the Seal statewide in 2011; over 10,000 seniors earned Seals upon graduation in 2012. That same year, the state of New York enacted similar legislation and Seals were adopted there, as well as in Texas and Illinois in 2013. In 2014, New Mexico, Washington, Minnesota, Louisiana and the District of Columbia adopted the Seal and the following year another six states did so – Virginia, Indiana, Nevada, Hawaii, Wisconsin and Utah. Variance among states' adoption of Seals, especially in terms of what constitutes bilingualism, is broad. In some cases, language proficiency assessment scores are sufficient to earn a Seal (Florida, Hawaii, Indiana, Maryland, Minnesota, Nevada, Rhode Island, Texas and Virginia), while in others (California, Colorado, Florida, Louisiana, North Carolina and Texas) only a minimum grade point average and completion of four years of coursework (Davin & Heineke, 2017) are required.

Although the increase in Seals may represent widespread interest in and support for multilingualism among growing numbers of communities, their adoption is often framed in the construct of World Language Education, in some cases with few connections for students whose home and/or heritage language(s) is/are situated as an essential part of earning Seals (Davin & Heineke, 2017; DeLeon, 2014). Amid the widespread implementation of Seals of Biliteracy, stakeholders and others must steadfastly acknowledge and work to deconstruct and combat contradictory sociopolitical perspectives and language ideologies that assign value to the attainment of multilingualism by monolingual white students, while also separately implicitly positioning language minoritized learners as deficient and in need of remediation. One way of doing so, as recounted by De Costa (2019), is to confront and decolonize 'elite multilingualism' through employing a linguistic ecology framework, or an ecology-of-language paradigm (Hornberger, 2002; Phillipson & Skutnabb-Kangas, 1996).

Elite multilingualism

Elite multilingualism can be conceived of as something 'that is performed, an enacted practice that reflects the unequal nature of different bilingual situations which exclude "small" [i.e. non-dominant] languages and language varieties, including minority "languages"' (De Costa, 2019: 2, citing Brennan, 2018: 160). It is socially constructed and sustained through pervasive emphasis on instituting *distinction* among speakers of particular languages – those of either the elite majority or marginalized minority, such that 'individuals actively attempt to set themselves apart from others' (De Costa, 2019: 2). Employing an ecological approach to elite multilingualism provides opportunities to interrogate the power in relationships and the interaction among speakers and learners of languages occupying spaces to which value has been assigned, deprived or some combination.

In drawing a distinction between ecology-of-language and diffusion-of-English paradigms, Phillipson and Skutnabb-Kangas (1996: 436) define the former as constituting: (1) a human rights perspective; (2) equality in communication; (3) multilingualism; (4) maintenance of languages and cultures; (5) protection of national sovereignties; and (6) promotion of foreign language education. Dual language education policies and implementation operating within an ecology-of-language paradigm should, for example, incorporate strategic, explicit and frequent acclaim for minority language(s), to reposition the inherent dominance and hegemony of English.

Henderson and Palmer (2020: 22) used 'a language ecology perspective' to investigate teachers as language policymakers in dual language bilingual education settings, and in doing so, 'embrace an understanding of language as practice'. Based on educator case studies, one recommendation they espouse is that districts allow 'schools to select and/or design program models that fit their local needs... they would need to invest deeply in professional development... and flatten leadership structures to allow teachers with the most understanding of bilingual education and biliteracy development to have agency' (Henderson & Palmer, 2020: 115).

Dual language programs

In recent years, there have been striking increases in new dual language programs across the country. In North Carolina, for example, 59 dual language programs exist, 37% of which were opened between 2013 and 2018 and the city of Dallas offers 56 dual language programs (Ingram, 2018). The first Haitian Creole-English bilingual program was launched in an immigrant-dense area of Boston in 2018 (Ingram, 2018). In Delaware, Governor Jack Markell launched a World Language Expansion Initiative in 2011. In discussion of its language immersion programs, he declared

> I want two things. I want students from Delaware to be able to go anywhere and do any kind of work they want to do, and I also want to attract businesses from around the world, to say, 'You want to be in Delaware because, among other things, we've got a bilingual work force'. (Harris, 2015: n.p.)

In the 2020/2021 school year, 44 schools house dual language immersion programs in Chinese and Spanish at 15 sites across the state (Dual Language Immersion Program Locations, 2020). Public schools in Portland, Oregon, offer dual language programs in Chinese, Japanese, Russian, Spanish and Vietnamese, and Minnesota administers 70 immersion and dual language programs, a third of which have been created within the last 10 years. However, the issue of positioning educators as arbiters (Johnson & Johnson, 2015) and interpreters (Moore, 2014) of language education policy implementation has been increasingly emphasized in recent research.

Language ideologies

Johnson and Johnson (2015: 223) centrally situate language ideologies amidst dual language educators' appropriation of top-down language policies, noting

> dominant-group language ideologies act as a template with which policymakers justify policies that restrict educational access and privilege particular ethnolinguistic groups (cf. Shohamy 2006; Wiley 1996). Social agents with access to institutional power tend to make policy decisions in line with dominant discourses that sustain and normalize linguistic, economic, and ethnic/social hierarchies (Ball 2006).

Based on interviews with teachers in a dual language bilingual program that required strict language separation, Henderson (2017: 31) distinguished between expressed assimilationist, versus pluralist language ideological perspectives and identified among two teachers 'a dynamic interplay between agency and structure'. Given the implicit nature of ideologies that may either achieve or undermine intended goals and consequences of dual language education, it is valuable to address the sociopolitical context of language education program development and implementation.

Sociopolitical consciousness

Perhaps antecedent to the concept of 'critical' consciousness among stakeholders involved in dual language education programs (Cervantes-Soon *et al.*, 2017), a sociopolitical consciousness calls on educators and students to 'critique implicit and explicit hegemonic language education policies that can result in subtractive schooling (Valenzuela, 1999)' (Freire, 2016: 48). Freire (2016: 37) describes dual language students as *nepantleras/nepantleros* 'to stress the importance of contesting language education policies and practices that overlook students' linguistic practices and socio-realities in the nepantla' and 'emphasize the everyday language crossing, the linguistic border experience, and the in-between and overlapping of Spanish and English language experiences of Latina/o students' (Freire, 2016: 39). Freire (2016: 38) refers to the scholarly contribution by Jaramillo and McLaren (2011: 60), who 'called nepantla "an intermediary space sin rumbo (a "borderland" of "betwixt-and-between") . . . In nepantla, las indigenas began to undo the trauma of colonization"'.

The development of sociopolitical consciousness among pre- and in-service educators in dual language education settings is necessary 'to fight against oppressive language education policies' (Freire, 2016: 45) and engage in emancipatory dialogue with students to nurture their own sociopolitical consciousness. Conversely Freire asserts, when dual language educators and students have not adopted sociopolitical consciousness, they instead operate based on 'naive consciousness' 'which ignores the combination of hegemonic forces in school and society' (Freire, 2016: 47). Similarly, Alfaro *et al.*, discuss 'the critical process of continuous learning and unlearning, conscious thinking and rethinking, and the commitment to change practice based on new understandings' (2014: 21) as part of university-school collaboration in a pre-service dual language educator preparation program.

As an extension of educators' development of sociopolitical consciousness, Freire (2020: 233) refers to 'the term conscientization [which] calls for lessons individuals learn related to injustice and inequity affecting minoritized populations. These calls can be stepping stones toward the development of sociopolitical consciousness and social justice commitment.' Conscientization acknowledges privilege and *microagressions* related to race and can be 'extended to include culture, disability, gender, sexuality, poverty, and religion (Sue *et al.*, 2010) to recognize conscious as well as unconscious offenses (Sue *et al.*, 2007)' (Freire, 2020: 233).

Dual language immersion in Utah

Utah's approach to language immersion has been particularly scrutinized since it created statewide dual language immersion (DLI) through the passage of Senate Bill 80 in 2007, which established a critical languages program, and Senate Bill 41 in 2008, which modified the Critical Languages Program and established a pilot Dual Language Immersion Program. These 'international education initiatives' began with Chinese, French and Spanish. As of the 2018/2019 school year, 224 DLI programs were reported, 113 in Spanish, 65 in Chinese, 30 in French, 13 in Portuguese, 2 in German and 1 in Russian. In the 2017/2018 school year, about 5% of students were enrolled in a DLI program in Utah. Although English learners enroll at higher rates than monolingual English speakers, they make up only 41% of students in DLI settings and 5% of those in one-way programs (Steele *et al.*, 2019).

Although Utah's student population is only 1% of the overall US student body, it makes up 20% of students in Mandarin dual language programs (Bench, 2019; see Sung & Tsai, 2019). The state's 2008 law was supported by then Governor Jon Huntsman, Jr, who is fluent in Mandarin, after time spent overseas in Taiwan (Bench, 2019). Utahans speak more languages than any other state's residents – 130 (Bench, 2019).

Flores (2015) referred to the country's overall embrace of language immersion as having been 'Columbused' by 'ignoring the history of Latin[x] activism' that produced bilingual-bicultural education.

The DC immersion movement

In 2014, only 13 elementary schools in Washington, DC, offered dual language programs (Chandler, 2014), and none were available 'east of the river' – a reference to the Anacostia. Just five years later, in 2019, the DC immersion movement reported 23 dual language one- and two-way programs (Damari *et al.*, 2019). These included 16 elementary, 4 middle and 3 high school programs, 1 multilingual program (an international school) and programs in Spanish, Mandarin, French/Spanish and Hebrew (Damari *et al.*, 2019: 13). But Carla Norde, an African-American native Washingtonian and parent 'tied the increasing popularity of dual-language programs to the city becoming more white and Hispanic' (Chandler, 2014), saying 'We have always been in that school, and we have never been pushing that agenda'. In 2018, 6 of the 10 charter schools with the longest waiting lists included multilingual programs (Stein, 2018).

Upon the opening of a new dual language program, African-American single mother Kristin Pugh complained that 'You are trying to push out the minority', adding that 'she believes that dual-language programs are more suitable for two-parent households who have enough time to help their children with their English and Spanish homework' (Stein, 2018, n.p.).

Little research has addressed the impact of expanding dual language programs on African American and other ethnic minority students. Palmer (2010) studied a dual language program strand within a larger school focused on classroom discourse patterns. One teacher remarked:

> 'On paper our school looks integrated and it's less integrated than you might think if you walk into different classrooms'. Although the entire school population is approximately 30 percent African American, on average dual-language classes contain only about five percent African American students, leaving the mainstream classrooms filled almost 50 percent African American students. (Palmer, 2010: 102)

Palmer's (2010) findings, echoing the District of Columbia parents' concerns, again stressed a fundamental question – bilingual programs, *for whom*? She emphasized the inherent paradox emerging in the expansion of dual language programs in states and districts across the country.

Native and tribal language programs

The US Census has estimated '5.2 million American Indian and Alaska Native people (1.7% of the population) and 1.2 million Native Hawaiian and other Pacific Islanders (0.4% of the population)' and 'reported 169 Native American languages spoken by 370,000 people' (McIvor & McCarty, 2017: 422, citing Siebens & Julian, 2011).

As Littlebear (2001) avowed

> Our languages mean much. They encompass whole linguistic solar systems of spiritual expression, whole galaxies that express universal human values like love, generosity and belonging, and whole universes of references that enable us to cope with an everchanging world. Because our elders are moving on, it is up to us to help strengthen our languages. When one elder journeys to the spirit world, a whole Smithsonian Institution's worth of information goes with him or her. We have to retain that information in our languages, and that is why language immersion is so vitally important. (Littlebear, 2001: 6–7)

Intergenerational language transmission plays a critical role for these communities' self-determination. Despite the weaponized use of schooling to strategically amputate the language, culture and cultural traditions of countless Native American and Indigenous children by the US government, Native and tribal language communities recognize and leverage the role schooling can play for language reclamation – through bilingual, trilingual and immersion approaches. 'Native American language immersion schools are Native language based with Native American and mainstream curricula and tribally/certified teachers, primarily tribal scholars' (Pease-Pretty On Top, 2001: 45).

New York City dual language programs

In 2018, the New York City Schools chancellor, Carmen Faria, launched 33 new pre-K dual language programs, more than doubling the existing number of programs. These included diverse languages such as Bengali, Italian, Mandarin, Russian, French, Haitian-Creole, Hebrew and Japanese (Amin, 2019). As Executive Director Steven Choi, of the New York Immigration Coalition remarked in 2018, 'In these difficult times for immigrant families, bilingual programs send a powerful message that families' home language is a valuable asset. These new programs are an important step in ensuring success for our emergent multilingual learners' (States News Service, 2018: 2). Manhattan Borough president, Gale A. Brewer, remarked 'Bilingual pre-K expansion is a welcome victory for all of New York's families. More languages offered and more bilingual pare-K seats overall mean that more families will be able to access the full benefits of pre-K' (States News Service, 2018: 1). As of December 2019, the city offered 671 bilingual programs in 13 languages (Amin, 2019).

French immersion advocate Dr Fabrice Jaumont (2017) declared a *bilingual revolution* and has produced a guidebook for communities' development of new language immersion programs. A *New York Times* report, however, traced the history of one middle school in the city, IS-293, Boerum Hill School for International Studies, which added a French program in 2015 with support from Jaumont. It reported that the new program prompted concerns from local families about the influx of white, wealthy students and the 'radically changed' racial dynamics.

Ongoing Activities in Language Education

With problematizing the future of dual language education positioned as a central consideration, despite the anti-immigrant sociopolitical rhetoric discussed in Chapter 1, ongoing and new initiatives are again today contributing to a possible future infrastructure for equitable access to and equity in bilingual programs. Examples of these are discussed in subsequent sections, intended not as representational, but rather illustrative of the field.

Californians Together

Despite the systemic dismantling of bilingual education and the 'sunsetting' of the BEA through the 1990s (Wiley, 2014), in the 21st century, advocates and movements made considerable strides. Californians

Together, formed 'in the aftermath of the Proposition 227 loss (1998)' (Gold, 2019, personal communication) 'is a vibrant coalition of over 20 education advocacy groups'. Founded by Shelly Spiegel-Coleman, Laurie Olsen and Rosalia Salinas, Californians Together led the statewide and later national campaigns for Seals of Biliteracy. More recently, its leadership launched the English Learner Leadership and Legacy Initiative (ELLLI), which was developed to pass on 'the legacy of how advocates for ELs have approached various sociopolitical challenges and to ensure that our Fellows were grounded in that history' (Gold, 2019, personal communication). Californians Together continues to play essential roles in fostering new education leadership for language minoritized learners; conducting policy-related research; supporting biliteracy programs and emergent bilingual education overall; and providing support for educators and administrators dealing with the current traumatization of immigrant children and their families.

English Learner Leadership and Legacy Initiative

The ELLLI, a collaborative effort of both Californians Together and the California Association of Bilingual Education (CABE), launched in 2015. It fosters expertise among fellows 'equipped to advance proactive projects... and respond effectively to political challenges at state and local levels' (Ou, 2015).

> The goal of the initiative is to develop a new generation of strong, well-informed, skilled, courageous and activist leaders to build and sustain the movement for educational equity and excellence for English Learners. The EL Leadership and Legacy curriculum will provide an advocacy framework, historical context, lessons from the past, immersion in research, mentor-ship and skill development to inspire and prepare advocates to work at multiple levels (state, district, community) to establish strategic action agendas, move policy and practice, develop and leverage research, work with media, and build and mobilize coalitions championing the right to quality education for English learners. (Ou, 2015)

Mentors for the ELLLI program include both currently active and retired advocates representing a broad range of backgrounds and positionality within the field of language minority schooling and the development and implementation of language education policy; for example, the former president of the California Latino School Board Association, former CABE board members, a civil rights attorney, school board members, current and former district and county administrators and California State University and other university faculty members, current and emerita. ELLLI is directed by Ruth Barajas, who has worked as a school and district-based educator and leader. She facilitates interactions among fellows and mentors and oversees the development of case studies for publication and dissemination regarding advocacy around language minority equity and language rights.

Dual Language Education of New Mexico

Dual Language Education of New Mexico (DLeNM) is a 'grassroots' organization based in Albuquerque, New Mexico, that gained non-profit status in 2000. Its mission is 'to develop, support, and advocate for high-quality dual language enriched education in New Mexico and beyond' (Dual Language Education of New Mexico, 2020). It hosts virtual learning and webinar events; provides programmatic supports, resources and instructional supports; and conducts advocacy activities for dual language programs. As of 2020, DLeNM employs 16 full-time, 2 part-time and 3 intern staff. Since 2008, DLeNM has also administered a student leadership initiative, which supports linguistically and culturally diverse youth to

> Embrace language, culture, and history as a source of power and responsibility; and embrace the invitation to lead as a way to build partnerships with each other for future advocacy and the betterment of our communities. (Dual Language Education of New Mexico, 2020)

The genesis of DLeNM was a series of five small pilot grants awarded to schools by the New Mexico State Education Agency for the creation of bilingual programs, based on findings from the 1991 Ramírez Report (Rogers, 2020, personal communication). These were distributed across the state. As programs were being developed and implemented, leaders collaborated closely to learn from one another and share resources, strategies and lessons learned. At the end of the first year, staff from each of the five programs were invited to come together for a statewide meeting. Although 30–35 attendees were expected, roughly 90 showed – this was the first convening that led to the annual La Cosecha Bilingual Education Conference. DLeNM estimated that in 2019, over 90% of La Cosecha attendees were school or district-based educators and 58% were teachers (Dual Language Education of New Mexico, 2020).

National Association of Bilingual Education

The National Association for Bilingual Education (NABE) was founded in 1975 by Dr Albar Peña, who was the first director of the Office of Bilingual Education, and incorporated as a non-profit in April 1976. With support from affiliates in 18 states, NABE represents 5000 members. Its mission is 'to advocate for educational equity and excellence for bilingual/multilingual students in a global society' (NABE, 2020). Its *Bilingual Research Journal*, first known as the *NABE Journal*, was founded in 1976; editor of the first 1977 volume was Alma Flor Ada (Flores, 2008).

NABE has played a pivotal role in impacting bilingual education policy. Its Washington-based contacts have been and remain high-reaching – for example, Edward Kennedy spoke at the 1981 NABE conference in Boston and Mrs Barbara Bush attended the 1983 meeting in Washington, DC (Flores, 2008). NABE runs institutes, creates and disseminates resources, provides professional development, conducts leadership and advocacy activities, publishes materials, hosts events and offers a learning portal, among myriad other activities. It may be most well-known for its annual NABE Conference, which brings together members to attend, share and collaborate around presentations and in other meetings. In April 2021, NABE will host its 50th Annual International Conference in Houston, Texas.

Native Language Reclamation

Jackson and Whitehorse De Laune (2018) share experiences co-teaching a course referred to as 'Kiowa College' that 'meets to practice the Kiowa language and learn Kiowa ways that include oral tradition, songs, military and women's societies, protocol, ceremony, history and values' (p. 38), most often around storytelling. They frame 'storytelling and community listening as a means of recovery and resistance' – 'Kiowa story performs transrhetorical resistance by moving meaning across temporal, spatial, and cultural locations and thereby creating relationships across these sites in order to form the broader movements upon which decolonization depends' (p. 41).

American Indian Language Development Institute

Founded 'with support from the National Endowment for the Humanities' by Lucille Watahomigie and Leanne Hinton in 1978 and housed since 1990 at the University of Arizona, the mission of the American Indian Language Development Institute (AILDI) is to provide critical training and strengthen efforts to revitalize and promote the use of Indigenous languages across generations' (AILDI 2019 Annual Report: 2). Initially, 'it was intended to develop a Yuman Language Workshop targeting Digueno, Havasupai, Hualapai, Mohave and Yavapai language communities' (AILDI History, n.d.). It brought together Native language communities and academic linguists 'to examine their languages and to create writing systems and teaching materials' (AILDI History, n.d.). In 2019, it hosted five workshops with 85 participants from 11 Tribal Nations (AILDI Annual Report, 2019). It also partners with the University of Montana and Chief Dull Knife College on Collaborative Language Planning Project, a grant from the National Science Foundation 'creating a network of support for Montana tribal college language instructors and activists' (AILDA Annual Report, 2019: 2). AILDI has been 'Cited by the U.S. Department of Education as one of ten outstanding programs for minority teacher preparation' and 'continues to be the standard-bearer for Indigenous language education' (AILDA Annual Report, 2019: 1).

First Nations Development Institute

The First Nations Development Institute 'improves economic conditions for Native Americans through direct financial grants, technical assistance and training, advocacy and policy' (First Nations Development Institute, n.d.). Programs include stewarding Native lands, nourishing Native foods and health, advancing housing and community asset-building strategies, strengthening tribal and community institutions, investing in Native youth and achieving Native financial empowerment.

Its Native Language Immersion Initiative (NLII) 'aims to build the capacity of and directly support Native American language-immersion and culture-retention programs' (First Nations Development Institute, n.d.). NLII was launched in 2017 through a $2.1 million grant from the National Endowment for the Humanities and matching funds from the Lannan, Kalliopeia and NoVo foundations. In its first two years, it awarded $2.185 million to 25 grantees representing 17 languages across 14 grade levels (Native Language Immersion Initiative, 2019: 3). Discussing why language is important for Native communities, Board Chair Benny Shendo, Jr, affirmed

> *Language is a core part of who we are as Indian people.* Each of us has our respective languages that connect us to our place of birth, teach us how to pray, and show us who we are as Indian people. *Language is sacred.* (Native Language Immersion Initiative, 2019: 2)

Shendo described a 'renaissance of Indigenous languages' across the country (Native Language Immersion Initiative, 2019: 2) and noted 'Each tribe and language is different. It's important to respect those differences and the different ways they choose to revitalize languages' (Native Language Immersion Initiative, 2019: 2).

The NLII funds programs in 14 states, with most grantees in New Mexico, South Dakota, Washington and Wisconsin and most applicants from Montana and Washington (Native Language Immersion Initiative, 2019: 7). Its success demonstrates how language immersion and other school-based programs can facilitate language reclamation for Native and tribal language communities. However, in its first two years, it was only able to fund 10% of applicants – 'which highlights the tremendous ongoing need for more funding for language programs' (Native Language Immersion Initiative, 2019: 3).

America's Languages Caucus

The America's Languages Caucus was created in November 2019 by Co-Chairs, House Representatives David Price of North Carolina (Democrat) and Don Young of Alaska (Republican) 'to develop a national strategy to raise awareness about the importance of world language learning and international education' (Joint National Committee for Languages National Council for Languages and International Studies, n.d.). It was prompted by findings from the 2017 American Academy of Arts and Sciences, Commission on Language Learning Report, *America's Languages: Investing in Language Education for the 21st Century*, reference to which is integrated in Wiley's (2021) Foreword to this volume. The report 'makes clear that the United States needs significantly more bilingual and biliterate citizens to help ensure national security, promote economic job growth, and develop the potential of every American student' (David E. Price, 2019, n.p.). Its legislative agenda includes a series of developed Acts, including the Supporting Young Language Learners' Access to Bilingual Education (SYLLABLE, described below), Biliteracy Education Seal and Teaching (BEST), and Esther Martinez Native American Languages Program Reauthorization Acts.

Strengthening Bilingual Education

Based on a better understanding of the infrastructure for bilingual education on a national scale, and with the accomplishments of innumerable educators, advocates and others in expanding bilingual programs, possible future endeavors may cultivate the orchestration of new infrastructure. A variety of next steps are discussed in this final section.

Convening

A symposium composed of leading scholars and activists in fields related to bilingual education and language education could serve to identify necessary pathways to dual language education that privilege minority students and overtly acknowledge and combat the intrinsic hegemonies and white monolingual power structures embedded in dual language programs. The initial meeting could involve scholars, activists and advocates with the goal of devising a mission for dual language education that at its core concerns strategies for integrating sociopolitical consciousness into the development and implementation of dual language programs. The symposium could produce proceedings that establish solidarity applicable to real-world stakeholders in districts and systems of schooling responsible for the creation of new and oversight of existing dual language programs.

A second series of meetings involving various state stakeholders could address current and anticipated local and national needs in areas related to dual language bilingual education and language education more broadly. These may be similar to the National Education Association (NEA) conference that occurred in Tucson in 1966, attended by educators, district leaders, administrators, regional representatives, as well as activists, and importantly, was keynoted by politicians equipped to write and sponsor legislation supporting language programs. Attendees could contribute on behalf of key member organizations in the areas of language minority schooling and language education, including for example, NABE and DLeNM. Vitally, faculty from Institutes of Higher Education (IHEs), which prepare educators to work in dual language, language minority and language education programs could be invited – in the long term, these faculty may play a critical role in helping to feed the pipeline of educators to support the language educational needs of students in early childhood through (ideally) postsecondary dual language bilingual settings.

Among appropriate congressional representatives to include is Raul Grijalva, coincidentally House of Representatives member from the Tucson area, who has for many years been among few in Congress consistently sponsoring legislation in support of emergent bilingual learners and dual language education. Most recently, on February 6, 2020, Representative Grijalva sponsored Supporting Young Language Learners' Access to Bilingual Education Act, or the SYLLABLE Act, which would provide $15 million in dual language flagship grants. The purposes of grants would be

> To develop innovative strategies for DLI programs serving children from low-income families, including English learners and minority children.
>
> To provide those programs with consistent support from pre-school through fifth grade.
>
> To improve school readiness of children and to enhance biliteracy and bilingualism skills.

'The SYLLABLE Act recognizes the importance, supports dual language programs in low-income communities, and ensures that every child has access to new educational opportunities that prepare them for a successful future', asserted Grijalva (2020).

Regional technical assistance centers

The creation of regional technical assistance centers could lead responsiveness efforts to local education agencies (LEAs) and state education agencies (SEAs) regarding needs in the areas of language educational programs. Technical assistance centers could serve small or larger areas, depending on the density of the programs and language types in a particular vicinity. In the 1981/1982 school year, for example, Title VII funded 19 bilingual education service centers. Some served a handful of states, such as that housed at the Florida International School of Education in North Miami, which served Florida, Georgia, South Carolina and North Carolina. Others, like the center at Hunter College, supported needs from New York City, as well as local Nassau and Suffolk counties. Two locations at the University of New Mexico and Arizona State University exclusively served Native American language education programs (Reisner, 1983).

Materials development centers

Materials development centers' responsibilities could include the creation of curricula, resources for professional development and, importantly, new assessments for both levels of proficiency in numerous languages, as well as content in languages other than English. These may include, for example, Spanish proficiency for students in DLE programs, French or Chinese proficiency for students in one-way world languages, or Navajo or Ojibwe in one-way American Indian immersion programs. In addition, content assessments could be developed to assess students' knowledge and skills in math, science, social studies and language arts in target languages for dual language programs.

Educator pathways

A well-established, long-standing critical need area for bilingual programs is educator preparation, expertise and professional development. Specially designed academic programs, particularly those offered through IHEs for pathways for dual language educators, administrators and leaders would be essential for a new national infrastructure to promote bilingual dual language schooling. As was the goal with the BEA and Title VII teacher training and fellowships, programs should target not only mainstream educators, but also school, district, university and field-based leaders.

Post-Baccalaureate

Given the current national teacher shortage and more acute dearth of English as a second language (ESL) and dual language educators, there could be periods during which dual language programs' personnel are under-prepared for their positions. To address this deficiency, post-baccalaureate programs integrated in, and articulated with, IHEs, could provide accessible opportunities for educators to obtain the necessary supports for successful teaching in dual language bilingual programs. Typically, Post-Baccalaureate Certificate programs are smaller units than master's degrees and convey credits that can be applied toward a future master's- or doctoral-level program.

Para-educators

Perhaps among school systems' most untapped resources are the expertise brought to schools by paraprofessional staff. Despite rampant teacher turnover, especially in urban areas, paraprofessionals are those school staff who often reside in and are a part of school communities. In some cases, these individuals may be particularly important because they serve as links between families and schools. Pathways to initial teacher certification for para-educators that account for para-educators' full-time employment could be highly beneficial in contributing to a dual language bilingual educator pipeline.

Fellowships at IHEs

Among the most important features of the programs created under the BEA and Title VII were tuition reduction, compensation and job placement through grants and fellowships for feeding bilingual educator pipelines. Equally, if not more critical, was the policy for provision of salary reimbursement to IHEs for the creation of director positions to administer university-based fellowship programs. One approach to the distribution of fellowship monies was to focus on students with earned master's degrees who completed doctoral programs. Job placement obligations for graduates to, in turn, become administrators employed by IHEs in the fellowship programs themselves, established a cadre of professors with impact on language minorit(ized) schooling. Title VII fellowship graduates continue to play leading roles in bilingual and language education programs in universities, states and districts across the country. The fellowships in a way entrenched expertise in educational institutions – from LEAs to SEAs, and IHEs, in research-oriented and non-profit organizations, policymaking and advocacy groups, governmental agencies and beyond. The extent of their impact on language educational programs was untold; reestablishment could have a colossal impact on recreating concentration of qualified educators dispersed across levels of schooling and the field.

New bilingual dual language education policymaking

The Office of Civil Rights' interpretation of J. Stanley Pottinger's May 25, 1970, memo prioritizing bilingual education as in compliance with Title VI of the Civil Rights Act marked the first major injection of policymaking that later also emerged in the *Lau v. Nichols* decision. Shirley Hufstedler's August 1980 Notice of Proposed Rulemaking extended beyond the *Lau* Remedies, mandating bilingual education in certain circumstances. A secretary of education under a new administration, under a president such as Joe Biden, could potentially again create policy similar to the 1970 and 1980 actions, to require school districts provide bilingual dual language education as the instructional priority for emergent bilingual students. If an act such as this transpired, it could be the dawn of a new day for language rights and bilingual dual language education in the United States.

References

Abrams, C. (1955) How to remedy our 'Puerto Rican Problem'. *Commentary* 19 (2), 120–127. See https://www.commentarymagazine.com/articles/charles-abrams/how-to-remedy-our/ (accessed 21 January 2020).

Acosta, I. (2015). *A family's linguistic memoire: Painting a multigenerational family portrait of Spanish maintenance and loss*. Master's Thesis. Sacramento, CA: California State University, Sacramento. Retrieved December 14, 2020 from http://csus-dspace.calstate.edu/bitstream/handle/10211.3/163244/2015AcostaIsabel.pdf?sequence=3

Adams, D.W. (1995) *Education for Extinction: American Indians and the Boarding School Experience, 1875–1928*. Lawrence, KS: University of Kansas Press.

Alfaro, C., Durán, R., Hunt, A. and Aragón, M.J. (2014) Steps toward unifying dual language programs, common core state standards, and critical pedagogy: Oportunidades, estrategias y retos. *Association of Mexican-American Educators* 8 (2), 17–30.

Alvarez, A. (2014) *Native America and the Question of Genocide*. Lanham, MD: Rowman & Littlefield.

American Academy of Arts and Sciences (2017) *America's Languages: Investing in Language Education for the 21st Century*. Commission on Language Learning. Cambridge, MA: American Academy of Arts and Sciences. See https://www.amacad.org/sites/default/files/publication/downloads/Commission-on-Language-Learning_Americas-Languages.pdf (accessed 12 January 2020).

American Indian Language Development Institute (2020) *Annual Report Fiscal Year July 1, 2019-June 30, 2020*. Retrieved January 3, 2020 from https://aildi.arizona.edu/sites/default/files/data/annual%20report%20brochure_20_v2_0.pdf.

American Indian Language Development Institute, *History*. Retrieved January 3, 2021 from: https://aildi.arizona.edu/content/history.

Amin, R. (2019) NYC education officials exploring dual language programs for 3-year-olds. *Chalkbeat New York*, 6 December.

Andersson, T. (1971) Bilingual education: The American experience. *The Modern Language Journal* 55 (7), 427–440.

Arawak Consulting Corporation (1977) *National Bilingual Clearinghouse Conferences, October/November 1976*. Washington, DC: National Institute of Education, US Department of Health, Education and Welfare.

Arias, M.B., Delgado, M.T., de Porcel, A. and Irizarry, R. (1977) Response to AIR Study 'Evaluation of the Impact of ESEA Title VII Spanish/English Bilingual Education Program'. Written testimony prepared for the Congressional Record, presented during the Hearings of the Subcommittee on Elementary, Secondary, and Vocational Education of the Congress of the United States.

Arias, M.B. and Wiley, T.G. (2015) Forty years after Lau: The continuing assault on educational human rights in the United States with implications for linguistic minorities. *Languages Problems and Language Planning* 39 (3), 227–244.

Author (1978) *Guide to Title VII ESEA Bilingual Bicultural Programs 1977–78.* Austin, TX: Dissemination and Assessment Center for Bilingual Education.
Author (2018a) Key facts about charter schools. Charter schools in perspective. See http://www.in-perspective.org/files/CharterSchoolsInPerspective_GuidetoResearch_KeyFacts.pdf (accessed 2 March 2020).
Baker, C. and Wright, W.E. (2017) *Foundations of Bilingual Education and Bilingualism* (6th edn). Bristol: Multilingual Matters.
Baker, K.A. and de Kanter, A.A. (1981) *Effectiveness of Bilingual Education: A Review of Literature.* Washington, DC: Office of Planning, Budget and Evaluation, US Department of Education.
Baker, K.A. and de Kanter, A.A. (1983) An answer from research on bilingual education. *American Education* 19 (10), 40–48.
Balderrama, F.E. and Rodríguez, R. (2006) *Decade of Betrayal: Mexican Repatriation in the 1930s.* Albuquerque, NM: University of New Mexico Press.
Ball, S.J. (2006) *Education Policy and Social Class.* New York, NY: Routledge.
Ballotpedia (n.d.) Charter school statistics for all 50 states. See https://ballotpedia.org/Charter_school_statistics_for_all_50_states (accessed 3 June 2020).
Barbian, E., Gonzales, G.C. and Mejía, P. (eds) (2017) *Rethinking Bilingual Education: Welcoming Home Languages into our Classrooms.* Milwaukee, WI: Rethinking Schools.
Barik, H. and Swain, M. (1975) Three year evaluation of a large scale early grade French immersion program: The Ottowa study. *Language Learning* 25, 1–30.
Beauchamp, Z. (2013) The inside story of the Harvard dissertation that became too racist. *ThinkProgress.* See https://thinkprogress.org/the-inside-story-of-the-harvard-dissertation-that-became-too-racist-for-heritage-3a14238f662e/ (accessed 5 February 2020).
Becker, W.C. and Gersten, R. (1992) A follow-up of follow through: The later effects of the direct instruction model on children in fifth and sixth grades. *American Educational Research Journal* 19, 75–92.
Bench, J. (2019) You Want Hope for U.S.-China Relations? Utah is the Gold Standard. *China Law Blog.* See http://utah-newspapers.com/news/you-want-hope-for-us-china-relations-utah-is-the-gold-standard/ (accessed 9 September 2020).
Berman, A. (2017) Jeff Sessions claims to be a champion of voting rights, but his record suggests otherwise. *The Nation Blogs.* See https://www.thenation.com/article/archive/as-attorney-general-jeff-sessions-would-be-a-threat-to-civil-rights/ (accessed 17 November 2020).
Bialystok, E. (2009) Components of executive control with advantages for bilingual children in two cultures. *Cognition* 112 (3), 494–500. See http://www.sciencedirect.com/science/article/pii/S0010027709001577 (accessed 25 August 2019).
Bilingual Education Act, Pub. L. No. (90-247), 81 Stat. 816 (1968).
Bilingual Education Act, Pub. L. No. (93-380), 88 Stat. 503 (1974).
Bilingual Education: Hearings Before the Special Subcommittee on Bilingual Education of the Committee on Labor and Public Welfare, United States Senate, Ninetieth Congress, First Session, on S. 428 (1967) Washington, DC: Government Printing Office.
Bilingual Education Act Hearings (1974) *Before the General Subcommittee on Education of the Committee on Education and Labor, House of Representatives, 93rd Congress, 2nd Session, on H.R. 1085, H.R. 2490, and H.R. 11464.* Washington, DC: Government Printing Office.
Bilingual Education Hearings, Part 3 (1977, June 7–9) *Hearings before the Subcommittee on Elementary, Secondary, and Vocational Education of the Committee on Education and Labor, House of Representatives, 95th Congress, 1st Session on H.R. 15 to Extend for Five Years Certain Elementary, Secondary, and Other Education Programs.* Washington, DC: US Government Printing Office.

Birman, B.F. and Ginsberg, A.L. (1983) Introduction: Addressing the needs of language-minority children. In K.A. Baker and A.A. de Kanter (eds) *Bilingual Education* (pp. ix–xxi). Lexington, MA: Lexington Books.

Blanton, C.K. (2004) *The Strange Career of Bilingual Education in Texas, 1836–1981*. College Station, TX: Texas A&M University Press.

Blanton, C.K. (2014) *George I. Sánchez: The Long Fight for Mexican American Integration*. New Haven, CT: Yale University Press.

Borjas, G.J. (2016) Yes, immigration hurts American workers. *Politico*. See https://www.politico.com/magazine/story/2016/09/trump-clinton-immigration-economy-unemployment-jobs-214216 (accessed 5 February 2020).

Brennan, S. (2018) Advocating commodification: An ethnographic look at the policing of Irish as a commercial asset. *Language Policy* 17, 157–177.

Brisk, M. (1978) *Bilingual Higher Education Programs: Their Impact on Institutions and Community*. Los Angeles, CA: National Dissemination and Assessment Center, California State University.

Brown, M. and Brown, A. (2019) Legacy set free: Emancipating the works of Oscar Brown, Jr. *University of Chicago Journal*. See https://www.journals.uchicago.edu/doi/pdfplus/10.1086/704022 (accessed 13 January 2020).

Bucchioni, E. (1982) The daily round of life in the school. In F. Cordasco and E. Bucchioni (eds) *The Puerto Rican Community and Its Children on the Mainland* (pp. 201–238). Metuchen, NJ: Scarecrow Press.

Buckley, J. and Schneider, M. (2005) Are charter school students harder to educate? Evidence from Washington, D.C. *Educational Evaluation and Policy Analysis* 27 (4), 365–380.

Burt, K. (2007) The tangled political roots of Hispanics. *Hispanic Link Weekly Report* 25 (43). See http://www.kennethburt.com/tangled.pdf (accessed 13 November 2019).

Butvilofsky, S. A., & Gumina, D. (2020). The possibilites of bilingualism: Perceptions of bilingual learners in Arizona. *Bilingual Research Journal* 43 (2), 196–211.

Cabinet Committee on Opportunities for Spanish Speaking People (1971, 21–25 June) Washington, DC: Task Force on Education.

Califano Jr, J.A. (1981) *Governing America: An Insider's View from the White House and the Cabinet*. New York: Simon and Schuster.

Cárdenas, J.A. (1977) *The AIR Evaluation of the Impact of ESEA Title VII Spanish/English Bilingual Education Programs: An IDRA Response with a Summary by Dr. Jose A. Cardenas*. San Antonio, TX: Intercultural Development Research Association.

Cárdenas, J.A. (1994) *All Pianos Have Keys and Other Stories*. San Antonio, TX: Intercultural Development Research Association.

Cazden, C.B. (1992) *Language Minority Education in the United States: Implications of the Ramírez Report. Educational Practice Report: 3*. Santa Cruz, CA: University of California Santa Cruz, National Center for Science Teaching and Learning. Washington, DC: Office of Educational Research and Improvement.

Center for Applied Linguistics (1973) *The Linguistic Reporter* 15 (3), 2.

Cervantes, R.A. (1979) An exemplary *consafic chingatropic* assessment: The AIR report. *Bilingual Education Paper Series* 2 (8). Los Angeles, CA: National Dissemination and Assessment Center, CSU Los Angeles.

Cervantes-Soon, C.G., Dorner, L., Palmer, D., Heiman, D., Schwerdtfeger, R. and Choi, J. (2017) Combating inequalities in two-way language immersion programs: Toward critical consciousness in bilingual education spaces. *Review of Research in Education* 41 (1), 403–427.

Chandler, M.A. (2014) Language immersion programs growing in D.C., but only west of the river. *Washington Post* blogs. See https://www.washingtonpost.com/blogs/local/wp/2014/12/01/language-immersion-programs-growing-in-d-c-but-only-west-of-the-river/.

Coady, M.R. (2020) *The Coral Way Bilingual Program*. Bristol: Multilingual Matters.

Coballes-Vega, C., Espinosa-Paris, C. and Marra, A.F. (1979) Title VII (Bilingual Education) fellowship program: A preliminary report. *Bilingual Education Paper Series* 2 (9). Los Angeles, CA: National Dissemination and Assessment Center, California State University.
Coleman, J.S., Campbell, E.Q., Hobson, C.J., McPartland, J., Mood, A.M., Weinfeld, F.D. and York, R.L. (1966) *Equality of Educational Opportunity*. Washington, DC: U.S. Department of Health, Education and Welfare, Office of Education. See https://babel.hathitrust.org/cgi/pt?id=umn.31951000810429b&view=1up&seq=3 (accessed 11 July 2019).
Collier Jr, J. (1988) Survival at Rough Rock: A historical overview of Rough Rock Demonstration School. *Anthropology and Education Quarterly* 19, 253–269.
Collier, V. and Thomas, W.P. (2004) The astounding effectiveness of dual language education for all. *NABE Journal of Research and Practice* 2 (1), 1–20.
Collier, V.P. (1992) A synthesis of studies examining long-term language minority student data on academic achievement. *Bilingual Research Journal* 16 (1&2), 187–212.
Combs, M.C. (2008) Urquides, María (1908–1994). In J. Gonzalez (ed.) *Encyclopedia of Bilingual Education, Volume II* (pp. 869–870). Los Angeles: Sage.
Committee on Education and Labor (1974) Bills to Amend Title VII of the Elementary and Secondary Education Act of 1965 to Extend, Improve, and Expand Programs of Bilingual Education, Teacher Training, and Child Development., House of Representatives, 93rd Cong. 81 (Testimony of Rosa Guas de Inclán).
Conde, C. (ed.) (1970) *The Spanish-Speaking People of the United States*. Washington, DC: Cabinet Committee on Opportunities for Spanish Speaking People.
Conde, Y.M. (1999) *Operation Pedro Pan: The Untold Exodus of 14,048 Cuban Children*. New York: Routledge.
Connell, C. (1980) New department opens up shop today. Education chief background rich. *Tuscaloosa News*, 4 May. AP.
Cotto, R. and Feder, K. (2014) *Choice Watch: Diversity and Access in Connecticut's School Choice Programs*. New Haven, CT: Connecticut Voices for Children.
Cox, P. (2001) *Ralph W. Yarborough: The People's Senator*. Austin, TX: Center for American History at the University of Texas at Austin.
Crawford, J. (2004) *Educating English Learners: Language Diversity in the Classroom*. Los Angeles, CA: Bilingual Education Services.
Cubberly, E.P. (1909) *Changing Conceptions of Education*. Boston, MA: Houghton Mifflin Company. See https://archive.org/details/changingconcepti00cubbuoft/page/n1 (accessed 11 July 2019).
Cummins, J. (1992) Bilingual education and English immersion: The Ramírez Report in theoretical perspective. *Bilingual Research Journal* 16 (1–2), 91–104.
Damari, R.R., Bertelli, V., Pulupa, C. and Silver, L. (2019) Demographics and equity of dual language immersion programs in Washington, DC. DC Language Immersion Project and National Foreign Language Center, University of Maryland. See http://dcimmersion.org/wp-content/uploads/2019/11/FULL-Demographics-and-Equity-Report-November-2019.pdf (accessed 7 November 2019).
Danoff, M.N., Coles, G.J., McLaughlin, D.H. and Reynolds, D.J. (1977/1978) *Evaluation of the Impact of ESEA Title VII Spanish/English Bilingual Education Programs: Overview of Study and Findings*. Palo Alto, CA: American Institute for Research.
Davies, G. (2007) *See Government Grow: Education Politics from Johnson to Reagan*. Lawrence, KS: University Press of Kansas.
Davin, K.J. and Heineke, A.J. (2017) The Seal of Biliteracy: Variations in policy and outcomes. *Foreign Language Annals* 50, 486–499.
De Costa, P.I. (2019) Commentary: Elite multilingualism, affect and neoliberal-ism. *Journal of Multilingual and Multicultural Development* 40, 453–460. https://doi.org/10.1080/01434632.2018.1543698

de Jong, E., Gort, M. and Cobb, C.D. (2005) Bilingual education within the context of English-only policies: Three districts' responses to Question 2 in Massachusetts. *Educational Policy* 19 (4), 595–620.

de la Luz Reyes, M. (ed.) (2011) *Words Were All We Had: Becoming Biliterate Against the Odds*. New York: Teachers College Press.

DeBoer, P.A. (1968) History of the early compulsory school attendance legislation in the State of Illinois. PhD dissertation, University of Chicago.

DeLeon, T.M. (2014) The new ecology of biliteracy in California: An exploratory study of the early implementation of the State Seal of Biliteracy. Loyola Marymount University. See http://pqdtopen.proquest.com/doc/1620743509.html?FMT=ABS (accessed 1 April 2017).

Demmert, W.G. (2008) Native American Languages, Legal Support For. In J.M. González (ed.) *Encyclopedia of Bilingual Education, Vol. 2* (pp. 589–593). Thousand Oaks, CA: Sage.

Department of Health, Education and Welfare (1969) *Malabar Reading Program for Mexican-American Children, Los Angeles, California*. Washington, DC: Government Printing Office.

Department of Justice (2018) Attorney General Announces Zero-Tolerance Policy for Criminal Illegal Entry. Department of Justice, Washington, DC. See https://www.justice.gov/opa/pr/attorney-general-announces-zero-tolerance-policy-criminal-illegal-entry (accessed 11 February 2020).

Devarajan, K. (2018, 12 September) Ready for a linguistic controversy? Say 'Mmhmm'. National Public Radio. See https://wamu.org/story/18/09/12/ready-for-a-linguistic-controversy-say-mhmm/ (accessed 10 June 2020).

Development Associates (1973) *A Process Evaluation of the Bilingual Education Program, Title VII, Elementary and Secondary Education Act, Volume 1*. Washington, DC: US Department of Health, Education and Welfare.

Development Associates (1978a) *A Study of the State of Bilingual Materials Development and the Transition of Materials to the Classroom*. Submitted to Office of Planning, Budgeting and Evaluation, US Office of Education, Department of Health, Education and Welfare; submitted by Development Associates. Washington, DC: Office of Planning, Budgeting and Evaluation.

Development Associates (1978b) *A Study of the State of Bilingual Materials Development and the Transition of Materials to the Classroom*. Arlington, VA: Development Associates. Contract No. DHEW 300-76-0358.

Dickerson, C. (2020, Oct. 21). *Parents of 545 Children Separated at the Border Cannot Be Found*. The New York Times. Retrieved December 16, 2020 from https://www.nytimes.com/2020/10/21/us/migrant-children-separated.html

Dickinson, E.E. (2016, winter) Coleman Report set the standard for the study of public education. *Johns Hopkins University Magazine*. See https://hub.jhu.edu/magazine/2016/winter/coleman-report-public-education/ (accessed 11 July 2019).

Dual Language Education of New Mexico (2020) What we do. See https://www.dlenm.org/what-we-do/ (accessed 9 September 2020).

Dual Language Immersion Program Locations (2020) See https://www.doe.k12.de.us/Page/3080 (accessed 23 November 2020).

Dyson, O.L., Jeffries, J.L. and Brooks, K.L. (eds) (2020) *African American Culture: An Encyclopedia of People, Traditions, and Customs*. Santa Barbara, CA: ABC-CLIO, LLC.

ED Facts (1990) *Information about the Office of Bilingual Education and Minority Language Affairs*. Washington, DC: US Department of Education.

Education of the Spanish Speaking (1972, June 8 and 14) *Hearings Before the Civil Rights Oversight Subcommittee (No. 4). 92nd Congress, 2nd Session*. Washington, DC: US Government Printing Office.

Ellis, F. (1954) German instruction in the public schools of Indianapolis, 1869–1919. *Indiana Magazine of History* 50, 119–138, 251–267, 357–380.
Epstein, A. (2018) *Miracle Child: The Journey of a Young Holocaust Survivor*. Boston, MA: Academic Studies Press.
Epstein, N. (1977) *Language, Ethnicity, and the Schools: Policy Alternatives for Bilingual-Bicultural Education*. Washington, DC: The Institute for Educational Leadership.
Escamilla, K. (2018) Growing up with the Bilingual Education Act: One educator's journey, *Bilingual Research Journal* 41 (4), 369–387.
Escamilla, K. and Hopewell, S. (2008) Amendment 31 (Colorado). In J.M. González (ed.) *Encyclopedia of Bilingual Education, Volume I* (pp. 24–28). Thousand Oaks, CA: Sage.
Evans, C. (2008) Andersson, Theodore (1903–1994). In J. González (ed.) *Encyclopedia of Bilingual Education, Volume I* (pp. 28–29). Thousand Oaks, CA: Sage.
Ewing, J.A. (1918) Education in California during the pre-statehood period. *Annual Publication of the Historical Society of Southern California* 11, 51–59.
Facing History and Ourselves (n.d.) America and the Holocaust. See https://www.facinghistory.org/defying-nazis/america-and-holocaust (accessed 11 July 2019).
Fee, M., Rhodes, N.C. and Wiley, T.G. (2014) Demographic realities, challenges, and opportunities. In T.G. Wiley, J.K. Peyton, D. Christian, S.C.K. Moore and N. Liu (eds) *Handbook of Heritage, Community, and Native American Language Education in the United States: Research, Policy and Practice* (pp. 6–18). London: Routledge.
Feffer, J. (2019) The 'Great Replacement' is a genocidal playbook. *The Nation*. See https://www.thenation.com/article/archive/white-supremacist-great-replacement/ (accessed 5 February 2020).
Feinberg, L. (1981) Reagan denounces Carter's proposed rules on bilingual education. *The Washington Post*, 4 March.
Finley, T. (2017) Emmett Till's cousin urged Jeff Sessions to make civil rights cases 'a priority'. *The Huffington Post*, 28 March. See https://www.huffpost.com/entry/emmett-tills-jeff-sessions-civil-rights_n_58dab9a2e4b0cb23e65bf99e (accessed 17 November 2020).
First Nations Development Institute (n.d.) Strengthening Native American communities and economies. See https://www.firstnations.org/ (accessed 9 September 2020).
Fishman, J. (1966) *Language Loyalty in the United States: The Maintenance and Perpetuation of Non-English Mother Tongues by American Ethnic and Religious Groups*. The Hague: Mouton.
Flores, B.M. (2008) National Association for Bilingual Education In J.M. González (ed.) *Encyclopedia of Bilingual Education, Volume II* (pp. 571–574). Los Angeles, CA: Sage.
Flores, N. (2015) Has bilingual education been Columbused? (blog post). See https://educationallinguist.wordpress.com/2015/01/25/columbising-bilingual-education/ (accessed 19 June 2020).
Flores, N. (2016) A tale of two visions: Hegemonic Whiteness and bilingual education. *Educational Policy* 30 (1), 13–38.
Forbes, S. and Lemos, P. (1981) The history of American language policy. In *Immigration Policy and the National Interest: Staff Report to the Select Commission on Immigration and Refugee Policy*. Washington, DC: Government Printing Office.
Foreign Language Annals (2016) ACTFL celebrates it first fifty years. *Foreign Language Anals* 49 (4), 642–646.
Freire, J.A. (2016) Nepantleras/os and their teachers in dual language education: Developing sociopolitical consciousness to contest language education policies. *Association of Mexican American Educators (AMAE) Journal* 10 (2), 36–52.
Freire, J.A. (2020) Conscientization calls: A White dual language educator's development of sociopolitical consciousness and commitment to social justice. *Education and Urban Society* 53 (2), 231–248. https://doi.org/10.1177/0013124520928608.

Freire, J.A., Valdez, V.E. and Delavan, G.M. (2017) The (dis)inclusion of Latina/o interests from Utah's dual language education book. *Journal of Latinos and Education* 16 (4), 276–289.

Gaarder, A.B. (1967) Bilingual Education Hearings Before the Special Subcommittee on Bilingual Education of the Committee on Labor and Public Welfare, U.S. Senate, 90th Congress, 1st Session on S. 428, Part 1, May 18, 19, 26, 29 and 31.

Gaarder, B.A. (1977) Political perspectives on bilingual education. Unpublished manuscript.

Gándara, P. (2015) Charting the relationship of English learners and the ESEA: One step forward, two steps back. *Journal of the Social Sciences* 1 (3), 112–128. https://www.muse.jhu.edu/article/605403.

Gándara, P. and Ee, I. (2018) U.S. Immigration Enforcement Policy and Its Impact on Teaching and Learning in the Nation's Schools. Civil Rights Project/*Proyecto Derechos Civiles*, Los Angeles. See https://www.civilrightsproject.ucla.edu/research/k-12-education/immigration-immigrant-students/u.s.-immigration-enforcement-policy-and-its-impact-on-teaching-and-learning-in-the-nations-schools/Immigration-enforcement-on-schools-093018.pdf (accessed February 13, 2020).

Gándara, P. and Hopkins, M. (2010) *Forbidden Language: English Learners and Restrictive Language Policies*. New York: Teachers College Press.

García, O. and Sung, K.K. (2018) Critically assessing the 1968 Bilingual Education Act at 50 years: Taming tongues and Latinx communities. *Bilingual Research Journal* 41 (4), 318–333.

Genesee, F., Lindholm-Leary, K., Saunders, W. and Christian, D. (2005) English language learners in U.S. schools: An overview of research findings. *Journal of Education for Students Placed at Risk* 10 (4), 363–385.

Gersten, R. and Woodward, J. (1985) Structured immersion for language minority students: Results from a longitudinal evaluation. *Educational Evaluation and Policy Analysis* 7 (1), 75–79.

Gold, N. (2019, December) Telephone call to discuss Cervantes' (1979, *Consafic Chingatropic* [Crevantes, 1979] publication).

González, G. (2008) Troike, Rudolph C., Jr. (1935–). In J. González (ed.) *Encyclopedia of Bilingual Education, Volume II* (pp. 860–861). Thousand Oaks, CA: Sage.

González, J.M. (1978) Bilingual education: Ideologies of the past decade, In H. LaFontaine, B. Persky and L.H. Golubchick (eds) *Bilingual Education* (pp. 24–32). Wayne, NJ: Avery Publishing Group.

González, J.M. (2008) Title VII, Elementary and Secondary Education Act, Key Historical Marker. In J.M. González (ed.) *Encyclopedia of Bilingual Education*, Volume II (pp. 833–837). Thousand Oaks, CA: Sage.

González, J.M. (2011) Words were all we had: Reflections on becoming biliterate. In M. de la Luz Reyes (ed.) *Words Were All We Had: Becoming Biliterate Against the Odds* (pp. 26–35). New York: Teachers College Press.

Gorena, M. (2008) National Clearinghouse for Bilingual Education. In J. González (ed.) *Encyclopedia of Bilingual Education, Volume II* (pp. 574–576). Los Angeles, CA: Sage.

Grant, M. (1917) *The Passing of the Great Race*. New York: Charles Scribner's Sons.

Gray, T. (1977) *Response to the AIR Study 'Evaluation of the Impact of ESEA Title VII Spanish/English Bilingual Education Program'*. Arlington, VA: Center for Applied Linguistics.

Green, P.E. (2008). *Méndez v. Westminster*. In J. M. González, *Encyclopedia of bilingual education*, Vol. 2, 549–551.

Grijalva, R. (2020) Rep. Grijalva introduces SYLLABLE Act to promote access to dual language immersion programs. See https://grijalva.house.gov/press-releases/rep-grijalva-introduces-syllable-act-to-promote-access-to-dual-language-immersion-programs/ (accessed 3 September 2020).

Gutiérrez, J.A. (2011) The Chicano movement: Paths to power. *The Social Studies* 102, 25–32.
Hakuta, K. (1986) *Mirror of Language: The Debate on Bilingualism*. New York: Basic Books, Inc.
Halperin, S. (1978) Foreword. In N. Epstein (ed.) *Language, Ethnicity, and the Schools: Policy Alternatives for Bilingual-Bicultural Education* (pp. v–vi). Washington, DC: Institute for Educational Leadership, The George Washington University.
Harris, E.A. (2015) Dual-language programs are on the rise, even for native English speakers. *The New York Times*, 8 October. See https://www.nytimes.com/2015/10/09/nyregion/dual-language-programs-are-on-the-rise-even-for-native-english-speakers.html (accessed 3 September 2020).
Havighurst, R.J. (1978) Indian education since 1960. *The Annals of the American Academy of Political and Social Science* 436, 13–26.
Hebert, J.G. (2016) Why I told the senate that Jeff Sessions thought civil rights groups were 'un-American'; My job was threatened if I said what I knew about Sessions, but I did it anyway. Now he's poised to lead the Justice Department. *Washington Post Blogs*, 22 November. See https://www.washingtonpost.com/posteverything/wp/2016/11/22/my-testimony-about-jeff-sessionss-racist-remarks-kept-him-from-becoming-a-judge/ (accessed 29 January 2020).
Heiman, D. and Yanes, M. (2018) Centering the fourth pillar in times of TWBE gentrification: 'Spanish, love, content, not in that order'. *International Multilingual Research Journal* 12 (3), 173–187. https://doi.org/10.1080/19313152.2018.1474064
Heiman, D. and Murakami, E. (2019) 'It Was Like a Magnet to Bring People In': School administrators' responses to the gentrification of a two-way bilingual education (TWBE) program in Central Texas. *Journal of School Leadership* 29 (6), 454–472. https://doi.org/10.1177/1052684619864702
Henderson, K.I. (2017) Teacher language ideologies mediating classroom-level language policy in the implementation of dual language bilingual education. *Linguistics and Education* 42, 21–33.
Henderson, K.I. and Palmer, D.K. (2020) *Dual Language Bilingual Education: Teacher Cases and Perspectives on Large-Scale Implementation*. Bristol: Multilingual Matters.
Hesla, K., White, J. and Gerstenfeld, A. (2019) A rowing movement: America's largest charter public school communities. National Alliance for Public Charter Schools, New Orleans, LA. See https://files.eric.ed.gov/fulltext/ED595146.pdf (accessed 29 January 2020).
Hinton, L. (2001) Federal language policy and indigenous languages in the United States. In L. Hinton and K. Hale (eds) *The Green Book of Language Revitalization in Practice* (pp. 39–44). San Diego, CA: Academic Press.
Hinton, L. (2001) Teaching methods. In L. Hinton and K. Hale (eds) *The Green Book of Language Revitalization in Practice*. San Diego: Academic Press.
Holan, A.D. (2019) In context: Donald Trump's 'very fine people on both sides' remarks (transcript). *Politifact*. See https://www.politifact.com/article/2019/apr/26/context-trumps-very-fine-people-both-sides-remarks/ (accessed 10 February 2020).
Hornberger, N.H. (2002) Multilingual language policies and the continua of biliteracy: An ecological approach. *Language Policy* 1 (1), 27–51.
Howard, E.R., Lindholm-Leary, K.J., Rogers, D., Olague, N., Medina, J., Kennedy, B., Sugarman, J. and Christian, D. (2018) *Guiding Principles for Dual Language Education* (3rd edn). Washington, DC: Center for Applied Linguistics.
Ingram, N. (2018) In these bilingual classrooms, diversity is no longer lost in translation. *The Christian Science Monitor*.
Inter-agency Committee on Mexican American Affairs (1968) *The Mexican American: A New Focus on Opportunity*. Washington, DC: Government Printing Offices. See https

://babel.hathitrust.org/cgi/pt?id=txu.059173026971484&view=1up&seq=1 (accessed 22 November 2019).

InterAmerica Research Associates (1979) *Strengthening Bilingual Education*. Washington, DC: National Clearinghouse for Bilingual Education. Pursuant to contract NIE 400-77-0101.

J.A. Reyes Associates, Inc. (1978) *Bilingual Education: Quality Education for All Children. Annual Report of the National Advisory Council on Bilingual Education, November 1, 1975*. New York: Arno Press.

Jackson, R.C. and Whitehorse DeLaune, D. (2018) Decolonizing community writing with community listening: Story, transrhetorical resistance, and Indigenous cultural literacy activism. *Community Literacy Journal* 13 (1), 37–54.

Jaramillo, N. and McLaren, P. (2011) Rethinking critical pedagogy: Socialismo nepantla, and the Specter of Che. *Critical Science & Education* 11, 51–82.

Jaumont, F. (2017) *The Bilingual Revolution: The Future of Education is In Two Languages*. Brooklyn, NY: TBR Books.

Johnson, D.C. and Johnson, E.J. (2015) Power and agency in language policy appropriation. *Language Policy* 14, 221–243.

Jorge, A., Suchlicki, J. and de Varona, A.L. (eds) (1991) *Cuban Exiles in Florida: Their Presence and Conditions*. Miami, FL: Transaction Publishers.

Keilar, B., Jones, A., Simon, D., Schneider, J., Nobles, R., Walsh, J., Brown, R. and Elam, S. (2017) President Trump defends executive order on immigration ban; protests across U.S. airports on immigration ban; President Trump reorganizes national security council; soldier killed in Yemen; Hollywood's reaction to President Trump's travel ban. Aired 5–6pm ET. CNN. See https://www.cnn.com/2017/01/29/politics/donald-trump-executive-order-statement/index.html (accessed 4 February 2020).

Kelley, D.Q. (2015) Commonplace African-derived English words. In M.J. Shujaa and K.J. Shujaa (eds) *The Sage Encyclopedia of African Cultural Heritage in North America*. Los Angeles, CA: Sage.

Kipp, D.R. (2000) *Encouragement, Guidance, Insights, and Lessons for Native Language Activists Developing Their Own Tribal Language Programs*. Browning, MT: Piegan Institute's Cut-Bank Language Immersion School.

Kirsch, N. (2018) Blackwater's dark prince return. *Forbes*, 4 April. See https://www.forbes.com/return-of-erik-prince/#2247109250aa (accessed 29 January 2020).

Kloss, H. (1977/1998) *The American Bilingual Tradition*. Washington, DC: Center for Applied Linguistics.

Lado, R. (1993) A very sane man of la mancha. In C.A. Evans (eds) *Scholar with a Mission: The Career of Theodore Andersson and His Contributions to Language Education* (pp. 13–14). Washington, DC: National Clearinghouse for Bilingual Education.

Lake, R., Jochim, A. and Dearmond, M. (2015) Fixing Detroit's broken school system: Improve accountability and oversight for district and charter schools. *Education Next* 15 (1), 20. See http://www.pearltrees.com/u/104645359-accountability-oversight (accessed 29 January 2020).

Lambert, W.E. and Tucker, G.R. (1972) *Bilingual Education of the Children: The St. Lambert Experiment*. Rowley, MA: Newbury House.

Leap, W. (1983) *American Indian Language Development Institute*. Mimeo. Tempe, AZ: National Indian Bilingual Center, Arizona State University.

Leibowitz, A. (1971) *Educational Policy and Political Acceptance: The Imposition of English as the Language of Instruction in American Schools*. Washington, DC: ERIC Clearinghouse for Linguistics, Center for Applied Linguistics.

Lescott-Leszczynski, J. (2019) *The History of U.S. Ethnic Policy and Its Impact on European Ethnics*. Abingdon: Taylor & Francis.

Lillie, K.E., Markos, A., Estrella, A., Nguyen, T., Trifiro, A., Arias, M.B., Wiley, T.G., Peer, K. and Pérez, K. (2010) *Policy in Practice: The Implementation of Structured*

English Immersion in Arizona. Los Angeles, CA: University of California Los Angeles Civil Rights Project/Proyecto Derechos Civiles.
Littlebear, R. (2001) Introduction. In J. Pease-Pretty on Top (ed.) *Native American Language Immersion: Innovative Native Education for Children & Families* (pp. 5–14). Denver, CO: American Indian College Fund. See http://www.aihec.org/our-stories/docs/NativeLangugageImmersion.pdf (accessed 3 September 2020).
Logan, J.L. (1967) Coral Way: A bilingual school. *TESOL Quarterly* 1 (2), 50–54.
Lucas, P. (2000) Eola mau kākou I ka ʻōmakuahine: Hawaiian language policy and the courts. *Hawaiian Journal of History* 34, 1–27.
Macías, R.F. (1985) Language and ideology in the United States. *Social Education* 49 (2), 97–100.
Macías, R.F. (2014) Spanish as the second national language of the United States: Fact, future, fiction, or hope? *Review of Research in Education* 38, 33–57.
Macías, R.F. (2015) Bilingual Education, Politics of. In S. Oboler and D.J. González (eds) *The Oxford Encyclopedia of Latinos and Latinas in Contemporary Politics, Law, and Social Movements* (pp. 61–67). New York: Oxford University Press.
Macías, R.F. (2016) Language ideologies and rhetorical structures in bilingual education policy and research: Richard Ruiz's 1984 discursive turn. *Bilingual Research Journal* 39 (3–4), 173–199.
Mackey, W.F. and Beebee, V.N. (1977) *Bilingual Schools for a Bicultural Community: Miami's Adaptation to the Cuban Refugees*. Rowley, MA: Newbury House.
Margolis, R.J. (1968) *The Losers: A Report on Puerto Ricans and the Public Schools*. New York: ASPIRA.
Markos, A. (2013) Personal communication conducted during discussion regarding consulting contract with the Center for Applied Linguistics, Washington, DC.
Martínez, P.E. (2008) Lyons, James J. (1947–). In J.M. González (ed.) *Encyclopedia of Bilingual Education* (pp. 536–537). Los Angeles, CA: Sage.
Martínez, D. G. (2020, Winter). Arizona. *Journal of Education Finance* 45 (3), 261–263.
Martínez, R.A., Hikida, M. and Durán, L. (2015) Unpacking ideologies of linguistic purism: How dual language teachers make sense of everyday translanguaging. *International Multilingual Research Journal* 9 (1), 26–42.
Mavrogordato, M. (2012) Educational equity policies and the centralization of American public education: The case of bilingual education. *Peabody Journal of Education* 87 (4), 455–467.
McCarty, T.L. (1992) Federal language policy and American Indian education. Paper presented at the Annual Meeting of the American Educational Research Association, San Francisco, CA, 20–24 April.
McCarty, T.L. (2002) *A Place to be Navajo: Rough Rock and the Struggle for Self-Determination in Indigenous Schooling*. Mahwah, NJ: Lawrence Erlbaum.
McCarty, T.L. (2013) *Language Planning and Policy in Native America: History, Theory, Praxis*. Bristol: Multilingual Matters.
McCarty, T.L., Nicholas, S.E. and Wigglesworth, G. (2019) A world of Indigenous languages: Resurgence, reclamation, revitalization and resilience. In T.L. McCarty, S.E. Nicholas and G. Wigglesworth (eds) *A World of Indigenous Languages: Politics, Pedagogies and Prospects for Language Reclamation* (pp. 1–26). Bristol: Multilingual Matters.
McField, G.P. (2006) The many faces of structured English immersion. *International Journal of Foreign Language Teaching* 2 (2), 2–22.
McField, G.P. (2008) Proposition 227 (California). In J.M. González (ed.) *Encyclopedia of Bilingual Education, Volume II* (pp. 691–696). Los Angeles, CA: Sage.
McField, G.P. (ed.) (2014) *The Miseducation of English Learners: A Tale of Three States and Lessons to Be Learned*. Charlotte, NC: Information Age Publishing.
McIvor, O. and McCarty, T.L. (2017) Indigenous bilingual and revitalization immersion education in Canada and the USA. In O.L. García and S. May (eds) *Bilingual*

and Multilingual Education. Encyclopedia of Language and Education (3rd edn, pp. 1–17). Cham: Springer.

Milk, R.D. (2008) Peña, Álbar Antonio (1931–1993). In J. González (ed.) *Encyclopedia of Bilingual Education, Volume II* (pp. 652–653). Los Angeles, CA: Sage.

Miron, G. and Gulosino, C. (2013) *Profiles of For-Profit and Nonprofit Education Management Organizations: Fourteenth Edition—2011–2012*. Boulder, CO: National Education Policy Center. See http://nepc.colorado.edu/publication/EMO-profiles-11-12 (accessed 29 January 2020).

Modern Language Association (2020) Kenneth W. Mildenberger Prize. See https://www.mla.org/Resources/Career/MLA-Grants-and-Awards/Award-Submissions-and-Nominations/Competitions-for-MLA-Publication-Awards/Biennial-Prizes-with-Competitions-in-2021/Kenneth-W.-Mildenberger-Prize (accessed 4 June 2020).

Molina, J.C. (1978) National policy on bilingual education: An historical view of the federal role. In H. LaFontaine, B. Persky and L. Golubchick (eds) *Bilingual Education* (pp. 16–23). Wayne, NJ: Avery Publishing Group Inc.

Molina, J.C. and Chavez, R.M. (1978) Bilingual education: A federal happening. *NABE* 2 (1), 21–24.

Montoya, J. (1974) U.S. Congress, Senate, Senator Montoya's address to bilingual education conference: Remarks by Senator Mondale, 93rd Cong., 2nd Sess., 22 March, *Congressional Record*, 120: S1231.

Moore, S.C.K. (ed.) (2014) *Language Policy Processes and Consequences: Arizona Case Studies*. Bristol: Multilingual Matters.

Moore, S.C.K. (2008) *Lau v. Nichols*, enforcement documents. In J.M. González (ed.) *Encyclopedia of Bilingual Education, Volume I* (pp. 510–515). Thousand Oaks, CA: Sage.

Moore, S.C.K., Fee, M., Ee, J., Wiley, T.G. and Arias, B. (2014) Exploring bilingualism, literacy, employability and income levels among Latinos in the United States. In R.M. Callahan and P.C. Gándara (eds) *The Bilingual Advantage: Language, Literacy and the US Labor Market* (pp. 45–76). Bristol: Multilingual Matters.

NABE (2020) NABE's mission. See http://nabe.org/about-nabe/nabes-mission/ (accessed 9 September 2020).

Natanson, H., Cox, J.W. and Stein. P. (2020) Trump's rhetoric has changed the way hundreds of kids are bullied in classrooms; The president's rhetoric has changed the way hundreds of children are harassed in American classrooms, *The Post* found. *Washington Post Blogs*, 13 February. See https://www.msnbc.com/craig-melvin/watch/washington-post-the-president-s-rhetoric-has-changed-the-way-hundreds-of-children-are-harassed-in-american-classrooms-78767685992 (accessed 2 March 2020).

National Advisory Council on Bilingual Education (1977) *Annual Report*. Washington, DC: National Advisory Council on Bilingual Education.

National Advisory and Coordinating Council on Bilingual Education (1985) *New Directions in the Late '80s: The Ninth Annual Report National Advisory and Coordinating Council on Bilingual Education*. Washington, DC: US Department of Education.

National Alliance for Public Charter Schools (2016) A Growing Movement: America's Largest Charter Public School Communities and Their Impact on Student Outcomes: 11th Annual Edition. See http://www.publiccharters.org/sites/default/files/migrated/wp-content/uploads/2016/11/enrollment-share-web1128.pdf (accessed 3 June 2020).

National Clearinghouse for Bilingual Education (1979) *Strengthening Bilingual Education: A Report from the Commissioner of Education to Congress and the President*. Rosslyn, VI: US Office of Education, Department of Health, Education and Welfare.

National Education Association (1966) *The Invisible Minority: Report of the NEA-Tucson Survey on the Teaching of Spanish to the Spanish-Speaking*. Washington, DC: Department of Rural Education, National Education Association.

National Park Service (n.d.) *American Latino Theme Study: The Making of America National Park Service.* Washington, DC: Washington, DC: U.S. Department of the Interior. See https://www.nps.gov/heritageinitiatives/latino/latinothemestudy/educat ion.htm#_edn10 (accessed 2 September 2020).

Native Language Immersion Initiative (2019) *These are Our Stories.* Longmont, CO: First Nations Development Institute. See https://www.firstnations.org/wp-content/uploads /2019/10/NLII-report-Oct-2019-for-web.pdf (accessed 9 September 2020).

Nazaryan, A. (2017) Betsy DeVos is coming for your public schools. *Newsweek*, 27 January. See https://www.newsweek.com/betsy-devos-trump-education-department -538533 (accessed 17 November 2020).

Nieto, S. (ed.) (2000) Puerto Rican students in U.S. schools: A brief history. In S. Nieto (ed.) *Puerto Rican Students in U.S. Schools* (pp. 5–38). Mahwah, NJ: Lawrence Erlbaum.

Nieto, S. (2011) On learning to tie a bow, and other tales of being biliterate. In M. de la Luz Reyes (ed.) *Words Were All We Had: Becoming Biliterate Against the Odds* (pp. 15–25). New York: Teachers College Press.

Office of Management and Budget (2020) A budget for America's future: Fiscal year 2021. Office of Management and Budget, Washington, DC. See https://www.whitehouse.go v/wp-content/uploads/2020/02/budget_fy21.pdf (accessed 11 February 2020).

Ou, V. (2015) *English Learner Leadership & Legacy Initiative.* Long Beach, CA: Californians Together. See https://www.californianstogether.org/english-learner-leadership -fellowships/ (accessed 2 March 2020).

Palmer, D. (2010) Race, power, and equity in a multiethnic urban elementary school with a dual-language 'strand' program. *Anthropology & Education Quarterly* 41 (1), 94–114.

Panetta, L. and Gall, P. (1971) *Bring Us Together.* Philadelphia, PA: J.B. Lippincott Company.

Parrish, T., Linquanti, R., Merickel, A., Quick, H., Laird, J. and Esra, P. (2002) *Effects of the Implementation of Proposition 227 on the Education of English Learner, K-12: Year 2 Report.* San Francisco, CA: WestEd.

PBS/Frontline (2020) America's Great Divide: Steve Bannon. See https://www.pbs .org/wgbh/frontline/film/americas-great-divide-from-obama-to-trump/transcript/ (accessed 12 February 2020).

Pease-Pretty On Top, J. (2001) *Native American Language Immersion: Innovative Native Education for Children & Families.* Denver, CO: American Indian College Fund. See http://www.aihec.org/our-stories/docs/NativeLangugageImmersion.pdf (accessed 9 September 2020).

Pedraza-Bailey, S. and Sullivan, T.A. (1979) Bilingual education in the reception of political immigrants: The case of Cubans in Miami, Florida. In R.V. Padilla (ed.) *Bilingual Education and Public Policy in the United States* (pp. 376–394). Ypsilanti, MI: Eastern Michigan University.

Peña-Hughes, E. and Solis, J. (1980) ABCs (unpublished report). McAllen, TX: McAllen Independent School District.

Peterson-Withorn, C. (2019) Inside Betsy DeVos' billions: Just how rich is the Education Secretary. *Forbes*, 24 July. See https://www.forbes.com/sites/chasewithorn/2019/07/24 /inside-betsy-devos-billions-just-how-rich-is-the-education-secretary/#4bd06f473b0e (accessed 29 January 2020).

Phillipson, R. and Skutnabb-Kangas, T. (1996) English only worldwide or language ecology? *TESOL Quarterly* 30 (3), 429–452.

Predaris, T. (1983) The National Clearinghouse for Bilingual Education. *Educational Perspectives* (pp. 29–32). Rosslyn, VA: National Clearinghouse for Bilingual Education.

Public Law 85-864, Statute 72, 1580. The National Defense Education Act of 1958.

Ramírez, J., Pasta, D., Yuen, S., Ramey, D. and Billings, D. (1991) *Final Report: Longitudinal Study of Structured English Immersion Strategy, Early-Exit, and Late-Exit*

Bilingual Education Programs for Language-Minority Children, Vol. II. (Prepared for US Department of Education). San Mateo, CA: Aguirre International.

Ramírez, J.D. (1992) Longitudinal study of structured English immersion strategy, early-exit and late-exit transitional bilingual education program for language-minority children (Executive summary). *Bilingual Research Journal* 16, 1–62.

Rand, C. (1958) *The Puerto Ricans.* New York: Oxford University Press. See http://www.pps.net/cms/lib8/OR01913224/Centricity/Domain/85/DLI_Year_4_Summary_Nov2015v7.pd

Reifle, S.R. and Goldsmith, R.P. (1978) *Summary Report on the National Assessment Survey of Title VII ESEA Basic Project Directors' and Teachers' Needs for the Products and Services of the National Network of Centers for Bilingual Education.* Austin, TX: Dissemination and Assessment Center for Bilingual Education. See http://hdl.handle.net/2027/txu.059173025437513 (accessed 26 July 2019).

Reisner, E.R. (1983) *Building Capacity and Commitment in Bilingual Education: A Practical Guide for Educators.* Washington, DC: Evaluation, Dissemination, and Assessment Centers for Bilingual Education. See https://files.eric.ed.gov/fulltext/ED255602.pdf (accessed 23 February 2020).

Resnick, S. (2012) VIDEO: Peter Brimelow attacks multiculturalism at CPAC. *Colorado Independent*, 9 February. See https://www.coloradoindependent.com/2012/02/09/video-peter-brimelow-attacks-multiculturalism-at-cpac/ (accessed 13 January 2020).

Reyes, X.A. (2000) Return migrant students: Yankee go home? In S. Nieto (ed.) *Puerto Rican Students in U.S. Schools* (pp. 39–67). Mahwah, NJ: Erlbaum Associates.

Richwine, J. (2009) IQ and immigration policy. Dissertation submitted as part of Doctor of Philosophy. Harvard University, Cambridge, MA.

Richwine, J. (2017a) Contra Acosta, longtime immigrants struggle with English literacy. *National Review Online.* See https://cis.org/sites/cis.org/files/richwine-literacy.pdf (accessed 5 February 2020).

Richwine, J. (2017b) Immigrant literacy: Self-assessment vs. reality. Center for Immigration Policy, Washington, DC. See https://cis.org/sites/cis.org/files/richwine-literacy.pdf (accessed 5 February 2020).

Riley, P. (2019) Richard Spencer's racist 'octaroons' tirade is peak white supremacy idiocy. *Newsone*, 4 November. See https://newsone.com/3892326/richard-spencer-octaroon-tirade-white-supermacy/ (accessed 13 January 2020).

Rivers, B. (2020) The president's budget defunds Department of Education, Humanities, State Department. Joint National Committee for Languages and International Studies, Garrett Park, MD. See https://www.languagepolicy.org/post/the-president-s-budget-defunds-department-of-education-humanities-state-department (accessed 17 November 2020).

Roessel, R. A. (1977). *Navajo education in action.* Chinle, AZ: Navajo Curriculum Center, Rough Rock Demonstration School.

Rogers, D. (2020, June 17) Personal communication conducted via Zoom.

Rojas, P.M. (1946) Reading materials for bilingual children. *The Elementary School Journal* 47 (4), 204–211.

Rojas, P.M. (1948) The teaching of English as a modern foreign language. *College English* 9 (6), 322–326.

Rojas, P.M. and Robinett, R.F. (1963) Progress Report on Ford Foundation Projects. See https://ufdcimages.uflib.ufl.edu/AA/00/06/60/59/00001/AA00066059_00001.pdf (accessed 4 June 2020).

Roosevelt, T. (1915) Americanism. Address delivered before the Knights of Columbus, Carnegie Hall, New York, 12 October. See https://vdare.com/posts/guest-post-by-teddy-roosevelt-americanism-october-12-1915 (accessed 11 July 2019).

Rosenberg, E. (2018) 'The Snake': How Trump appropriated a radical black singer's lyrics for immigration fearmongering. *The Washington Post*, 24 February. See https://www

.washingtonpost.com/news/politics/wp/2018/02/24/the-snake-how-trump-appropriated-a-radical-black-singers-lyrics-for-refugee-fearmongering/ (accessed 13 January 2020).

Rotberg, I. (2014) Charter schools and the risk of increased segregation. *Phi Delta Kapan* 95 (5), 26–31.

Ruíz, R. (1984) Orientations in language planning. *NABE Journal* 8 (2), 15–34. doi: 10.1080/08855072.1984.10668464

Salazar, J.J. (1998) A longitudinal model for interpreting thirty years of bilingual education research. *Bilingual Research Journal* 22 (1), 19–30. doi: 10.1080/15235882.1998.10668671

Saldaña, L.P. (2013) Teachers' memories of schooling: The sociocultural injuries and the mis-education of Mexican teachers in the barrio. *Association of Mexican-American Educators (AMAE) Journal* 7 (1), 58–72.

San Antonio Hearings (1968, December 9–14/1969) *Hearings Held in San Antonio, Texas*. Washington, DC: Commission on Civil Rights/Government Accountability Office.

San Miguel Jr, G. (2004) *Contested Policy: The Rise and Fall of Federal Bilingual Education Policy in the United States 1960–2001*. Denton, TX: University of North Texas Press.

Sappiens, A. (1979) Spanish in California. *Journal of Communication* 29 (2), 72–83.

Saville, M.R. and Troike, R.C. (1971) *A Handbook of Bilingual Education, revised edition*. Washington, DC: Teachers of English to Speakers of Other Languages.

Schlossman, S.L. (1983) Is there an American tradition of bilingual education? German in the public elementary schools, 1840–1919. *American Journal of Education* 19 (2), 139–168.

Schneider, S.G. (1976) *Revolution, Reaction, or Reform: The 1974 Bilingual Education Act*. New York: L.A. Publishing Company, Inc.

Schudel, M. (2019) John Tanton, architect of anti-immigration and English-only efforts, dies at 85; The 'most influential unknown man in America' was condemned for leading white nationalist hate groups. *Washington Post Blogs*, 21 July. See https://www.washingtonpost.com/local/obituaries/john-tanton-architect-of-anti-immigration-and-english-only-efforts-dies-at-85/2019/07/21/2301f728-aa3f-11e9-86dd-d7f0e60391e9_story.html (accessed 5 February 2020).

Seal of Biliteracy (n.d.) Frequently asked questions. See https://sealofbiliteracy.org/faq/ (accessed 3 September 2020).

Secada, W.G. (1987) This is 1987, not 1980: A comment on a comment. *Review of Educational Research* 57 (3), 377–384.

Sharpes, D.K. (1979) Federal education for the American Indian. *Journal of American Indian Education* 19 (1), 19–22.

Shear, M.D., Benner, K. and Haberman, M. (2018) How anti-immigration passion was inflamed from the fringe. *The New York Times*, 19 June. See https://www.nytimes.com/2018/06/18/us/politics/immigration-children-sessions-miller.html (accessed 5 February 2020).

Shohamy, E. (2006) *Language Policy: Hidden Agendas and New Approaches*. London and New York: Routledge.

Siebens, J. and Julian, T. (2011) *Native North American Languages Spoken at Home in the United States and Puerto Rico: 2006–2010*. (American Community Survey Briefs.) Washington, DC: U.S. Census Bureau.

Silva, D. (2018) 'Like I am trash': Migrant children reveal stories of detention, separation. NBC News.com, 29 July. See https://www.nbcnews.com/news/latino/i-am-trash-migrant-children-reveal-stories-detention-separation-n895006 (accessed 13 February 2020).

Sinclair, J. (2018) 'Starving and suffocating': Evaluation policies and practices during the first 10 years of the U.S. Bilingual Education Act. *International Journal of Bilingual Education and Bilingualism* 21 (6), 710–728.

Singh, K. (2008) *Casteñeda v. Pickard*. In J.M. González (ed.) *Encyclopedia of Bilingual Education, Vol. 1* (pp. 114–116). Thousand Oaks, CA: Sage.

Skrentny, J.D. (2002) *The Minority Rights Revolution*. Cambridge, MA: The Belknap of Harvard University Press.

Smith, M.E. (1942) Effect of bilingual background on college aptitude scores and grade point ratios earned by students at the University of Hawaii. *Journal of Educational Psychology* 33, 356–364.

Smith, M.M. (2001) Remembering Mary, shaping revolt: Reconsidering the Stono Rebellion, *The Journal of Southern History* 67 (3), 513–534.

Southern Poverty Law Center (2019) Hate at school. Teaching tolerance, Montgomery, AL. See https://www.splcenter.org/sites/default/files/tt_2019_hate_at_school_report_final_0.pdf (accessed 17 November 2020).

Span, P. (1995) The many lives of Stanley Pottinger. *The Washington Post*, 13 May. See https://www.washingtonpost.com/archive/lifestyle/1995/05/13/the-many-lives-of-stanley-pottinger/57bd1250-9066-4406-9665-69b168a59248/ (accessed 21 February 2020).

Spolsky, B. (1970) Literacy in the Vernacular: The Navajo Reading Study. Paper presented at the Council of Anthropology and Educator Symposium on Cognitive and Linguistic Studies, 69th Annual Meeting of the American Anthropological Association, San Diego, California, 19 November.

Spolsky, B. (2004) *Language Policy*. Cambridge: Cambridge University Press.

States News Service (2018) Chancellor Fariña announces 33 new pre-K dual language programs. See https://www.schools.nyc.gov/about-us/news/announcements/contentdetails/2018/01/17/chancellor-fari%C3%B1a-announces-33-new-pre-k-dual-language-programs (accessed 18 February 2020).

Steele, J.L., Slater, R.O., Zamarro, G., Miller, T., Li, J., Burkhauser, S. and Bacon, M. (2017) The effects of dual language immersion programs on student achievement: Evidence from lottery data. *American Educational Research Journal* 54 (1), 282–306.

Steele, J.L., Watzinger-Tharp, J., Slater, R., Roberts, G. and Bowman, K. (2019) Student performance under dual language immersion scale-up in Utah. Utah State Board of Education. See https://www.schools.utah.gov/file/10d447ed-5b6e-4071-a7b0-28aa6719bb1c (accessed 28 February 2020).

Stein, P. (2018) Are dual-language programs in urban schools a sign of gentrification?; One D.C. elementary school is divided about the future of its campus. *Washington Post Blogs*. See https://www.washingtonpost.com/local/education/are-dual-language-programs-in-urban-schools-a-sign-of-gentrification/2018/07/03/926c4a42-68c2-11e8-9e38-24e693b38637_story.html (accessed 23 August 2020).

Stephens, D. (1983/1984) President Carter, the Congress, and NEA: Creating the Department of Education. *Political Science Quarterly* 98 (4), 641–663.

Stoller, P. (1976) The language planning activities of the U.S. Office of Bilingual Education. *International Journal of the Sociology of Language* 11, 45–60.

Stratford, M. (2020) 'Preach it, sister!' Why the Trump base loves Betsy DeVos. *Politico*, 6 February. See https://www.politico.com/news/2020/02/06/preach-it-sister-why-the-trump-base-loves-betsy-devos-111535 (accessed 17 November 2020).

Strauss, V. (2016) Obama's real education legacy: Common core, testing, charter schools. *The Washington Post*, 21 October. See https://www.washingtonpost.com/news/answer-sheet/wp/2016/10/21/obamas-real-education-legacy-common-core-testing-charter-schools/ (accessed 30 January 2020).

Strauss, V. (2020) In State of the Union, Trump makes clear his aversion to public schools. *Washington Post Blogs*, 5 February. See https://www.washingtonpost.com/education/2020/02/05/state-union-trump-makes-clear-his-aversion-public-schools/ (accessed 11 February 2020).

Sue, D.W., Capodilupo, C.M., Torino, G.C., Bucceri, J.M., Holder, A.M.B., Nadal, K.L. and Esquilin, M. (2007) Racial microaggressions in everyday life: Implications for clinical practice. *American Psychologist* 62 (4), 271–286.

Sue, D.W., Rivera, D.P., Capodilupo, C.M., Lin, A.I. and Torino, G.C. (2010) Racial dialogues and White trainee fears: Implications for education and training. *Cultural Diversity and Ethnic Minority Psychology* 16 (2), 206–214.

Sung, K. and Tsai, H.-M. (2019) *Mandarin Chinese Dual Language Immersion Programs*. Bristol: Multilingual Matters.

Targeted News Service. (February 14, 2019 Thursday). Governor Ducey Signs Legislation to Improve Outcomes for English Language Learner Students. Targeted News Service.

Terry, R.M. (2016) *A History of ACTFL: A Review of Current Progress in Teaching Foreign Languages*. Alexandria, VA: ACTFL.

Thomas, W.P. (1992) An analysis of the research methodology of the Ramírez study. *Bilingual Research Journal* 16 (1&2), 213–245.

Thomas, W.P. and Collier, V.P. (2002) *A National Study of School Effectiveness for Language Minority Students' Long-Term Academic Achievement*. Santa Cruz, CA: Center for Research on Education, Diversity & Excellence.

Thornton, J.K. (1991) African dimensions of the Stono Rebellion. *American Historical Review* 96 (4), 1101–1113.

Tireman, L.S. (1944) Bilingual children. *Review of Educational Research – Education of Exceptional Children and Minority Groups* 14 (3), 273–278.

Tireman, L.S. and Watson, M. (1943) *La Communidad*. Albuquerque, NM: University of New Mexico Press.

Todd, Z. (2019) Last man standing: The immigration insurgent who survived the Trump White House. Public Broadcasting System: Frontline, 22 October. See https://www.pbs.org/wgbh/frontline/article/last-man-standing-stephen-miller-white-house/ (accessed 10 February 2020).

Torres, A. (1985) Teachers and question of bilingual education. *Chicago Tribune*, 16 November. See https://www.chicagotribune.com/news/ct-xpm-1985-11-16-8503190460-story.html (accessed 23 January 2020).

Toth, C.R. (1990) *German-English Bilingual Schools in America: The Cincinnati Tradition in Historical Context*. New York: Peter Lang.

Trende, S. (2012) The case of the missing white voters. *Real Clear Politics*. See https://www.realclearpolitics.com/articles/2012/11/08/the_case_of_the_missing_white_voters_116106-2.html (accessed 10 February 2020).

Triay, V.A. (1998) *Fleeing Castro: Operation Pedro Plan and the Cuban Children's Program*. Gainesville, FL: University Press of Florida.

Troike, R.C. (1978) *Research Evidence for the Effectiveness of Bilingual Education*. Rosslyn, VA: National Clearinghouse for Bilingual Education.

Uddin, A. (2018) It's time we talk about the 'Trump Effect' on kids. *Teen Vogue*, 19 January. See https://www.teenvogue.com/story/its-time-we-talk-about-the-trump-effect-on-kids (accessed 13 February 2020).

Ujifusa, A. (2016) First-ever education secretary had a groundbreaking tenure at the department. *Education Week*, 13 April.

US Civil Rights Commission (1972) *The Excluded Student: Educational Practices Affecting Mexican-Americans in the Southwest*. Washington, DC: US Commission on Civil Rights Clearinghouse.

US Congress, Senate Committee on Labor and Public Welfare (1973) Education Legislation of 1973, *Hearings before a Subcommittee on Education of the Senate Committee on Labor and Public Welfare on S. 1539*, 93rd Congress, 1st Session, p. 2600.

U.S. Government Accountability Office (2013) Education needs to further examine data collection on English language learners in charter schools. Government Accountability Office, Washington, DC. See https://www.gao.gov/assets/660/655930.pdf (accessed 30 January 2020).

US House of Representatives (1978) *Excerpt of a Report on the Education Amendments of 1978, H.R. 15. Committee on Education and Labor*. Washington, DC: US Government Printing Office.

US Office of Education (1979) *Annual Evaluation Report on Programs Administered by the Office of Education Fiscal Year 1979*. Washington, DC: US Office of Education, Department of Health, Education and Welfare.

US Office of Education (1980) *Strengthening Bilingual Education: A Report from the Commissioner of Education to the Congress and the President*. Rosslyn, VA: National Clearinghouse for Bilingual Education.

Valdés, G. (1997) Dual-language immersion programs: A cautionary note concerning the education of language-minority students. *Harvard Educational Review* 67 (3), 391–429.

Valente, J. (1980) Mrs. Carter, education chief visit Bilingual Oyster School. *The Washington Post*, 8 May. See https://www.washingtonpost.com/archive/politics/1980/05/08/mrs-carter-education-chief-visit-bilingual-oyster-school/0440affc-16ae-4560-a634-8b73a1e78870/ (accessed 19 February 2020).

Vales, L. (2018) Trump twisting meaning of The Snake lyrics, say Oscar Brown Jr.'s daughters. See https://www.cnn.com/2018/02/27/politics/the-snake-africa-oscar-brown-jr-daughters-trump-don-lemon-cnntv/index.html (accessed 13 January 2020).

Verhoeven, L. (1991) Acquisition of biliteracy. *AILA Review* 8, 61–74.

Wagner, S. (1981) Historical background paper for bilingual/biculturalism conference. In J. Bartell (ed.) *The New Bilingualism*. New Brunswick, NJ: Transaction Books.

Watahomigie, L.J. and McCarty, T.L. (1994, Winter) Bilingual/bicultural education at peach springs: A Hualapai way of schooling. *Peabody Journal of Education* 69 (2), 26–42.

Weinberg, M. (1995) *A Chance to Learn: A History of Race and Education in the United States*. Long Beach, CA: California State Long Beach University Press.

Weinberg, M. (1997) *Asian-American Education: Historical Background and Current Realities*. New York: Routledge.

Whiteman, H. (1986) Historical review of Indian education: Cultural policies United Sates Position IX Inter-American Indian Congress, Santa Fe, New Mexico, October 28–November 1, 1985. *Wicazo Sa Review* 2 (1), 27–31.

Wiley, T.G. (1996) Language planning and policy. In S.L. McKay and N.H. Hornberger (eds) *Sociolinguistics and Language Teaching* (pp. 103–147). Cambridge: Cambridge University Press.

Wiley, T.G. (1998) The imposition of World War I-era English-only policies and the fate of German in North America. In T. Ricento and B. Burnaby (eds) *Language and Politics in the United States and Canada* (pp. 211–241). Mahwah, NJ: Lawrence Erlbaum.

Wiley, T.G. (2000) Continuity and change in the function of language ideologies in the United States. In T. Ricento (ed.) *Ideology, Politics, and Language Policies: Focus on English* (pp. 67–85). Amsterdam: John Benjamins.

Wiley, T.G. (2004) Language policy and English-only. In E. Finegan and J.R. Rickford (eds) *Language in the USA: Perspectives for the Twenty-First Century* (pp. 319–398). Cambridge: Cambridge University Press.

Wiley, T.G. (2014) Distinguished Scholarship and Service Award Lecture. American Association of Applied Linguistics Annual Conference. Portland Marriott Downtown Waterfront, Portland, OR.

Wiley, T.G. (2019) The rise, fall, and rebirth of bilingual education in California and the ongoing American dilemma. In T. Ricento (ed.) *Language Politics and Policies: Perspectives from Canada and the United States* (pp. 135–152). Cambridge: Cambridge University Press.

Wiley, T.G. (2020) Afterword: On contested theories and the value and limitations of pure critique. In J. MacSwan and C. Faltis (eds) *Codeswitching in the Classroom* (pp. 268–281). London/Washington, DC: Routledge and the Center for Applied Linguistics.

Wiley, T.G. (in press) The grand erasure: Whatever happened to bilingual education? And the retreat from language rights. In J. MacSwan (ed.) *Language(s): Multilingualism and Its Consequences*. Bristol: Multilingual Matters.

Wiley, T.G. and Lukes, M. (1996) English-only and standard English ideologies in the United States. *TESOL Quarterly* 3, 511–530.
Wiley, T.G. and Wright, W.E. (2004) Against the undertow: Language-minority education policy and politics in the 'age of accountability'. *Educational Policy* 18 (1), 142–168.
Wiley, T.G., Lee, J.S. and Rumberger, R. (eds) (2009) *The Education of Language Minority Immigrants in the United States*. Bristol: Multilingual Matters.
Williams, B.A. (1980) Government suggests new regulations in bilingual education. *The Associated Press*, 5 August.
Williams, C. (1939) *Factories In the Fields*. Boston, MA: Little and Brown.
Willig, A.C. (1985) A meta-analysis of selected studies on the effectiveness of bilingual education. *Review of Educational Research* 55, 269–317.
Wilson, W.H. (2014) Hawaiian: A Native American language for a state. In T.G. Wiley, J.K. Peyton, D. Christian, S.C.K. Moore and N. Lui (eds) *Handbook of Heritage, Community, and Native American Languages in the United States* (pp. 219–228). Washington, DC/New York: Center for Applied Linguistics/Routledge.
Wilson, W.H. and Kamanā, K. (2001) '*Mai Loko Mai O Ka 'I'ini:* Proceeding from a Dream'. In L. Hinton and K. Hale (eds) *The 'Aha Pūnana Leo Connection in Hawaiian Language Revitalization* (pp. 147–176). San Diego, CA: Academic Press.
Wise, A.E. (1974) *Legislated Learning: The Bureaucratization of the American Classroom*. Berkeley, CA: University of California Press.
Wollenberg, C.M. (1975) All deliberate speed: Segregation and exclusion in California schools: 1855–1975. Unpublished doctoral dissertation, University of California, Berkeley.
Wong, K.K. and Nicotera, A.C. (2004) 'Brown v. Board of Education' and the Coleman Report: Social science research and the debate on educational equality. *Peabody Journal of Education* 79 (2), 122–135.
Wooten, K. (1941) Anglo-Latin-American Spanish class. *Texas Outlook* 25, 14–16.
Wright, W.E. (2008) Proposition 203 (Arizona). In J.M. González (ed.) *Encyclopedia of Bilingual Education, Volume II* (pp. 684–688). Thousand Oaks, CA: Sage.
Wright, W.E. (2019) *Foundations for Teaching English Language Learners: Research, Theory, Policy, and Practice* (3rd edn). Philadelphia, PA: Caslon Publishing.

Index

A Better Chance to Learn, 1975: 50, 75
Advisory Committee, Bilingual Education: 2, 51, 54, 70-74, 81
Affirmative ethnicity: xii, 99
Amendment 31 (See English-Only Movement, Colorado)
American Indian Language Development Institute: 136
American Institutes of Research (AIR) Report: 100-107
America's Languages Caucus: 137-138
America's Languages: Investing in Language Education for the 21st Century (2017): xv, xvi, 138
Americanization movement: xii, xiii, xiv, xv, xvi, 23, 25-27
Andersson, Theodore: 47-48, 51-53
Appropriations (for bilingual education, See Funding)
Arizona, language education
    English Language Development four-hour block: 122-123
    Proposition 203, 2000: 13, 122-123
    Senate Bill 1014, 2019: 123
ASPIRA of New York, Inc. v. Board of Education: 64-65

Baker de Kanter Report: 115-116
Bell, Terrell: 113
Bennett, William: 61, 118
Border separation, families: 2, 5-7
Brown v. Board of Education: 27, 54, 58

Cabinet Committee on Opportunities for Spanish-Speaking People: 58, 61
California, language education
Proposition 227: 13, 122, 127, 134
Proposition 58: *xiv*, 13, 122
Californians Together: 127-128
Cárdenas, José A.: 82, 100, 101-103
Carter, Jimmy: 110-112, 114
Casateñeda v. Pickard: 114-115, 118
Center for Applied Linguistics: 22, 31, 62, 65, 71-72, 104-105, 130
Centers, Resource: 87-97
    Dissemination and Assistance Centers: 91-93, 95
    Materials Development Centers, 91-95
    Training Centers, 91-93, 95-97
Cervantes, Robert: 105-107
Civil Rights Act: 35, 54, 58, 59-61, 63-64, 66, 114, 141
Clearinghouse, Bilingual: *xiv*, 3, 68, 70, 81, 83-87
Coleman Report, The: 35-37
Commission on Civil Rights: 55, 59, 75
Committee on Mexican-American Affairs: 58-59
Committee on Opportunities for Spanish-Speaking People: 58-59, 61-62
Coral Way School/bilingual program: 41-43, 71
Consafic Chingatropic: 105-107
Cuba
    Miami refugees: 33-34, 41-43

De Inclán, Rosa Guas: 71-72
Department of Education, US: 16-20, 70, 87, 110-114
Department of Health, Education and Welfare (DHEW): 57-61, 104, 105, 110-111

Development Associates: 88-89, 105-107
DeVos, Betsy: 16-17
Division of Bilingual Education: 61, 83
    1971 Guidelines: 61
Dual Language Education of New Mexico: *vii,* 135

Ecology-of-language: 128
Elite multilingualism: 128-129
English-only, contemporary: *xiv, xv,* 13, 74, 97, 114, 115-116, 121
    Arizona, Proposition 203: 122-123
    California, Proposition 227: 122
    Colorado, Amendment 31: 121-122
    Massachusetts, Question 2: 123-124
English-only, historical: *xiii, xiv,* 24, 45, 112
English-only movement: 121-124
English immersion (See Sheltered/Structured English Immersion)
English Learner Leadership and Legacy Initiative: 134-135
Epstein, Noel: *xii,* 98-100, 101, 113
Epstein Report, The: 98-100

Fellowships, for bilingual educators: 70, 76-81, 140
First Nations Development Institute: 137
Fries Linguistic Readers: 41-43

German schools, *xii,* 21-23, 25-26
González, Josué: 21, 50-51, 108-110
Grijalva, Raul: 139

Hawaiian: 39
Hualapai: 69
Hufstedler, Shirley: 63, 111-113

Intercultural Development Research Association: 101-103
Invisible Minority, The: 34, 43

Johnson, Lyndon B.: 34, 36-37, 49, 50, 53-56

Kennedy, Edward: 63-64, 66-67, 101, 136

Language Opportunity for Our Kids (LOOK) Act, 2017: 123-124

Laredo, Texas language education: 44-46, 47, 52
Lau v. Nichols, 1974: 65, 112, 114, 141
Lau Remedies: 64, 66, 112, 114, 118, 141
Las Voces Nuevas del Sudoeste: 46-47
Lyons, James J.: 114

Malabar Program, The: 39-41
May 25, 1970 Memo: 59-61, 63, 112, 141
    Division of Bilingual Education 1971 Guidelines: 61
Méndez v. Westiminster School District, 1946: 27
Mexican
    Immigration: 31-32
    Student movements: 34-35, 46-48
Miller, Stephen: 10-11, 12-14, 16
Molina, John: 74, 83, 85

National Advisory Committee on Mexican-American Education: 54-56
    Published Reports: 55
National Association of Bilingual Education: 135-136
National Clearinghouse for Bilingual Education (National Clearinghouse for English Language Acquisition): 68, 83-87
National Defense Education Act: 29-31
National Education Association: 43-49, 111, 138
National Network, The (National Network Centers for Bilingual Education): 89-97
Nativism: *xiii,* 26
Navajo language program
    Rock Point, Arizona: 75
    Rough Rock, Arizona: 37-39
New York City
    Pre-K12 bilingual programs: 132
    Historical bilingual programs: 33, 50, 65, 91
Nieto, Sonia: 50
Nixon, Richard: 53, 56-57, 58-59, 65, 106-107
    Approach to Bilingual Education
    Notice of Proposed Rulemaking

1980, Shirley Hufstedler's Notice of Proposed Rulemaking: 112

Office of Bilingual Education (OBE): 68, 69-70, 82, 108-110
Office of Bilingual Education and Minority Affairs (OBEMLA): 70
Office of Civil Rights: *xiv*, 56-57, 65, 118, 141
Office of English Language Acquisition: 70
O'Malley, Michael: 104

Para-educators: 140
Peña, Albar: 52-53, 135-136
Post-Baccalaureate: 140
Pottinger, Stanley J.: 59-61, 112, 141
Puerto Rico: 34, 41-43, 89
Rican-Americans: 32-33, 35, 37, 65, 75
Proposition 203 (See English-Only Movement, Arizona)
Proposition 227 (See English-Only Movement, California)

Question 2 (See English-Only Movement, Massachusetts)

Ramírez Report, The: *xv*, 119-121, 135
Reagan, Ronald: *xiv*, 61, 74, 98, 113-114, 118
Reauthorizations, Title VII
  1974: 55, 63, 66, 69, 72, 76, 81, 83, 98
  1978: 73, 83, 107-108, 115
  1984: 117-118
  1988: 74, 117-118
Resource Centers: 68, 87-97, 109
  Materials Development Centers: 87-88, 92-95
  Dissemination and Assessment Centers: 87-88, 95

Training Resource Centers: 87-88, 95-97
Rock Point Navajo program: 75
Rough Rock Navajo program: 37-39
Rojas, Pauline Martz: 28-29, 41-43
Ruiz, Richard: 116-117

Seal of Biliteracy: 124, 127-128
Sessions, Jeff: *xiii*, 5-7, 10-11, 11-12, 14, 16
Slavery, Languages: 24
  Language Restriction: 24
Spanish
  Language history: 24-25
Spanish for Spanish Speakers: 44
Supporting Young Language Learners' Access to Bilingual Education (SYLLABLE) Act: 137-138
Strengthening Bilingual Education, 1980: 108-110
Structured/Sheltered English Immersion: 13, 115-116

Task Force on Education: 61-62
Teacher training, bilingual programs
Training, bilingual educator: 68-69, 70, 72-74, 76-81
Troike, Rudolph C.: 31, 37, 62, 71-72
Trump, Donald: *xii, xiv,* 4-5
  Rhetoric in schools: 5-7

Urquides, María: 43-44
Utah, Dual Language Immersion programs: 127, 131

Valdés, Guadalupe: 126
Voices of the Southwest: 43-46

World War I: *xii, xiii, xiv,* 27, 48
World War II: 27-29, 31, 48

Yarborough, Ralph: 29, 48-49, 52

Lightning Source UK Ltd.
Milton Keynes UK
UKHW020858180321
380560UK00003B/93